"SO MUCH MORE THAN THAT"

A British Family Journey of Football, Industry, War and Migration

Hannah Grainger Clemson

First published by Pitch Publishing, 2023

Pitch Publishing
9 Donnington Park,
85 Birdham Road,
Chichester,
West Sussex,
PO20 7AJ
www.pitchpublishing.co.uk
info@pitchpublishing.co.uk

A CIP catalogue record is available for this book
from the British Library.

ISBN 978 1 80150 418 8

Typesetting and origination by Pitch Publishing
Printed and bound in Great Britain by TJ Books Ltd, Padstow

Contents

Acknowledgements 6

1. Introduction 7

2. Clan feuds and home turf 20

3. Castles, coalmining, and digging up raw
   Scottish talent 44

4. Civil war, aspiration, and royal approval for
   Birmingham's jewellers. 65

5. Precious objects and professional attitudes 92

6. Fighting for a better life 113

7. Gang violence, family welfare,
   and women's rights 134

8. Guns, gold, and a new Football League 162

9. War horses and fair wages 190

10. Scotland's steel and playing football
    in Flanders Fields 216

11. A long way from St Andrew's 245

12. Entertainment, emigration, and keeping the home
    fires burning 274

13. Peace, building a business, and forever Villa . . . 297

14. Family duty and a football legacy 321

Bibliography 344

Index 348

For my parents, who resolved their sporting differences to bring up my brother and me with love and determination, and to value family, team, and community.

And for all those who came before them.

Acknowledgements

I AM so grateful to many people – friends and strangers – who helped and inspired me on this journey: writers and publishers giving advice; knowledgeable researchers sharing their findings in blogs and articles; patient volunteers and employees of local and national archives responding to my many requests; Margaux and Fiona for reading my drafts and sending notes; enthusiastic local historians digging out better images and nuggets of information; my relatives near and far who shared their own memories and photographs; team-mates and colleagues who let me go on about 'the book' and encouraged me to keep at it. Thank you all.

Chapter 1

Introduction

'So much more than that'

Bill Shankly, the Liverpool FC manager from my ancestors' village in Scotland, was on a TV chat show in May 1981. 'Somebody said that "football's a matter of life and death to you",' he recalled to the show host. 'I said, "Listen, it's more important than that."'

Any passionate player or manager might smile and nod in agreement, and so might any football fan. You could even replace the word 'football' with many sports or activities that communities of people come together to do, support, and celebrate.

To me, the 'more than that' also signifies that our lives are rarely one-dimensional. Whatever might be occupying our thoughts on one particular day, there is always something else bubbling away in the back of our minds. We might also have different personalities depending on the environment. The quiet person in the office might be saving their energy to become a demon in training that night. The kid who struggles in the classroom might be a genius outside with a ball.

The different parts of our lives can also be intertwined. Whom we meet and spend time with may be influenced by our hobbies or our work. Travel and experiencing new places may be dictated by a need to go where the work is, or the good fortune to be on holiday, or simply to go to an away game. Families, communities and whole nations will pass on a love of particular cultural forms – sports, music, other pastimes – to their children who will then remould it in their own preferred style.

The book title deliberately paraphrases Shankly's words, rather than directly quoting him. I wanted to refer to all the different ways in which our lives and those of our families can be shaped: where we live, our relationships, our work, sport and other pursuits, and also by national and international events. For Shankly, the 'more than' might refer specifically to the coal and iron community that he grew up in, like so many of my ancestors and thousands upon thousands of families through the centuries in Britain. Other football legends, such as Pat Crerand and Jock Stein, have spoken publicly about how players coming from the mining areas were brought up to look after one another and they took that fighting friendship out onto the pitch. As Shankly is quoted to have said, they started their careers 'mining for coal and came up with silver'.

What is this book about?

This book is about the lives of men and women, boys and girls, in England and Scotland from the 17th to the mid-20th century. Some of these are members of my family. None of my ancestors were or are well-known, although some of them knew famous people. None of them did anything particularly world-changing or out of the ordinary. They could be very much like the family of someone reading this book. In fact, the people my family lived near to and worked and fought alongside could very well be the ancestors of some readers. But, even if not, those generations are still connected to us in the present day in long chains of events and circumstances. We are who we are because they were who they were.

This book is about how these people's homes and professions developed in and around the industrial heartlands of England and Scotland. For the most part, they were not wealthy. They lived in small dwellings in heavily populated areas. They were coalminers, metalworkers, gunmakers, and jewellers. They cleaned other people's homes and clothes. They tended to other people's farms and fought in other people's wars.

It is also about the development of modern association football and how this was bound up with industrial and social developments. Key characters find their way into the stories: professional footballers, club board members and presidents, mill owners, Football Association officials, and the occasional lord, king or queen. Aston Villa and Birmingham City feature most of all, these being the favoured clubs of the two main branches of my family. However, well over 100 other clubs also have their important place, including: West Bromwich Albion; Wolverhampton Wanderers; Sheffield FC; Crystal Palace; Manchester United; Motherwell; Dick, Kerr Ladies; Borussia Dortmund; and Bill Shankly's own Glenbuck Cherrypickers.

Why did you want to research and tell your family story?
I have always been interested in history. As young children, we were lucky to be taken on numerous field trips by my state primary school. This being the West Midlands, it was the castles of Kenilworth and Warwick, the Lunt Roman Fort, Coventry Cathedral, and 'Shakespeare's' Stratford-upon-Avon. For our teachers, it was never about memorising dates of battles or the names of political leaders. It was about the lives and experiences of ordinary people and the community leaders who helped and influenced them. We drew pictures

of old buildings and imagined what it felt like to inhabit them. We dressed in Victorian costumes and learned how to add up 'old money' with chalk and slate. We stood in formation as Roman soldiers and wrote letters home as Second World War evacuees. We developed empathy and a sense of community identity; a sense of our local history. Being a multi-cultural community, we also learned stories from other continents and religions. We celebrated Diwali as well as Christmas.

Decades before laptops, we read books in the library, went to museums, and watched well-worn VHS tapes of *How We Used to Live* (Yorkshire Television) on the school's single TV and video player. When we went to sing carols at a care home – we called them 'Old People's Homes' – we asked them about their own childhoods. I loved watching *This Is Your Life* (Thames Television), fascinated that even famous celebrities had ordinary school friends and aunts and uncles they had not seen for a long time and that they could become nostalgic about the most ordinary details. More recently, the internet and subscription sites have boosted amateur genealogy, making it much quicker and easier to find out if our family have always lived in the local area or if they have been involved in some dramatic past event. Programmes such as the BBC's *Who Do You Think You Are?* have also added to the rise in family history projects.

For many decades, my sense of family extended only as far back as my grandparents. Of my grandfathers, I only ever knew one of them who also passed away when I was too young to have ever had a grown-up conversation with him. My grandmothers told me some stories of their lives, but these were also when I was younger and it never occurred to me to write them down. I suppose, in the innocence of youth, it did not occur to me that there would not be another opportunity to ask.

Perhaps I am now at that time in my own life where my perspective has shifted. It is no longer just about me and my ambitions and where I am going. I want to know where I have come from over generations past. My father (the Birmingham City side of the family) has passed away and so my mother (the Aston Villa side) is the main source of collective family memory, and even she admits that what she remembers is limited to the more recent generations. Perhaps the global pandemic and sudden increased loss of life also prompted a broad societal reflection on who we (all) are and what is truly important to us.

The family and other historical research could have been enough personal satisfaction – just to know for myself. Indeed, that is really how it began. But then I wanted to share it with others in my family and also see if they could add to it. I wanted to give them the same satisfaction I had in discovering an interesting fact or a mysterious blank. I was experiencing the thrill of making connections between the national and local landmarks and events I knew about and members of my own family who had been nearby when such things were being built and taking place. The more I dug into the lives of my own ancestors, the more I was also adding pieces of other families' lives. The more I learned, the more I wanted to share the stories with a wider community in the same way I had heard them in school. I thought that if I shared these quite ordinary stories about quite ordinary people, it might trigger an interest or memory in someone else in a positive way.

Why did you want to write about football and social history?
Football has always been part of my family's life. One of my earliest memories is kicking a ball in the tiny back yard of my grandparents' bungalow in Birmingham. My brother and I spent Sundays hanging out and drinking lemonade at

the clubhouse where my father was captain while the men towered over us with their dimpled-glass pint tankards of beer; the classic style with the handles. It smelt of muddy boots and cigarette smoke as one could still puff away indoors back then. As Sunday was for playing football, we had Saturday lunch as a family instead, listening to the matchday build-up on the radio. By five o'clock you knew whether the rest of the weekend and following week would be upbeat. In the seasons when Villa and Birmingham were in the same division, you would also know whether there would be a little bit of mockery from one parent to the other. You knew whether or not you could hold your head high at school on Monday morning. There was even a rousing school assembly hymn ending with the line 'And a win for my home team'. You always hoped that one came up on a good Monday.

As I started to research my family history and looked in parallel at developments in football, I was struck by the similarities with today's sporting issues. As recently as 2021 the football community was collectively horrified by the proposal of a breakaway European League. How could a few clubs think that they were so special as to only want to play each other? How could a few individuals be so greedy for more money as to engineer this and ignore the needs of the ordinary fan? And yet, in the 1880s, the creation of the Football League must have seemed this way too. Most of us cannot imagine earning the kind of money that professional footballers do today and still their agents negotiate for more, justified by notions of market value and relatively short playing careers. In the late 19th and early 20th centuries, there were also the same debates, leading to tense player meetings and union disputes.

For me, there was an important overarching story to be told about 'the beautiful game' and how it evolved as witnessed by the ordinary folk who lived alongside it – outsiders and yet part of the fabric. Football is not the same without its supporters and amateur players. We have learned this during the pandemic. We have felt its absence and the players have felt ours. Football was prescribed as a necessary part of soldier recovery in the First World War and the wartime halt on matches lasted only a few months in the Second World War before a temporary league started up again. Viewers of *The English Game* (produced by 42, released by Netflix in 2020) may be forgiven for thinking that this is mostly about clubs in England. However, the title – proven by the plot of the television show – is ironic: it is not monocultural. The influence of Scottish players and businessmen on the formal game was enormous in the late 19th and early 20th centuries. But the origin of clubs in churches, factories, and bars also resonates in other countries, as I found when tracing my grandfather's steps across Belgium and Germany.

Sports researchers Adam Benkwitz and Gyozo Molnar argue, 'Far from being passive cultural beings, the working classes, from the beginnings, actively negotiated the development of their own emergent football culture.'[1] Football was a necessary winter alternative to cricket. Organised sport also fitted the religious ideal of young men who were 'strong in body, pure in heart, faithful to friends, family and country and knew their duty before God'. However, rather than being promoted by a higher authority, it is argued that the ordinary members of communities organised themselves into teams as suited their own lives and interests. By 1880, there were 214 cricket teams in Birmingham alone: 64 were church teams, 16 were

---

1 Adam Benkwitz and Gyozo Molnar (2017). The emergence and development of association football: influential sociocultural factors in Victorian Birmingham, *Soccer & Society*, 18:7, pp.1027-1044.

pub teams, 25 came from places of work. Once the football season extended beyond March, players – and supporters – then had to make a choice.

Seeing history through my ancestors' eyes, it has been important to balance the stories of the professional players with those of the fans. I wanted to draw more attention to the people and the emotion of the football terraces that J.B. Priestley wrote about in his 1929 novel, *The Good Companions*:

'It turned you into a member of a new community, all brothers together for an hour and a half ... you had escaped with most of your mates and your neighbours, with half the town, cheering together, thumping one another on the shoulders, swapping judgments like Lords of the Earth, having pushed your way through a turnstile into another and altogether more splendid life, hurtling with Conflict and yet passionate and beautiful in its Art.'

Football crowds and terraces were understood as joyful places to be, away from the hardship of work and the horrors of war. It is argued that this changed in the latter half of the 20th century as those in positions of power became concerned and suspicious about the close-knit people that the football grounds contained. There was an obvious overlap with the communities that were enduring financial and social hardship and it was these people – the miners, the factory workers – that the authorities perceived as needing to be increasingly controlled. This was *Peaky Blinders* territory. Tensions increased as the ordinary supporter was suspected, condemned, and penned in by external rule-makers. It was counterintuitive and counterproductive to a sport which, yes, has some structure but is also of-the-moment grassroots stuff; 'jumpers for goalposts'. Football's enduring appeal relies on and celebrates the ordinary person and their friends watching their humble 'one of our own' heroes in flashes of improvised genius. This is why I wanted to go back to the start of it all: with the kids, the families, and the local entrepreneurs who made it happen.

I am aware of my own gender when writing the stories but only to the extent of trying to give equal voice to the females in my family and wider community. This was a challenge given that the details of women's lives feature much less in official records. If a woman did not have a trade other than 'domestic duties' – being a housewife – there would be nothing in the census or trade directories to give a sense of her competences or interests. I have not set out to put forward a particularly feminist perspective on history, although women's rights are mentioned as a key part of social change in the early 20th century. Along with descriptions of home life and having children, I have included the emergence, and the decline, of ladies' football teams. Their existence pleasantly surprised me and the attitude of the English and Scottish football associations to exclude them disappointed me. However, I leave the reader to reflect for themselves whether or not they agree with the FAs' actions. The only moment I faltered was when it was suggested to me that my book 'might not be credible enough' for some men to read. To that I can only say that I am a fan of football, and have been all my life, as have the men and women in my family for generations. I hope that to write as a genuine fan is good enough.

Despite being quite ordinary members of society, there are odd tales and rumours surrounding my family that also inspired the research. The first is the friendship between my Scottish grandmother's family and that of William McGregor, legendary Aston Villa committee member and 'father' of the Football League. This connection is one that started me on the long journey of discovering many more links between Scottish and English football and industry.

My grandmother also delighted in saying that the famous Robert Burns, national poet of Scotland, was a friend of our ancestors. This always seemed rather far-fetched and I am not sure that anyone really believed her. However, history reveals not one but two or more possible connections by circumstance. If only my grandmother were still here to tell her tale.

Other stories are the mysterious twists and unfortunate ends to my ancestors' lives: theft, witchcraft, prison, battlefields, disappearance. Perhaps they are not epic enough for a new Netflix series but it was real life.

How did you go about writing the book – what were the steps and challenges?

I started, as many do, with a subscription to an ancestry website. I was lucky that other relatives – in my close and more distant family – had also made a start in checking census, birth and marriage records. As a warning to those starting out, this can quickly turn into quite an obsession. Many nights after work, training, and food, I would log in with the intention of a quick browse. After a particular success I would then be spurred on to find 'just one more' relative or factual detail to add to the tree, and then one more, dragging me into a black hole until the wee hours of the morning.

Digital records also have to be carefully checked. Census records have original errors from poor handwriting and manual copying mistakes. Digital databases made from these also have typed errors. Other amateur internet site users sometimes make a link between their relative and yours when they coincidentally have the same name, and were born in the same year and city, but are not the same person. One click and you can end up attached to the wrong tree. It can also be frustrating when dealing with popular names that bring up more than 1,000 search results. The monthly subscription costs to these various sites also adds up over time.

The next step was to choose the people and the stories to base the chapters on. Guided by geography, there were three distinct industrial areas: around Glasgow in the south of Scotland; around Sheffield and Manchester towards the north of England; and around Birmingham in central England. Chronologically, there were also distinct eras in the development of football: before the Football Association and rules that gave more structure; the early years of the Football League; before and during the world wars; and the postwar era (1950s–1960s).

I then chose family units across the different branches of the family tree and across the generations that seemed to fit with and complement the stories of developing industry and football. For each family unit, I followed the path of their personal history and then added in the details of local history and any relevant sporting stories. Doing so then opened up even more questions about a particular family member or about the industry in which they worked. After a while, the stories could only go so far when based on information generated online. I needed to come home: to walk down the same streets, and look through family photos. I retrieved national and regional archive material, went to the National Football Museum, visited the very helpful people at Birmingham, Manchester, and Edinburgh city libraries, and reconnected with relatives who might be able to fill in the other gaps.

I sent over 100 emails to historians, creatives, and media specialists to enquire about image copyrights. I babbled on to friends and begged them to proofread chapters. I am truly indebted to every single person for their patience and mutual passion.

How should the book be read?

Ever since deciding to write book chapters, I had an idea that I wanted the reader to be able to make sense of the stories depending on their own memories and interests. There should be no fixed start and end point.

The chapters are present in a rough chronological order according to the years that the main characters were alive. Like the adventure books I loved as a child, I would encourage the reader then make a free choice at the end of each chapter: to continue through history to the next generation; to read a different chapter about the same industry or town; or simply to skim through the many pictures or anecdotes about particular sporting events.

What I hope is that the reader does not see this as just about my own family or football team. From my travels and from my little life so far, I sense that we are all connected in some way, and, even if not, we try to be. It is part of our human, communal nature that our ears prick up when we hear a familiar place or event talked about: 'I don't suppose you know so-and-so?' 'Do you remember when this happened?' 'Oh, yes, I [or he, or she] was there too!' Even if we have never met, and do not even speak the same language, we can still dance along to music together or have a kick-about if someone brings a ball. I hope that every reader is able to find a moment to smile or be nostalgic when they come across something they can relate to.

Finally, I hope that reading the book can be both an enjoyable trip into the past but also a way of reflecting on how society and sport are today. There are so many issues raised by looking at the past that it can shine a light on what we think is currently important: what is a fair salary? What kinds of conditions are some people living in? How can we best educate and feed children? Who stands up for the rights of those who do not have a voice? What does being 'professional' mean? How can sport improve our mental and physical wellbeing? These are big questions and no less important are all the others: who is on the team sheet for the next game? When did the bibs last get washed? Will we have enough points to stay up?

If there is one thing that my amazing journey through history has constantly reminded me, it is that, however lost you feel, there is a community somewhere looking out for you. And if the sporting losses come a little too often, there is always next season.

#UTV

Chapter 2

Clan feuds and home turf

Near Edinburgh (1600–1850s)

1600s	George Cuninghame and Marion Whyte	
	Andrew Cuninghame and Marion Crawford	
	Edward Cunningham and Margaret Godrell	
	Edward Cunningham and Janet Hill	William Walker
1700s	John Cunningham and Helen Aitkin	Thomas Walker and Janet Broun
	James Cunningham And Elizabeth Walker	
	James Cunningham And Elizabeth Nisbet	

Lines of known ancestors from 17th- and 18th-century Scotland. Bold denotes key people referred to in the chapter.

JAMES CUNNINGHAM, my five-times great-grandfather, was born at the beginning of March 1762 in Kirkliston, Scotland. Kicking and screaming his way into the world, he had just missed the festivities of Shrove Tuesday, the day before Lent when village and town communities cooked up their fatty foods and enjoyed local pastimes.

In both Scotland and England, this feast day typically included a local game of 'Foot-Ball'. That same year was also the first recorded fixture between the parishes of St Michael and St Paul in Alnwick, Northumberland, just over the border. The annual game is still played to this day and, just as it was back then, there can be over 100 players in each team. The goalposts are about 400 yards apart (four times the size of today's pitches) and the simple objective is to score two 'hales'. There are few other rules except that, after the game, the ball is traditionally thrown into the river and whomever swims in and carries it out on the other side can keep it.

FOOT BALL, KINGSTON-UPON-THAMES,
SHROVE TUESDAY, FEB. 24TH, 1846.

A traditional Shrove Tuesday game of 'Foot Ball'.

Kirkliston is a small town to the west of Edinburgh, now overshadowed by the international airport, but with a long history and not a quiet one.

The ancient name of the town was Liston, probably from the British word 'llys' meaning court or manor, and the Old English word 'tun' meaning town or farmstead. Britons (the indigenous people from before the Roman invasion) would have been the earliest inhabitants of the area, with Angles (descended from Germanic immigrants) later arriving from Northumberland. In the 13th century the name was recorded as Temple Liston, referring to the Knights Templar, who owned the Barony of Liston at the heart of the parish. The Knights Templar were a rich, powerful, and multinational Catholic military order – imagine Apple or Amazon today but with an army of skilled soldiers and the support of the Pope; or imagine that a successful corporation like Microsoft had their own football team in the Premier League.

The prefix Kirk (church) first appeared in the village name in the 14th century, after the Knights Templar had been disbanded and their lands confiscated. This was also a rather nasty event, not long after the original 'Auld Alliance' – an agreement between France and Scotland to oppose England. The Knights were not only rich and powerful, they also had a private initiation ceremony which meant that many people were suspicious of their secret club. The French King Philip pounced on an opportunity to get rid of them. He needed to erase his debt with the Knights, who had previously assisted him in his war against the English. Playing along with the public rumours, he had the Knights arrested, tortured, and many burned at the stake, and he also demanded that other countries helped to bring down this large organisation of religious men.

This sudden relegation of the Knights from the top division of society was not the first time that Kirkliston was under the international spotlight. It was the location of the first recorded parliament in Scottish history and the Estates of Scotland met there in 1235, during the reign of Alexander

II. In June 1298 King Edward I of England made camp at the town on his way to fight Sir William Wallace at the Battle of Falkirk, part of the Scottish War of Independence. Just to keep the historical records straight, this is not Proud Edward of the 'Flower of Scotland' anthem of the rugby, football, and Commonwealth Games teams. That song (from the 1960s) refers to the victory of the Scots, led by Robert the Bruce, over King Edward II of England at the Battle of Bannockburn in 1314.

A map showing the road between Livingston and Edinburgh in 1767. Newliston is marked to the north and was Lord Stair's new mansion built one mile outside of Kirkliston. Reproduced with the permission of the National Library of Scotland.

As a boy growing up in the countryside, James might have been told that his family line could be traced back to George Cuninghame, who married Marion Whyte in Edinburgh in 1620. The end of the English Civil War (1651) brought Scotland under the rule of Oliver Cromwell and his parliament, and anyone who was against that was at risk. This was then followed by a dangerous period of resistance by some Scots to acknowledging the new king, Charles II, as head of the kirk (church), which was also punishable by death. Finally, the Glorious Revolution meant that Scotland

and England were linked but separate countries, each with their own parliament, which had authority over the Crown. For ordinary working families, the 'ill years' famine of the 1690s forced many from their rural homes into the urban centres, meaning that Edinburgh was becoming a rabbit warren of streets and alleyways under the shadow of its castle. It was the second largest city in Britain, bustling and crammed with merchants and goldsmiths. Rather than try to profit from this social change, my family decided to move in the opposite direction, to the relative tranquillity of the countryside.

By the mid-17th century, the Cunningham family name was already caught up in some serious local gossip in Kirkliston. The parish records describe how the Smiths and the Cunninghams were not on good terms. One day, in 1668, the quiet village street erupted as Mrs Smith and her daughters confronted Mrs Cunningham and her daughters. The large bosom of Mrs Smith heaved with rage and her face turned as red as the hair on the Cunningham girls. The other villagers hid by their doorways, muttering to each other, until one word of the screaming accusations by the women in the street stopped everyone in their tracks: 'witchcraft'.

The Cunningham women knew exactly what they were doing against the Smiths, and the Smiths in retaliation. They could use the accusation of witchcraft against neighbours for their own gain or popularity but it was a risky move. Witch trials were internationally famous and the Witchcraft Act of 1563 was used against thousands of people, including the most vulnerable in society: the old, the physically impaired, the mentally ill, and most of them women. The accused were locked in towers and dungeons, and tortured with ropes, thumbscrews, and spiked iron collars. Scottish folk were big on superstition and belief in the supernatural, and Scotland had around five times the number of cases than elsewhere in Europe (around 2,500 strangled or burned at the stake). Woe betide any misfit in the community being present at an unusual local event. 'Could witchcraft have had a hand in the shock result of last feast day's "fute ball" match?' 'Methinks I saw the wee old granny of the opposition striker hovering near the goalposts in the final minutes ...'

Such public accusations in the village could not be left without immediate action. The women were brought before the next church session, which was a disciplinary committee run by the parish elite. Mrs Cunningham and Mrs Smith may have been close to scratching each other's eyes out but, on this day, they had to smile sweetly at the priest and smooth their clean aprons. 'What, me, sir? Of course not, you must be mistaken.' The committee clerks, seemingly tired of this family feud decided to let the matter go and luckily so for the women. If it had gone further, it could have easily resulted in torture and one or more of the mothers or daughters being burned at the stake. The kirk ordered the families to remain in peace from that day forward, under caution of the large sum of £20 (around £2,275 today or the value of three horses at the time).

In fact, it was a football match that sparked the case of Anne Gunter.[2] Anne's father, Brian, had become enraged at a village match just outside Oxford and had killed two of the opposition – the Gregory brothers. The sister-in-law of the boys, Elizabeth Gregory, then made it her personal business to scream and swear at Brian at every opportunity from then on and declare public hatred of the man. This went on for a few years. Then his daughter, Anne, fell sick and Brian persuaded her to fake the symptoms of being bewitched that

---

2   The full story is described in J. Sharpe (2000), *The Bewitching of Anne Gunter, a Horrible and True Story of Deception, Witchcraft, Murder, and the King of England* (New York: Routledge)

he had read in a book. Anne agreed and put on a good act from her bed, trembling and saying that Elizabeth Gregory was responsible. Elizabeth was put on trial but the local judges were not convinced.

Brian Gunter was not giving up. Despite knowing full well that he had the blood of two young footballers on his hands, he was wealthy and he had good connections. He knew that King James was rather obsessed by stories of witches and presided personally over some trials. The king's actions and thirst for conquests have been likened to the sport of deer hunters, chasing lone individuals across the land with weapons and packs of hounds (his clerics).[3] Despite knowing deep down that the case was false, the King still took young Anne into his care and subjected her to dancing for him and all manner of other cross-examinations that led to more supposed witnesses being questioned. Eventually, Anne became tired of the performance and dropped her story but not before the public and the palace had enjoyed the full potential of the soap opera. What had begun as a relatively small incident at a football match had blown up into major social entertainment with reputations made and ruined, only to be forgotten about when the next big thing came along.

Over the course of the 15th century, four separate Acts of Parliament were issued which attempted to curtail 'fute-ball', highlighting its popularity as well the concerns about the violent nature of the game. Today's spectators would probably see more similarities in rugby football with scrummaging, and Gaelic football with hand-passing and shoulder-charging tackles. Despite the opposition by the authorities, Scotland seems to have also encouraged women

---

3   Described by historian Margaret Alice Murray in the chapter 'The "Devil" of North Berwick' in ed. B.P. Levack (1992) *Witchcraft in Scotland* (New York and London: Garland Publishing Inc)

Suspected witches kneeling before King James. The drawing comes from his own book Daemonologie *(1597), based on the trial of women from North Berwick in Lothian.*

to play football, at least initially. In the 18th century, football was allegedly linked to local marriage customs. Single women would play football games against married women. Single men would watch these games and use the evidence of their footballing ability to help them select prospective brides. In fact, ball games – and stick and ball games – go back thousands of years worldwide and certainly pre-date Christianity. Shinty – similar to hockey and Irish hurling – golf, and football all date back hundreds of years in Scotland.

Shinty is played with a long, curved stick – 'caman' – and a small hard ball. Like football, it was typically played without any formal rules on feast days by people within one community, sometimes competing against people from another community. Today, it is played mostly in the Highlands and on the west coast and is thought to have been brought to Scotland some time ago from Ireland alongside the Christian faith and Gaelic language. It was certainly regarded as a brutal game but with worthwhile prizes that could include a cask of whisky or the right to raid an opposing player's farm for good food without being stopped. Nottingham Forest in England was formed in 1865 from a 'shinny' (variation of the word shinty) team. They named themselves Forest after the Recreation Ground that they first played on.

Illustration of a game of shinty, published in The Penny Magazine, *1835. Image: The National Galleries of Scotland.*

Golf originated from a similar premise to shinty but without the mass team format. Players on the coast near Edinburgh were required to hit a pebble over sand dunes and around tracks using a bent stick or club. Some believe that the earliest golfers were actually shinty players having an individual skills practice on the beach. King James II banned both golf and football in 1457 by an Act of Parliament as his men were neglecting their military training in order to play. Disgruntled sportsmen would have to wait a few decades for their new king, James IV of Scotland, to approve of it and encourage its spread to England and France. The first golf club was formed at Leith in 1744 and the first 18-hole course in St Andrews in 1764.

Players at the Royal and Ancient Golf Club of St Andrews, Fife, Scotland, in 1798. Image: Hulton Archive.

While James's ancestors were engaged in petty village politics, over on the other side of Scotland lived the traditional rulers of the family, or 'clan': the rich in their castles. The sport of the Cunningham(e) clan Earls of Glencairn was unsurprisingly focused on fighting – or trying to compromise with – rival clan chiefs. Sadly, you will not find any romantic Highland *Outlander* heroes in my clan, but rather a line of men happy to switch allegiance depending on which team was most likely to win, or cause them the least amount of grief after the battle. And, yes, the Cunninghames were firing on the side of the British government forces at the Battle of Culloden (1746), rather than with the Jacobite rebels.

The area in Ayrshire where Clan Cunningham originates from got its name from the words 'cunny' or 'coney', meaning rabbit, and 'hame', meaning home: rabbit's home. This is hardly likely to strike fear into any visiting enemies, unless they are a fan of Monty Python's *Holy Grail* and know about the fictional Killer Rabbit of Caerbannog who attacks King Arthur and his knights.[4] Modern comedy films aside, even the centuries-old outside wall of Notre Dame Cathedral in Paris depicts a soldier running away from a particularly aggressive hare as part of the Final Judgement. Perhaps we should be more wary of these small herbivores after all? An 18th-century Cunningham coat of arms shows two coneys – this possibly being a play on words for king (Koenig in German) – and a unicorn to further indicate some royal association. Years later, the rabbits disappeared and the current clan crest sticks with the more impressive unicorn and the motto 'Over Fork Over'. In a similar way, sports and other community organisation badges would gradually take on an important role in publicly demonstrating their origins and member allegiance.

A quick run through the history of the clan gives a good idea of the type of men ruling the land. William Cunninghame, 4th Earl (1540–47), was initially loyal to the Crown but, when he witnessed the atrocities of the English, he joined the forces of the Reformation and played a significant part in the cause. James Cunninghame, 7th Earl (1581–1629), seemed to enjoy fighting so much that he completely undid his own father's life's work of friendship with the Campbells, Montgomeries, Boyds, and Wallaces. Local skirmishes reached a head with the murder of Hugh, 4th Earl of Eglinton. James promptly denied any knowledge

---

4   The Rabbit of Caerbannog is a fictional character in *Monty Python and the Holy Grail*. It viciously attacks King Arthur and the knights, killing and injuring several of them.

From left to right: 18th-century Cunningham coat of arms (Image: PJRCunningham, CC BY-SA 4.0 via Wikimedia Commons); a hare chasing a soldier – part of the façade of the Notre Dame Cathedral in Paris (Image: Thesupermat, CC BY-SA 3.0 via Wikimedia Commons); the Cunningham clan badge (Image: Celtus, CC BY-SA 3.0 via Wikimedia Commons).

of it and many of the Cunninghames and Montgomeries were killed or fled the country in the bloody 20-year aftermath.

William Cunninghame, 9th Earl (1631–64), was a supporter of King Charles I, just like Sir Thomas Holte was in his Aston Manor in Birmingham, despite many locals being against the monarchy (see Chapter 4). The Scottish parliament demanded that William give up his title. He soon realised that Scotland was being drawn into the feud between King Charles and the parliament in London, so William withdrew his support for the monarch. His title was restored but then he made the bold decision to fight with the Highland clans against General Monck and Cromwell when they invaded Scotland. Unfortunately, William's troops were forced to surrender and, when he returned home, he was thrown into prison anyway on charges of plotting. So much for trying to be on the winning side.

I feel a bit sorry for William Cunningham, 13th Earl (1734–75), and his own changing ways in light of public opinion. First, he installed a more liberal minister at Kilmarnock (a 'New Licht' supporting the voluntary nature of religion rather than for Church and State being formally connected) which caused part of the congregation to riot.

Then he hired an 'Auld Licht' minister which immediately upset the other believers. To top it all off, he married the daughter of a carpenter and travelling violinist, which the whole aristocracy certainly did not approve of.

It was the 14th Earl, William's son James, who met Robert Burns in Edinburgh where they became great friends and to whom one of Burns's poems is dedicated: *Lament to James, Earl of Glencairn.* James was a huge supporter and helped Burns to become a famous national poet. Unfortunately, none of the 14th Earl's generation were able to provide heirs and thus ended the line of the Earls of Glencairn.

Back in Kirkliston with the working-class Cunninghams, the town would have been constantly busy with trade and news of battle victories as it lies on the main route from Edinburgh and Linlithgow to Falkirk and Stirling. Mills were set up along the river to utilise water power. Weaving became a popular trade in the 17th century and a distillery was later built in 1795. Although there are no official records, the family would likely have been working in one of these mills or on the land. The tales of clan gossip are what my own ancestor, James, might have heard on the grapevine from those people travelling between Ayrshire and Edinburgh, including the same famous poet Robert Burns.

Portrait of James Cunningham, 14th Earl of Glencairn. Image: Dumfries Museum (Dumfries & Galloway Council).

Burns was on his travels in the summer of 1787 and, rather like using a permanent marker in a pub toilet cubicle, he was known to scratch his name or a short verse on tavern window panes. One such pane can be seen in the National Museum of Scotland.

When Robert stayed in Kirkliston, he was 28 years old, and gaining attention for his newly published works. James (my five-times great grandfather) was similarly a lad of 25 and perhaps they shared a whisky or two in the local tavern. My grandmother was fond of the family rumour that our ancestors were friends with the great poet, and here is perhaps one way in which that rather surprising claim came about, as well as other ancestors being neighbours of Robert's uncle in a different village (see Chapter 3). Equally possible is the scene as James was heading to the fields early the next morning:

'Here, laddie!' called down the innkeeper from a first-floor window. 'Dinnae ye be drinking with that poet til the wee hours? He scratched summat on ma windows!'

James half-smiled and shrugged, carrying round the corner only to see Robert climbing into the horse-drawn coach bound for Edinburgh.

'Ye travel safe!' James called out. 'An' what's this the innkeeper be bletherin' about windows?'

'Ah, consider that a gift,' replied Robert, laughing. 'And ye know the man who gave me the diamond-tipped stylus to do it?' James looked blank. 'Your clan chief, Cunningham, the Earl of Glencairn!' And with that, the carriage door slammed shut, and, with a wave, the poet Robert Burns was gone. James shook his head. His own clan causing mischief again. Best not to mention it to the innkeeper.

Some of James's other Kirkliston neighbours had their own claims to glory, although many of their exploits are perhaps not widely acceptable by today's standards. Archibald Dalzel was a doctor but ran several slaving depots in West Africa and he defended the slave trade, believing that it was an easy route to early retirement in comfort. One could legally own a slave in Scotland until 1778 and some wealthy families delighted in having a young 'black boy' or girl to wait on them. It was only in 1807 that Britain abolished the trading of slaves, although plantation slavery still existed in the colonies.

Another successful career man was Robert Liston. Having worked as a tutor and then secretary to a diplomat, he was given the rather impressive titles of envoy-extraordinary and minister-plenipotentiary to the United States of America in early 1796, just after the end of the War of Independence. Despite these grand adventures, he preferred to return to near Kirkliston in his old age.

Rather than try to make a life overseas (as his descendants later would), James married a local girl, Elizabeth Walker, and they made the countryside their home. Walker is an English and German surname derived from the Middle High German 'walker' (Scots 'waukin'), meaning a fuller of cloth. This was the process of thickening cloth with the hands or feet (later in mills) and soaking it in urine to cleanse it. Scotswomen would sing 'waulking' songs to keep a rhythm and pass the time as a group. The name Walker can also refer to an officer whose duty consisted of walking or inspecting a certain part of a forest.

The Walkers had been tenant farmers in the area since around 1745. In the 18th and 19th centuries, East Lothian's landed estates were divided into several farms, each with their own steading. The Walkers stayed for many years at Hiddlefaulds, a house and stables on the Kilpunt farm.

Detail of an 18th-century engraving of Scotswomen waulking (fulling) cloth and singing.

The region was regarded as the most advanced in Scottish farming at the time. Before the Industrial Revolution, a lot of work was to be found in the countryside and during the industry and population boom in the cities, agriculture remained important in supplying food to urban residents.

Farm buildings could be quite substantial and included cart and granary sheds, horse mills, cattle courts and 'doocots' (doves provided meat in winter). Workers included a foreman, bailies to look after cattle, ploughmen, a dairy maid, a housemaid, kitchen maids, and 'oot' women performing outdoor work. Children fed hens and brought food to the other workers. Stocks of dried heather helped to lights fires of peat (turf cut from local areas) which could be kept dry for winter fires. Water for drinking and cooking came from nearby wells and needed to be fetched every day. If there was a stream nearby, the family's clothes and blankets could be washed there or trampled in a large wooden tub and rinsed in a barrel of rainwater.

A distant family relative still possesses deeds, wills and letters from the time. The marriage contract between

An illustration of a Scottish Lowland farm in the 17th century with a small collection of buildings, surrounding land to be ploughed, and workers with horses. It is a section from The Prospect of the Abby of Dunfermling *by John Slezer, published in* Theatrum Scotiae, *1693. Reproduced with the permission of the National Library of Scotland.*

Elizabeth's grandparents in 1728 details a sizeable amount of land and money in hundreds of Scottish merks (the old currency) so we can assume that they were living comfortably. It took some time for this relative to deduce the right Elizabeth as the bride for James Cunningham as there was also a much younger cousin with the same name. Church records can blur truths about age and circumstances as well as provide hard evidence. In the case of the Walker family, Elizabeth's other cousin, John, was recorded in the Kirkliston parish registers as having 'irregularly' married Isabel Neil in 1816. This probably means 'quickly' without banns – the intention to marry – read aloud for three weeks previously as Isabel was already pregnant, giving birth to their first daughter three months later. Marrying in their situation was not unusual for the time, nor unusual throughout history. However, it says something about Kirkliston Church that they decided to write it down and make a public statement about the couple's behaviour before marriage, rather than keep it quiet.

In the 18th and early 19th centuries, sports and general leisure activities were limited to either rich folk, or whatever time poorer folk could spare from their long hours. This was when Saturday was still a normal and full working day. Sport also depended on whether the local church would permit such non-religious (from their perspective) activities on Sundays.

The simple game of 'quoiting' involved throwing metal rings – quoits – weighing 4kg or more, at a pin some 20 paces away. It was definitely a game for men more used to physical labour and typically involved some gambling and drinking on the side. Football required more time and more players. It has long been described as more of an annual event, taking place at Fastern's E'en (Shrove Tuesday – the day before Lent) or as part of the celebrations and break from work at Yule (winter festival in December which is at the same time as Christmas in the Christian religion). A poem by the Rev. John Skinner (born in the north of Scotland in 1721) gives a detailed and humorous account of a brutal village game, although he does not go so far as to call it immoral or sinful.

In the poem, one player bashes the head of another against the church wall. Another player, rather less skilled and lacking in strength, tries his best to kick the ball but lands on his backside. The game continues with several men both giving and receiving 'routs and raps'. Men of all trades get involved and many insults and shouts are added to the kicks and hits. Despite this, and the various incidents during the match involving notable individuals, the game eventually ends. As with any impromptu game, there is the typical call from some 'for hawf an hour's mair fun' but suddenly all are friends again and off for 'a pint o' Lillie's/Best ale'.

Having married in 1785, in the same kirk as they had both been christened, James and Elizabeth immediately set to their own Christian duty and had eight children over

Rob Roy, I wat he was na dull,
  He first leit at the ba',
Syne wi' a rap clash'd Geordie's skull
  Hard to the steeple-wa'.
Wha was aside but auld Tam Tull?—
  His frien's mishap he saw,—
Syne rair'd like ony baited bull,
  And wi' a thud dang twa
              To the yird that day.

The tanner was a piimpit bit,
  As flimsy as a feather,
He thought it best to try a hit,
  Ere a' the thrang shou'd gadyr:
He ran wi' neither fear nor wit,
  As fu' o' wind's a bladder;
Unluckily he tint the fit,
  And tann'd his ain bum-lether
              Fell weel that day.

Verses from 'The Monymusk Christmas Ba'ing' (Balling) by the Reverend John Skinner. The collection is titled Songs and Poems, *published in 1859 by W.L. Taylor.*

the following 20 years, all born locally. Their trades were typical of the agricultural villages in which they lived but, in the 19th century, the family started to follow the national shift in construction and industry: from manual labour and woodwork to coalmines and great iron works. One of their sons – also named James and my four-times great-grandfather – was registered as a joiner, which referred to a range of carpentry and woodworking trades. There would have been plenty of work: on the structural pieces of houses and farm buildings; making furniture; and crafting or repairing tools.

However much that son James was dedicated to his trade, once the lovely Elizabeth Nisbet caught his eye then the opportunities for distraction were endless. They married and settled down in Broxburn, another village west of Edinburgh. They had seven children in total, although the eldest daughter sadly died aged 12. In the next decade their safe little rural existence then seemed to come apart at the seams.

Peter (my three times great-grandfather – see Chapter 10) confessed to his father that he would not be following him into the carpentry trade but had heard of the new ironworks in the west and that he wanted to try working there. Many of his generation were doing the same and, all over the Lowlands, young farm labourers were moving to the towns to be replaced by seasonal workers coming down from the Highlands. And so Peter left, probably carrying his few possessions in a small wooden trunk that he or his father would have made in their cottage workshop. Some years later, James and Elizabeth took a long look at their own life in the agricultural community. 'Perhaps there is nothing much left for us here now.' 'Aye, and Peter sends word of his success. Perhaps we owe it to the other children to go there?' So it was that James and Elizabeth packed up their belongings and migrated west to Lanarkshire, south of Glasgow, with their younger children.

Whatever Peter had described to his parents and brothers, it was perhaps not the most honest picture of the landscape. While the Cunninghams were used to the slow pace of agricultural villages, they were about to arrive in a darker and more dramatic landscape that sounds more like inner-city Birmingham and Glasgow at the time, described by David Bremner in *The Industries of Scotland: Their Rise, Progress, and Present Condition* (published by A. and C. Black, 1869):

> 'Though Coatbridge is a most interesting seat of industry, it is anything but beautiful. Dense clouds of smoke roll over it incessantly, and impart to all the buildings a peculiarly dingy aspect. A coat of black dust overlies everything, and in a few hours the visitor finds his complexion considerably deteriorated by the flakes of soot which fill the air, and settle on his face.
>
> 'To experience Coatbridge it must be visited at night when it presents a most extraordinary spectacle … From the steeple of the parish church the flames of no fewer than 50 blast furnaces may be seen … The flames have a positively fascinating effect. Now they shoot far upward, and breaking off short, expire among the smoke; again spreading outward, they curl over the lips of the furnace, and dart through the doorways, as if determined to annihilate the bounds within which they are confined; then they sink low into the crater, and come forth with renewed strength in the shape of great tongues of fire, which sway backward and forward, as if seeking with a fierce eagerness something to devour.'

This area would later become a hotbed of sporting talent. It is often said that the scores of determined and physical athletes that it produced was a direct result of the harsh living and working conditions that their parents and grandparents had endured. The county of Lanarkshire alone would provide notable football names. Hughie Gallacher (Newcastle United captain) was from the mining town of Bellshill, that also attracted many immigrants from eastern Europe. Sir Matt Busby (Scotland international and Manchester United manager) came from the mining village of Orbiston

Lanarkshire footballing talent Hughie Gallacher, Matt Busby (Images: Colorsport), and George Graham (Image: Mirrorpix).

and was known for his deceptive dribbling skills. Robert McSkimming (1885–1952) was an iron moulder in his teenage years until he escaped to play professional football for Sheffield Wednesday and Motherwell. George Graham was born in a poor mining community near Coatbridge. He played initially for Aston Villa (1959–64) and other teams before managing Arsenal, Leeds and Spurs in the 1980s and 1990s. Jock Stein (Celtic and Scotland manager) both worked as a miner and played football for many years until he could finally turn professional in 1950. It is he who is quoted as saying, 'You go down that pit shaft, a mile underground. You can't see a thing. The guy next to you, you don't know who he is. Yet he is the best friend you will ever have. Mines were places where phonies or cheats couldn't survive for long.'

The town of Coatbridge was a popular destination for families escaping the famine in Ireland and Irish workers accounted for around a third of its population in the mid-19th century. Lanarkshire also attracted families from eastern Europe. Unfortunately, these migrations caused early religious tensions to develop between Catholics and Protestants as newcomers sought both work and accommodation. These tensions would later become highly visible in the rivalry between the supporters of Glasgow's two main football clubs, Celtic and Rangers. Celtic would be founded by Brother Walfrid, a member of the Roman Catholic order of Little Brothers of Mary as part of his charitable work among the poor Irish immigrants in Glasgow and their supporters would be Irish-Scots. Even though Rangers would be founded much earlier, in 1872, and with no particular religious basis, their supporters would be more likely to identify with Protestantism and the Orange institution, which supported the government suppression of the Irish Rebellion in 1798. In the 1920s, when the Orange order became more popular in Glasgow and some players even attended meetings, the club would then create an unwritten rule never to sign a Catholic player; a rule which would remain for decades.

New housing continued to be built in the Coatbridge area, but, even with the closure of some ironworks, the town was considered the most overcrowded place in Scotland by the early 20th century. This is where the family would stay for some generations until lured south to the industrial cities of Sheffield and Birmingham. When the younger James Cunningham passed away, he was buried back in Kirkliston alongside his beloved first daughter who had died in childhood. Elizabeth, however, stayed just outside Coatbridge with their son, Walker, who became an apprentice engineer and later an engine fitter in Glasgow. She lived until the grand age of 77, surrounded by many other members of the Cunningham clan who would eventually, for work and for war, be on the move again.

Chapter 3

Castles, coalmining, and digging up raw Scottish talent

Sanquhar and Glenbuck, Scotland (1770–1850s)

1600s		Robert McGhie and Janet Cunnon		
		Thomas McGhie and Janet Forrest		
	Robert and Isobel Russell	John McGhie and Janet Bell		
1700s	James Russell and Janet Reid	John McGhie and Agnes Lawcock		
	James Russell and Margaret Donaldson	James McGhie and Annabel Wilson	Donald McLeod and Helen Wilson	Robert Logan and Catharine Tudhope
	Robert Russell and Jean McGhie		Cornelius McLeod and Jean Logan	
1800s	Archibald Russell and Helen McLeod			

YOU MIGHT wonder what castles and coalmining have to do with the birth of sporting talent and its devoted communities. How did the windswept glens of the Scottish Lowlands produce such hardened and feisty footballers who would eventually dazzle the industrial cities down south?

The answer lies in its history of joining forces: to fight for freedom or to battle a whole day, literally through solid rock, for a few precious hours of leisure in return. Such determination was passed down through generations and prime examples of these communities lay south of Glasgow, on the border between Lanarkshire, Ayrshire, and the Dumfries and Galloway region.

When Robert Russell was born in 1770 in Sanquhar (pronounced sang-kuh), his father, James, and his mother, Margaret, had been married for just over two years and Robert was already their second son in that time.

Sanquhar is a small market town in the valley of the River Nith, which has been one of the main routes from central to southern Scotland during much of history. Sanquhar was well-known for its wool and weaving products. It was granted the status of a Royal Burgh in 1598 by King James VI that then encouraged trade in the area to flourish – so much so that the town gave its name to a popular style of pattern knitting which typically incorporated two different shades and geometric shapes. Until the end of the 18th century, the spinning of yarn was mostly done by women and the weaving done by men, although women were starting to take on this role. It could have been that Margaret supplemented the family income in this way, toddler Robert idly playing with balls of wool with his older brother, and baby Janet asleep in a basket by her feet.

The name Sanquhar – Seann Cathair in Scottish Gaelic – means 'old fort'. These days, aside from its castle ruins, a prime building of interest is its tiny post office. Established in 1712, it is believed to be the oldest working post office in the world, predating ones in Stockholm, Sweden (1720) and Santiago, Chile (1772). Another ancient building still standing is the Tolbooth, built in the 1730s by the 3rd Duke of Queensberry, and a site of tough criminal punishments. A large iron staple and ring still exists on the outer wall. This was known as the 'joggs' or 'jougs' to which criminals were attached by an iron collar. It held them captive on public display so that passing townsfolk could shout abuse or throw rotten eggs. It was last used in 1820 for a burglar who was so small – albeit ideal for breaking into houses – that he had to stand on a large stone for his neck ring to reach the wall fastening. He was locked there for two hours each day for three consecutive days, one of which was a market day, unfortunately for him.

Market days were a hive of activity with farmers and other tradespeople coming from all over to promote, exchange, and sell their goods. With plenty of trading activity on their doorstep, the local weavers enjoyed a relatively comfortable existence. They earned good wages and worked at their looms indoors, often at their homes. They could work whatever hours they wanted, and could take time off in the autumn to help farmers with their harvests. It is claimed that any time there was a noise in the streets the weavers would be the first ones to drop their work, run out, and begin gossiping about the matter.

One thing that could be said for the folk of Sanquhar is that they did not keep their opinions quiet. The 'Covenanters' were devoted to maintaining Presbyterianism as the only church organisation in Scotland. This dragged Scotland into England's civil wars between supporters of King Charles I and II and supporters of Cromwell and parliament in the 17th century, 100 years before the final Jacobite risings. Because Sanquhar was the only major town in the vast countryside, it was the ideal place for people to make their big political statements. The 'Sanquhar Declarations' were intended as the basis of religious freedom in Scotland. This was all well and good for those who wanted public attention. However, imagine being one of the many who were hunted down for their religious beliefs or rebellious acts against the king. Sanquhar's location along the river made it a useful navigation point for those who were trying to evade capture by soldiers across open territory. They would have hidden in safe houses and in the surrounding woodland. But when the town was also drawing attention to itself, one had to lie very low. The Rev. Richard Cameron, and his brother Michael, were killed after publicly calling for an end to the reign of Charles II.

Going back further, Sanquhar has a long history of rebellion. In the 13th century the Barons of Scotland were summoned by King Edward I to Scone, the ancient gathering place some 40 miles north of Edinburgh. This was

Mel Gibson in the 1995 film Braveheart, *based on the life of Sir William Wallace. Image: Moviestore Collection.*

in order to swear fealty (loyalty) to the Crown of England and sign the famous Ragman Roll. There were some that refused, including Sir William Wallace of Ellerslie and Sir William Douglas of Sanquhar. Douglas had never had a good relationship with the English, who imprisoned him and took his land on many occasions. He also fought with his own neighbours, abducting one girl, Eleanor, from another castle and marrying her. Douglas joined forces with William Wallace in rebellion, whose story was given Hollywood treatment – by which we might say majestic cinematography along with some historical inaccuracies – in Mel Gibson's 1995 film, *Braveheart*.

One action-packed event that could be the climax to many a good historic film is the time when Wallace helped his good friend Douglas to recover Sanquhar Castle, which was in the possession of the English. It was early in the morning, with the mist slowly rising from the surrounding fields. A simple but cunning plan had been devised and it was brave Thomas Dickson who had been chosen as the main playmaker. At that time of day, a few servants were starting their shift, and some early deliveries were commonplace. Apart from that, it was relatively quiet. Thomas tugged his hood a little further down over his face and tried to maintain a relaxed composure as his wooden cart rolled over the cobbles and up to the castle gates. Mercifully, they were open, but it was not the game plan to keep moving. Thomas brought the horse to a stop and it was then that suspicions were aroused.

'What business have you here, man?' asked the rough-faced, but tired, porter.

Thomas said nothing but whipped out his dirk (long dagger) and killed the porter where he stood. The gate wardens rushed to close the gates but it was impossible with the cart blocking the entrance. In dramatic solo fashion,

Thomas killed three gate wardens with an axe, leaving the coast clear for the waiting men to come through behind him. The castle was effectively retaken before the English defenders could rise from their beds. When 3,000 more English soldiers later arrived to lay siege to the castle, Thomas slipped out through a secret passage to alert William Wallace, who rescued the castle in full combat with his own troops. In a happy Hollywood-style ending, Thomas was later permitted to marry Douglas's daughter, Margaret. But, as history tells us, both Wallace and Douglas were to later die at the hands of the English, accused of treason.

Five hundred years after this event, when Robert was a growing boy, Sanquhar Castle was sadly already crumbling to ruin and life in the area was more about daily routine than epic battles. No doubt he went up there from time to time with the other village lads and recreated the old tales of rebellion.

The remains of Sanquhar Castle. Image: Phouka on Wikimedia (CC BY-SA 3.0).

Time passed, market days came and went, and Robert (my four times great-grandfather) married a local girl, Jean McGhie, on 19 March 1802 in Muirkirk. He was already

31 years old – no spring chicken as they say – but she was a bonny lass of 20.

The McGhie family are traditionally from Galloway, the coastal region in the south-west of Scotland. Similar to the Cunningham clan (that my Russell ancestor would eventually marry into), the McGhies tactically supported the king at all the right times in history. They thereby managed to acquire and keep their land and possessions during all the various periods of rebellion. However, a lack of male heirs meant that the estates were gradually sold off and the McGhies dispersed across the country and around the world.

The oldest surviving family picture of that line is of John McGhie and Agnes (nee Lawcock) who were the grandparents of Jean. They were married in Lesmahagow, which was a small village in an area popular with writers such as Sir Walter Scott and William Wordsworth. The portrait is very modest – nothing like the grand and colourful ones in larger houses – but they still had to have some disposable income to afford it. They are both wearing several layers of heavy clothing, no doubt as protection against the Lanarkshire weather. As a married lady, Agnes is wearing a 'mob cap', pleated around her face and decorated with a simple ribbon. With her large, dark eyes, she seems like a rather formidable woman. John seems like a gentle and thoughtful man, though he had clearly made a vain attempt to pull down a few strands to cover his receding hairline.

Muirkirk (Scottish Gaelic: Eaglais an t-Slèibh) means 'church of the moor'. It was another prominent stopping point on the road south from Glasgow, later to have rail connections supporting the iron and coal industries.

Muirkirk was also a place of poetry and folk music. As many people were illiterate, poems and songs were an important way of communicating local history, including sporting events and more rebellious acts. It was the home of

John and Agnes McGhie in around the year 1770 - the oldest surviving picture from our family album.

John Lapraik, a friend of – and also an early inspiration to – Robert Burns, the famous Scottish poet, who visited in 1785. This may be another of the ways in which my own family folklore connection to Burns has been fuelled. Burns was also a frequent visitor to Sanquhar, where Robert Russell had been born, as he was renovating a farm nearby and passed through on the way back to his wife in Ayrshire. He called Sanquhar 'Black Joan' in his ballad 'Five Carlins' in which local places are described as human characters.

The town was home to Isobel 'Tibbie' Pagan, who made a living by writing verses and singing. She was lame and used crutches but she had a sharp tongue and was a popular, unofficial landlady. She welcomed locals to her cottage, which acted as a 'howff', a meeting place where whisky and other drink was served. It is certainly possible that Robert Russell was a customer along with his pals and other local workers at the end of a long day. Although she never wed, Tibbie allegedly had a child by a man called Campbell who deserted her on the eve of their marriage.

51

As the daughter seems to have disappeared into the mists of time, this story might have been confused with that of her own father, as Tibbie was also supposedly illegitimate (born out of wedlock).

A map from the year 1804 showing Sanquhar and Muirkirk. Reproduced with the permission of the National Library of Scotland. These days, the M74 motorway follows the old road north from Douglas and Lesmahagow to Glasgow. Glenbuck Lock, where Robert and Jean moved to, is on the road going east between Muirkirk and Douglas.

Jean was clearly a strong and healthy woman herself, giving birth to 11 children at a steady rate of one every two years. By the time of their first child – James in 1804 – she and Robert were already living in Glenbuck (Scottish Gaelic: Gleann Buic), a small, remote village in the hills, three miles east of Muirkirk. It was here that the most famous and concentrated pool of Scottish footballing talent ever documented was born. But to understand how that could happen, one needs to know how the town grew, and suffered, and grew again.

A 'glen' is a valley. It is typically long and bounded by gently sloped concave sides, unlike a ravine, which is deep and bounded by steep slopes. The word strath is also used for a wider flat-bottomed valley formed from the flood plain of a river. A 'buck' is a male deer and as places or hills were sometimes named after the animals and flora found there, it can be assumed that deer is what the early settlers found, or kept with them in plentiful supply. So we have 'Glen-Buck', or 'valley where there are male deer' as the likely origin of the name.

Glenbuck is first known for its loch – not a natural one, but created in 1802 by James Finlay for his Catrine Lace Mill. This was not the first nor the last time that the Scottish landscape was radically altered in pursuit of industry and high profits. Elsewhere, the small island of Belnahua off the west coast was churned up with quarries 60ft deep and massive buildings and machines heaved on top. Next to beautiful Loch Maree in the Highlands, over 300 acres of trees were cut down to feed the hungry iron blast furnace. At Ravenscraig, to the east of Glasgow, the wasteland left behind by the steel works is big enough for 700 football pitches. Adding to this, the mass-scale sheep grazing and the deer herds for sport caused a big loss in forestry and a drastic change in the ecosystem across Scotland, which wider society is only just acknowledging today.

An illustration of Gartcloss Colliery around 1835, drawn by R. Findlater, shows the impact on the landscape. Image: North Lanarkshire Council/ CultureNL.

The loch at Glenbuck had been dense bog before its creation, meaning that the old road had always passed up on higher ground. 'Wee Darnhunch' was the old toll house for this earlier higher road and it was manned by none other than Robert Burns's maternal uncle, John Brown, in the 1790s. This again may have sparked Russell family pride in being associated with the famous poet. Glenbuck is mentioned in Burns's poem *The Brigs of Ayr* describing the River Ayr – 'Auld Ayr' – in winter flood threatening the New Brig:

> Aroused by blustering winds an' spotting thowes,
> In mony a torrent down the snaw-broo rowes;
> While crashing ice, borne on the rolling spate,
> Sweeps dams, an' mills, an' brigs, a' to the gate;
> And from Glenbuck, down to the Ratton-key,
> Auld Ayr is just one lengthen'd, tumbling sea-

Just these few lines give an insight into how harsh the conditions could be in the winter in rural Ayrshire and just how strong one had to be to thrive there.

Like other local towns and villages, weaving was a principal trade in the 18th century, before iron-making expanded. Unfortunately, the Glenbuck Iron Company hit early financial problems in the 1810s, which severely affected the village. Robert Russell had become a coalminer and so his income would have undoubtedly shrunk. Work in the village took some time to recover but it did so eventually by further exploiting the coal deposits.

In the 19th century the work was done mainly by hand. A 'hewer' cut the coal from the seam; a 'hurrier' moved carts of coal from the coal face to the shaft, sometimes with the use of ponies; and a 'trapper' (usually a conveniently small child) opened and closed trap doors to allow carts to pass through and to regulate ventilation. The hours were long and the conditions were dangerous. As mines expanded, the risk of accidents – flooding, falling roofs, and gas explosions – increased.

The mines dominated life in the towns, as described in *Griffiths' Guide to the iron trade of Great Britain* by Samuel Griffiths (1873):

'Under a constant cloud of black smoke, the vivifying rays of the sun being obscured here by the volumes of almost

An illustration of the entrance to a coalmine in the 19th century. It shows candles lighting the dim interior, a worker using a hand-held pick in the background, and a small child leading a pony back into the darkness to collect the next load. The image appeared in Griffiths' Guide to the iron trade of Great Britain *by Samuel Griffiths, published in 1873.*

material carbon floating in the atmosphere. On the one hand there is the destructive effect of the smoke on vegetation, on the other, of the injurious hydrochloric, sulphurous, and chlorine gas evolved from acid gases, numerous chemical works almost in the heart of this devoted township.

'Bright grates and fire-irons become rusty in a single night, and all household furniture, which is held together by appliances of iron, suffers much, and all other metals are damaged by these gases ... The workmen, on their return from work at the pits in the evening, show honourable traces of the useful labour they have performed, in the soiled garments and dirty faces they present. Vegetation succumbs altogether; scarcely a shrub, a tree, or a greenfield is to be seen, amid the general devastation of the surface, which presents itself for miles round.'

I would like to think of my family living in some comfort, even if they only had a modest house and a few belongings to be able to keep themselves happy and healthy. However, as a rural coalminer, it is likely that the Russell family home was sparse, just like their neighbours' and those of thousands of other families across the country. In the mid-19th century 71 per cent of Scottish homes had no more than two rooms. In Glasgow and Edinburgh, families of five or more lived in single-room homes. Around 8,000 families had homes with no windows. In Dundee, there were only five toilets for over 90,000 inhabitants and three of those were in hotels.

Coalminers' houses were sometimes found to be in a terrible state, as a 1842 report on the East of Scotland District to the Children's Employment Commission revealed:

'The hut itself is a wretched hovel, perhaps ten to twelve feet square, in which a family of from six to ten individuals are huddled together; two bedsteads ... a few stools ... and some damaged crockery ... fowls, occasionally a pig or a jackass, dogs, and whatever animals it may chance that they

Glenbuck village. Image: Jimmy Taylor/www.ayrshirehistory.com.

possess, share the room with the family; and the only objects of comfort which present themselves are the pot, and the fire over which it invariably hangs.

'All drainage and the filth ... of each cottage is accumulated before the door ... One of the witnesses informs us that his father said "that dung and filth paid for the whiskey", and I believe the purchase of whiskey is usual destination of the profit of the [dung].

'There exists a general want of cleanliness in the habits of the colliers, with exceptions of course; though I believe it is usual for them to wash their faces on in the day after labour, and sometimes the children follow the same example ... As might be expected, these hovels are infested with vermin, as are the persons of the children ... [The] storing of coals under the bed ... encourages domestic animals to resort there for their natural needs [and] this aggravates the impurity of the air.'

Aside from the ups and downs of its coal and iron industries, the village is most well-known for football and the two things are closely related. It was the birthplace in 1913 of the legendary Bill Shankly, who played football for Preston North End and Scotland before going on to manage

Liverpool. Shankly's four older brothers played for Glenbuck Cherrypickers, the local team, which was a bizarrely successful club and produced more than 50 professional footballers in its relatively short existence.

Bill Shankly (1913–1981). Image: PA Images.

Village societies and activities were a key part of Scottish rural life before the formalising of association football. The club was founded in the late 1870s by Edward and William Bone, among others. They originally called it Glenbuck Athletic and played in white jerseys and black trousers. There was no local football league at the time, but they frequently entered a team into cup competitions. Other fixtures were created by advertising in local papers. The players had to provide their own equipment and cover their own expenses, including a shilling a week towards the upkeep of the ground. The club archives provide further details:

'For away matches they travelled usually in a three-horse brake [wagon pulled by three horses]. On the cold dark nights of winter, the homeward journey was far from comfortable, and the players would often walk a good deal of the distance to ease their cramped limbs ... It was largely a family affair ... Sons succeeded their fathers, nephews their uncles, cousins and brothers played in the same team ... The Glenbuck team, with few exceptions, remained a team of Glenbuck lads, upholding the Glenbuck tradition.'[5]

It is believed that the club changed their name to the Cherrypickers because some of their men fought with the 11th Hussars in the Boer War and the regiment had this as their nickname. That story goes that the regiment was attacked while raiding an orchard of cherry trees at San Martin de Trebejo in Spain, during the earlier Peninsular War, and that they were recognisable by their cherry-red trousers after that. Another association of the term 'cherry-picking' is the process of sorting coal on a conveyor belt, which was also a common task for these mining men.

Players of the Glenbuck 'Cherrypickers'. Image by permission of East Ayrshire Council/East Ayrshire Leisure.

Of the numerous professional players who emerged, Alec Tait and Alec Buck went on to play for Tottenham Hotspur, winning the FA Cup Final with them in 1901. Apparently, on that day, the crowd was 114,815, the third-largest football

---

5   From *The Cherrypickers* by the Rev. M.H. Faulds and W.M. Tweedie junior, first published in 1951.

attendance in English history. Later in the year, the cup was brought to Glenbuck and exhibited in one of the shop windows. This would not have been the original trophy, made of gold, which was stolen in 1895 from a Birmingham shop window while in the temporary possession of Aston Villa. Fortunately the inhabitants of Glenbuck village were trusted with this new one for a brief outing. Other Cherrypickers also took their football boots south of the border, including Jock Bone, who played for Aston Villa, and John Crosbie who was with Birmingham City.

Sadly, with the decline of the mining industry and Great Depression in the early 20th century, the football club also started to struggle, with many leaving the village for other opportunities. It folded after the 1931 season. However, it was mining that had been at the root of its existence and success. One former player, Tom Hazle, explained to *The Scotsman* on 20 October 2015, 'Mining was the thing that made the football players in Glenbuck … It was the pit. We were desperate to get out of it.'

The Glenbuck Cherrypickers memorial and list of player names which stands at the edge of the now deserted village. Image: @Glenbuckls (Twitter).

Some decades before the birth of this football hotbed, and with the fashioning of Mr Finlay's new loch, the valley downstream had dried out enough to create a new road and, later, a railway line. Business-minded people will recognise that transport equals easier trade. Sports-minded people will be grateful for more accessible away fixtures.

Turnpike trusts were bodies set up by individual Acts of Parliament, with powers to collect road tolls for maintaining the principal roads in Britain from the 17th century. Many tollhouses were built by turnpike trusts in Scotland, as well as England and Wales, during the 18th and early 19th centuries. These tollhouses provided accommodation for a toll collector and were typically modest single-storey stone dwellings with a slate roof. While these people and places served to generate income to maintain and develop road routes for horse-drawn transport, they also acted as resting places for those on such long and arduous journeys. In Glenbuck, a cottage next to the loch became the new toll house and it was the Russell family who proudly moved in. The 1851 census also records that Robert's profession

A photograph of the lochside cottage in the 1970s, believed to be the new tollhouse where the Russells lived. Image: David Chatterton (CC SA-BY 2.0).

had officially changed from coalminer to 'Tollkeeper and Innkeeper'.

By this time, one of their youngest sons, Archibald (my three-times great-grandfather), had continued in the family trade of coalmining but had moved to live alongside many other mining families nearer to Muirkirk. Not to be outdone by neighbouring Glenbuck, the town would later boast at least two football teams, as well as bowling, curling, and quoiting clubs at the start of the next century. It would also produce Jimmy Weir, who played for Ayr United, Celtic, and Middlesbrough. He is reported to have been a very vocal team-mate: shouting loudly as he went in for crunching tackles while also being something of a Burns songs specialist off the pitch.

Also living with Archibald was his wife, Helen, and their two young children, as well as his older brother, William, a coal pit contractor.

Helen was a McLeod by birth and anyone who knew the tales of her (MacLeod) Highland clan would probably do anything to stay on the right side of her. Previous clan chiefs were called Alexander the Humpbacked (who had been mutilated by a battle axe), John the Speckled, and Norman the Wicked (who attacked his own clansmen for fighting on the other side of the Jacobite Rising). With their Norse blood, they were known for their violence. In one incident, in 1577, the MacLeods raided the island of Eigg and all of the terrified inhabitants, who were part of the MacDonald clan, hid in a cave. The MacLeods allegedly blocked the entrance with heather bushes and set light to them, killing hundreds of the people trapped inside. The next year, some of the surviving MacDonalds sailed to an island inhabited by the MacLeods, trapped them in their church and burned that to the ground. This might have settled the matter but the MacDonalds could not sail away as their boats were grounded in the low tide. The MacLeods who had not been at church ran down to the shore and murdered all of the MacDonalds in retaliation.

Helen had been a local girl. Her father was a coal cutter in Glenbuck, as were her brothers from the age of about 14. It was her grandparents and great-grandparents that had migrated down from different areas of the Highlands in the time known as the 'Clearances' when tenant farmers were being forcibly evicted, having their homes destroyed to make way for extensive sheep farming. Later, Archibald and Helen migrated back north to Cambusnethen, Lanarkshire, to where Helen's brothers were already working as coalminers in a booming industry. This rolling migration – of going where the work was – would also support the eventual spread of sporting talent to the cities.

Back in Glenbuck in the mid-1800s, all of Robert and Jean's other ten offspring had either left the family home

Alexander and Margaret Russell, around 1850. Alexander's son was influential in the Scottish oil-shale mining industry. His grandson then took the family skills abroad, emigrating with his whole family to Australia in 1879 to manage a mine. Image: Barbara Day.

or passed away, with the exception of one son. There is no photograph of Robert and Jean to see what they looked like, although there is one of Robert's brother and his wife Margaret, who were not far away in Muirkirk and continuing the family trade of mining.

Robert and Jean remained in the village, quietly – or perhaps not so quietly – enjoying the endless company of passing travellers or working locals. Robert was too old for heavy work and with his large family dispersed he might have enjoyed the profitable and sociable work of toll collecting. But even the roads were giving way to new invention. Having perhaps purposefully chosen a small and quiet place to live, Robert and Jean's little world was about to be upturned by another new industry boom and bigger steam trains ploughing through the village in their later years. And Scottish footballing talent would be dug up from the ground and shaped by rough labour before being scattered far and wide, just like its coal, to other places that demanded it.

A steam train running through Glenbuck. Image: Nally Murray/www.ayrshirehistory.com.

Chapter 4

Civil war, aspiration, and royal approval for Birmingham's jewellers

Aston and Birmingham (1600–1900)

1700s	William Swann and Sarah Millard		
	Thomas Swann and Elizabeth Gains		
1800s	James Swann and Mary Ann Spencer		Thomas Cox and Ann Caldicott
	Priscilla Swann	**Samuel Swann And Elizabeth Cox**	William Cox

BEFORE SPORTS clubs could exist, and before parishes and local communities could arrange to do friendly battle against each other in fixtures, society needed to organise itself into such places as towns and villages, and into trades. Inhabitants were bound together by living in close proximity but also by the work they did, often in support of the more powerful and wealthy landowner. Without necessarily being neighbours, the notion of 'societies', and what we understand as groups of people coming together with similar interests or a set of beliefs, has a long history. In ancient Greece and Rome there were groupings of people wanting to establish trade links or worship particular gods together. There were groups of people debating ideas. There were also 'burial societies' of which one could become a member to ensure a proper send-off for oneself.

Birmingham and the surrounding areas in the middle of England were similar in some ways to the Lowlands of Scotland. There were clans and castles. There was a need to make careful choices about swearing allegiance to the king (or queen) that would have unforeseen consequences for the survival of trade and sport. There was also rebellion – and punishment. The rise in popularity of football is thanks to the Church and to the existence of other sports, notably cricket. Football gifted a physical pastime to those who worked together or had similar social or spiritual ideals. The migration of individuals from the north also played its own special part.

To understand how society developed in the Midlands area of England, we need to take another leap further back in time to the *Domesday Book* of 1086. This was a survey, ordered by King William I (William the Conqueror), of every shire in England. In it one can find references to the small manors of Birmingham (Berminghame), Handsworth, Northfield, Yardley and Aston. The name Birmingham comes from the Old English Beormingahām, meaning the home or settlement of the Beormingas. This was a tribe or clan whose name literally means 'Beorma's people' and which is thought to be an early way of describing a community under Anglo-Saxon administration. Beorma could have been its leader at the time of the Anglo-Saxon settlement, a shared ancestor, or a mythical tribal figurehead. Place names ending in -ingahām are typical of main settlements that were established during the early Anglo-Saxon colonisation. This suggests that Birmingham was probably in existence by the early seventh century.

Surrounding settlements that developed later (when the population grew) had names ending in:

-tūn or 'ton'	farm
-lēah or 'leigh'	woodland clearing
-worð	enclosure
-field	open ground

While Fosse Way, the Roman road, is well known in Warwickshire and bypasses Birmingham, another of the Roman roads of ancient England ran from the Fosse Way at Bourton-on-the-Water in Gloucestershire, right through Birmingham, to Templeborough in South Yorkshire. In fact, a Roman pottery kiln was discovered in the garden of a resident in Wellington Road, next to the entrance for horses and traps to Aston Villa's first football ground in Perry Barr. Aston was first mentioned in the *Domesday Book* in 1086 as 'Estone', presumably because it was to the east of Birmingham. At the time, it boasted 30 villagers, a priest, a slave and 12 smallholders. This does not sound like a lot, but in fact it was bigger than Birmingham was at the time. However, by the mid-14th century it had become known as Aston-juxta-Birmingham (Aston beside Birmingham), forging a long-lasting link.

It was at this time that the Holte family began accumulating land. Sir Thomas Holte was an agent of Thomas Cromwell, the chief minister to King Henry VIII. Holte profited greatly from the Reformation (the dismantling of churches) although Cromwell lost his life and all property. A century later, in 1634, his grandson – also Sir Thomas Holte – completed the building of an impressive manor house as a grand symbol of his wealth and status. Fans of Aston Villa today will instantly recognise the name from their iconic stand of die-hard supporters – the Holte End – and the chant 'Holte Enders in the sky' taken from a rather aggressive song, in part directed towards rival Birmingham supporters. Turn back a few centuries and they would perhaps think twice about singing that name in the streets.

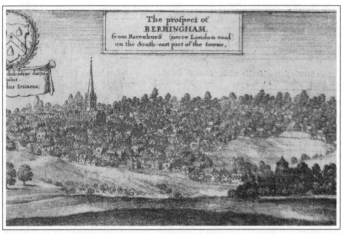

An engraving of Birmingham by Wenceslaus Hollar, published in 1656. Today the artist would be surrounded by cars on the busy ring road, near the Camp Hill roundabout. Image part of the University of Toronto Wenceslaus Hollar Collection.

Even though the folk of Coventry and Birmingham would later seek upper-class and royal approval for their gold and silver trade, in the 1600s they were not necessarily fans of King Charles I. This set them apart from the citizens living closer to London, who were more likely to be royalists. Birmingham's weaponry experts refused to make swords for the royalists but did make 15,000 of them for the supporters of parliament. The town's dislike of the monarchy was possibly fuelled by the fact that King Charles had not spared Warwickshire from paying shipbuilding tax during a period of recession. A quick glance at a map of Britain and you will see that Birmingham is a very long way from the coast in all directions, compared to other major towns and cities. Shipbuilding would have been the last thing on their minds and it is hardly surprising that they were angry.

Choosing to make a public show of royal support, and completely defying local opinion, Sir Thomas Holte invited King Charles to dine at his new Aston Hall in October 1642. The king travelled with not only aides and servants but also numerous soldiers. Once they had safely delivered the royal guests to the hall, the soldiers would have begun to smile among themselves and check how many coins they had between them in their leather pouches. Rather like away fans at an evening kick-off, the troops hurried into Aston to avail themselves of local hospitality, singing and jostling among themselves. The local innkeepers would have watched nervously from their doors at the approaching group. They would be glad of the extra income, but knew that they would be spending the night putting up with rowdy, drunken soldiers of a king that no one particularly liked.

If Aston managed to put on a good show for the visitors, their neighbours were not going to be such good hosts. When the king and his troops entered Birmingham, the rebellious locals took the opportunity to loot the royal luggage for any wealth in the form of plate and coins, claiming it for the opposition cause – the Parliamentarians.

A portrait of Sir Thomas Holte (1571–1654) in front of Aston Hall. Image: Birmingham Museums Trust. His sophisticated gloves are a deliberate artistic mark of wealth and fashion. Removing one allows the painter to show the equally elaborate lace cuffs and his elegant and 'pure' hand.

They ran off with it and stashed it at the garrison (military base) in the town of Warwick. This act of treason was not forgotten and the next year, the king's nephew, Prince Rupert, returned to Birmingham with 2,000 men and seeking revenge. A Parliamentarian pamphlet from April 1643 describes the events:

'They ran into every house cursing and damning, threatening and terrifying the poore Women most terribly, setting naked Swords and Pistols to their breasts, they fell to plundering all the Town before them, as well Malignants as others, picking purses and pockets, searching in holes and corners, Tiles of houses, Wells, Pooles, Vaults, Gardens and any other place they could suspect for money or goods, forcing people to deliver all the money they had ... The soldiers told the inhabitants that Prince Rupert had dealt mercifully with them, but when they came back with the Queen's army they would leave neither man, woman, nor child alive.'

It could be that this pamphlet had a hint of 17th-century social media 'fake news', making the raid sound more violent than it actually was, in order to incite further hatred of the Crown. Even if the author had exaggerated the events, it seemed to do the trick. The king was now the enemy and Aston Hall was a target.

Birmingham trade suffered in these Civil War years and Warwickshire villagers suffered equally by having to pay taxes to both sides of the conflict. At the end of 1643, over 1,000 Parliamentary troops (Roundheads) attacked Aston Hall as part of Civil War fighting and Sir Thomas Holte had to call for help from the local Royalist (Cavaliers) garrison at Dudley Castle. My ancestors, the Swann family, may have sided with those in Warwickshire hoping to bring down Holte and his fancy Aston Hall. However, if Thomas had not succeeded in defending his estate, there might have been nothing left to support the leisure time and sport of the local community in centuries to come.

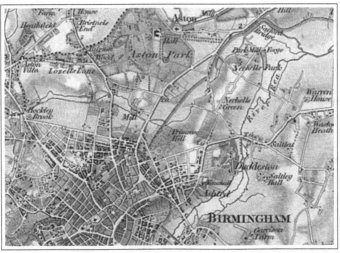

A map of Birmingham in 1834 showing the vast Aston Park to the north. My ancestors were living near to Hockley Brook, on the north-west side of town, and close to the original 'Aston Villa' (both marked). Image: Great Britain Historical GIS/University of Portsmouth (CC BY-SA 4.0).

My great-great-grandfather, Samuel Swann, was born in 1843 and lived in the parish of Aston, north-east of Birmingham, for most of his life. His father and grandfather were both born and lived in Atherstone, some 17 miles (six hours' walk) further east. Atherstone had been the main hat supplier to slave owners in America who, by law, had to provide their slaves with sun protection in the cotton fields. This profitable industry was then promptly ended by the 1843 slave emancipation and those specialist workers in Warwickshire had to seek new trades, adding to the massive influx into the cities in the 19th century.

Atherstone is famous for its traditional Shrove Tuesday Ball Game – another prime example of a mass village sporting event (see Chapter 2) – and it is highly likely that James and Thomas Swann (Samuel's father and grandfather) were enthusiastic participants in their day. It has been held each year since the 12th century and it takes place along the old Roman Road, involving hundreds of local players. The ball is much larger and heavier than an ordinary football, meaning that it cannot be kicked far, but it can be passed, grabbed, and ripped by hand. There are no goals and only a few rules. The game starts at 3pm when the ball is dropped from the window of the bank and finishes at 5pm. Rules state that no one is allowed to be killed but the ball can be deflated or hidden after 4.30pm. The person holding the ball at the end is the winner and can keep the ball.

Participants crush together in an attempt to win the Atherstone ball. Image: PA Images.

Just after he was born, Samuel's family were living in Great King Street in what is known as the Jewellery Quarter. His father was a silversmith and his eldest brother was a goldsmith, and so it was the ideal place for the family to be. Given that many men worked individually or in family partnerships, living in the same place meant easier access to resources; a sharing of the latest techniques; a discussion of any prevailing issues; and the possibility to attract customers away from their regular contacts.

Like many Birmingham trades at the time, the business of creating objects out of silver was located in thousands of individual homes and workshops, not just a few factories. The list of possible items was endless: shoe buckles, nutmeg graters, baby rattles, snuff boxes, as well as heaps of buttons and cutlery. The Birmingham Assay Office weighed and stamped the goods together with some form of the initial(s) of the maker. The hallmark symbol for Birmingham jewellery is an anchor, which might seem a strange choice for an inland city. However, the story goes that, in the 1770s, Birmingham and Sheffield had asked for their own Assay Office to avoid taking all of their goods on the long trek to Chester to be weighed and verified. The man in charge of the decision, Matthew Boulton, happened to be staying at the Crown and Anchor pub in London. He flipped a coin to decide their new symbol based on the name of the pub. Sheffield took a crown and Birmingham took an anchor.

Examples of Birmingham silverware and markings. Image: Birmingham Assay Office.

The working conditions for goldsmiths were the same, but this trade – in particular for jewellery – was suffering from a lack of interest. The fashionable and wealthy preferred to obtain theirs from France or Germany. Birmingham's jewellers knew that they needed to have someone with influence to endorse their products. They aimed high. In 1818 Aston Hall had been sold by the Holte family to James Watt junior, a 'nouveau riche' of the steam industry, and was visited by the future Queen Victoria in 1830. Ten years later, would she still remember it fondly and could she be convinced to admire the handiwork of the local Brummies?

So it was that, in the 1840s, skilled Birmingham workers got together and produced a collection of jewellery for Queen Victoria, which was displayed at the Town Hall. It was actually Prince Albert who inspected the collection and declared that the people of England need not always go abroad for such things when there are fine examples at home – and that the queen was sure to agree. With this unofficial royal seal of approval, Birmingham wasted no time in declaring it. Trade could expand, boosted also by the discovery of gold in Australia and California, known as the 'Gold Rush'. In 1854, legislation also added nine-, 12-, and 15-carat standards to the existing 18-carat and 22-carat standards. Gold jewellery could become cheaper and, therefore, more people could buy it and sell it.

The 1851 census records Samuel as attending school aged eight years old. Whether he actually went to school is another matter. Nearly 20,000 boys and girls were estimated to be working, with over 1,000 of these being eight to ten years old. The superintendent of the Baptist Sunday School in Samuel's road noted that most children were those of artisan (skilled worker, usually by hand) parents but that many did not send their children because of a lack of appropriate clothing. If he was not working for his father or running errands for his mother, Samuel might have escaped to play chase or another game in the streets. But missing his duties for too long would have earned him a clip round the ear, which he could accept with a cheeky grin if the street game had been worth it.

Children at work in a metalworking factory in 1910. Image: Rijksmuseum/ Europeana.

By the time Samuel was 18, in 1861, the family had literally moved up (north) in the world, but only less than a mile up the road, to Wheeler Street, just inside the parish of Aston. Samuel had found work in electroplating, which used the power of electricity to deposit metal on the surface of various types of objects. Elkington, Mason and Company was the big factory doing so at the time. Although already discovered long before, in the 1800s, it still must have felt technologically advanced compared to his family and contemporaries using more traditional tools in their home workshops. The firm used a new electroplating process developed by a local surgeon and, among many other items, supplied sports club, with medals and trophies.

The working class had little time for recreation, enduring long hours and only Sunday as the official day off if they

Elkington and Co. used electroplating for their silver-plated sports trophies and many other items. Image: Amoret Tanner Collection.

were employed. And, as always, there would have been other odd jobs to do and the family to look after. In the mid-19th century, Aston Hall and Park Company had taken over the estate from a completely private residence. They turned the grounds into something of a popular regional amusement park. Proud of his new job and wages, Samuel could have treated the family to a visit, and they would have been able to wander along the paths in their Sunday best clothes, marvelling at the music, circus acts, aquarium, and skating. These attractions faded over the decades and, by the 1870s, the hall itself had passed over to Birmingham Town Council to act as a museum and art gallery, while the Lower Grounds went their separate cultural way to continue to offer skating, cycling and, of course, football.

Football was not the only sport on display in Aston Lower Grounds: cricket was played, including by W.G. Grace (believed to be the greatest player of the 19th century), and even lacrosse was reportedly played by Iroquois tribes.

Aston Park being enjoyed by visitors. Smoke is visible from the factories in the distance. Sketch appears in Carl Chinn, Free to All: Aston Hall and Park – People Power in Victorian Birmingham, *published by West Midlands History.*

Cricket was the main organised sport of the time. Enville in the neighbouring county of Staffordshire claims to be the oldest Midlands club, dating from 1821, with Walsall, West Bromwich, and Wolverhampton all officially following in the 1830s. Knowing that cricket clubs were instrumental in supporting the emergence of football clubs, it is worth acknowledging their own history. Thomas Lord's famous cricket ground in the capital has been on the same site since 1814. But whatever London had, Birmingham wanted to prove it had too. In the early 19th century the Calthorpe Estate believed that Birmingham could become the new home of cricket because of its many railway links and large population. Construction began and became the now world-famous Edgbaston.

Nineteenth-century society – its politicians, church preachers, and poets – adored cricket. To them, it embodied the Christian moral values of endeavour and good sportsmanship. They thought that it promoted a sense of supreme British cultural product, not muddled with any other foreign influences, as far as the authorities knew or wanted to believe. It was celebrated as a spiritual ritual as much as an athletic pastime.[6] But for all the upper-class snobbery and 'gentlemanly' airs, people of all classes played, and village rivalry often forgot the moral code of proper behaviour.

Knowing also that modern football would owe so much to Scotland, it is worth pointing out that cricket was not exclusively an English affair. Completely removed from the romantic image of a quaint little village green, try picturing cricket in Glasgow in 1829. The first club was called Western and their rule book even included a section on making bets on the runs of other players.[7] They were playing on Glasgow's Green more than 40 years before the founders of Rangers would watch a football match being played there and decide to set up their own club. Like the Scottish poem about a village football match (see Chapter 2), there is also a poem about a cricket match featuring Western. *The Pump* was written by Andrew Jackson Macgeorge in 1835 and tells us how a mention in the local paper draws a crowd from all sections of society:

> The Chronicle had puffed the match, and from
> the town did pour
> A motley mob of all degrees, – squire,
> commoner, and whore;
> There was a swatch of all mankind, from saint
> down to sinner,
> Curdownie, – Clelland LL.D. – Stoddart – and
> Mr Jenner.

---

6   See Keith A. P. Sandiford (1983), 'Cricket and the Victorian Society', *Journal of Social History*, Vol. 17, No. 2 (Winter, 1983), pp. 303-317 (15 pages), Oxford University Press.

7   See Robert MacLean (2017), 'When cricket reigned supreme in Glasgow', University of Glasgow Library Blog, 20 March 2017.

It refers to aggressive behaviour by the 'Keelies' – a name for the more disreputable inhabitants of Glasgow. The poet then enjoys describing how one star player is late and causes some stress to his fellow team-mates – something that many amateur teams can relate to:

> Why do the players idly stand, their hands
> within their pockets?
> Why do their strained eye-balls gleam, like
> candles or sky-rockets?
> A master-spirit is not there – Bob Maxwell is
> not there;
> Tis that make Currie bit his nails, and Taylor
> tear his hair.

Reports printed in Scottish journals describe the cricketers as 'burly', well-built fellows who put a lot of physical effort into the game. The Glasgow players seemed to make up for their lack of skill with pure Scottish muscle. This was in contrast to the University of Glasgow cricket club which consisted of slim-built but proficient English students in the early years of the 1830s. It would take until 2018 for Scotland to beat England for the first time.

As for the spectators, a sketch by the same club member who composed the poem captures various heated discussions and an injured player in the background, together with fighting youths and an opportunistic pickpocket.

Back down south, the tiny form of Elizabeth Cox was taking her first steps in the world. Elizabeth was the youngest of six children born to Thomas Cox, a pan-maker, and his wife, Ann. Elizabeth grew up in the red-brick dwellings of Stourbridge, which was historically part of Worcestershire (11 miles directly west) and known for its glass-making. By the time she was 14 the family had moved to the centre of

'A motley group of all degrees' gather to watch cricket on Glasgow Green. Pen-and-ink sketch by Andrew Macgeorge, c.1835. Image: University of Glasgow Archives and Special Collections, Mu24-y.23.

Birmingham. Although the railways were fast-developing, it is more likely that they persuaded a neighbour who owned a horse and cart to load up their modest belongings and make their way slowly into the town.

Elizabeth had no trade initially, nor was she at school. She was simply listed in the census as 'unmarried', unlike the paid work that gave her older brothers some identity, or that of Henry the lodger who was also twice her age. There was another girl next door but she was the house servant and would have had little time for play or conversation. Elizabeth had to bide her time and help her mother to keep house as her 21st birthday came and went.

Finally, on Christmas Day, 1869, Elizabeth married Samuel Swann in the Parish Church of Edgbaston, witnessed by Elizabeth's eldest brother. On the very same day in the same church, Samuel's sister Priscilla married William Cox (Elizabeth's brother), witnessed by John Swann (Samuel's brother). Elizabeth's other two brothers – Joseph and Thomas – were both working in electroplating and so perhaps they had fun playing matchmaker with their colleague Samuel and capturing his rather pretty sister at the same time.

There were also another four weddings that happy day in 1869. During the 18th and 19th centuries, getting married on Christmas Day was popular up and down the country. This might seem like a romantic idea but it was also wholly practical. Christmas Day was the only day that most working-class people were guaranteed to have off and was sometimes offered at a cheaper price for a quick service, particularly in industrial cities. Bank Holidays were not introduced until 1871. The Swanns and Coxes seem to have got two for the price of one and on the only day they could all make it to celebrate properly. This was also before football fixture lists had to be consulted in advance of wedding planning – although it is a proud point that my parents still managed to watch a match at Villa Park on the afternoon of their ceremony.

Weddings could also be arranged quickly in order to make sure that the first child was born with the parents being married. This seems the case with Samuel and Elizabeth's first daughter, Marion, affectionately known as Minnie (or Aunt Minnie to my grandfather). She was born in Sheffield, another major industrial centre, just a few months after the wedding. When they returned to Birmingham, they shared the home of Elizabeth's father, now widowed, also with William Cox and Priscilla living there, plus baby Fred. This was Cherry Street, a small road that was part of the crowded working-class housing in the very heart of industrial Birmingham.

The spaces inside these houses were multi-functioning: the same room could be used for work (such as making jewellery), cooking, washing, eating and sleeping. Children, sometimes six or seven at a time, were piled together in one bed. To the outside eye of a health inspector this may have been shocking; to the residents it was a normal and sociable part of family life. Most of the parents' wages would be spent on food, rent, coal for the fire and sundries such as soap, candles, matches, clothing and tobacco. A typical diet was bread and dripping with potatoes and onions along with a small piece of meat or offal if and when they could afford it.

Concern for the state of these dwellings was printed in the local press:

'The air is heavy with a sooty smoke and with acid vapours, and here it is that the poor live – and wither away and die. How do they live? Look at the houses, the alleys, the courts, the ill-lit, ill-paved, walled-in squares, with last night's rain still trickling down from the roofs and making pools in the ill-sluiced yards. Look at the begrimed windows, the broken glass, the apertures stopped with yellow paper or filthy rags; glance in at the rooms where large families eat and sleep every day and every night, amid rags and vermin, within dank and mildewed walls from which the blistered paper is drooping, or the bit of discoloration called "paint" is peeling away. Here you can veritably taste the pestilential air, stagnant and mephitic, which finds no outlet in the prison-like houses of the courts; and yet here, where there is breathing space for so few, the many are herded together, and overcrowding is the rule, not the exception. The poor have nowhere else to go.'[8]

Birmingham was expanding year on year. It had a reputation to uphold and aspired to be more like its European counterparts. The house in Cherry Street no longer exists although the road does. The poorer housing was cleared at the end of the 1870s to make way for what was promoted

---

8   From J. Cuming Walters, 'Scenes in Slumland' (article series), *Birmingham Daily Gazette*, 1901.

as a 'Parisian-style boulevard', which is now Corporation Street. The Swanns' home in the slums was replaced by a new and impressive four-storey building in the 'arts and crafts' style. Architects working in this style included simple and natural decorative pieces to commercial and residential property, proving that even industrial buildings could be attractive. It was another way to celebrate the craftsmanship of the city and many of the movement's artists were socialists, promoting rights for workers. The building sitting directly where the Swanns lived contained the prestigious Graves Art Gallery where the Birmingham Art Circle was founded. This feels like a fitting legacy considering the skilled but humble goldsmith who once lived there.

Samuel and his family needed to get out in any case. Even in the sprawling town centre, the winters could be cold and the factory smoke lingered with the damp air. His growing family – four more children in the next ten years – needed more space than the one room in his father-in-law's old house. Evenings by candlelight brought whispered conversations with his wife. The Coxes had been generous

The fashionable Corporation Street in 1890 as it would become after the slum houses were demolished. Image: Copyright The Francis Frith Collection

hosts but the Swann family had to make their own way. So where would they go next? Start again in another metal-working town? Or return to Aston where the land was marked for new development and where there would be at least some familiar faces and green spaces? They chose the latter.

It was during one of those cold and dark winters, in early 1874, that young members of the Wesleyan chapel at Villa Cross were in need of a pastime until the summer brought around a new cricket season. There had been a Georgian country house in the area known as Aston Villa, although this had disappeared by then. The nearby chapel took its name from the house and it was the adult Sunday school that set up an amateur football team.

Some of the men – Jack Hughes, Frederick Matthews, Walter Price, William Scattergood – had discussed it at length under the yellow gas lamp in the road. None of them had much time off work, and certainly not in the sparse winter daylight. The fast and intense game of association football was ideal. They had already spotted a game being played in the meadow by Heathfield Road.

'What about trying our luck against the lads from Stafford Road Works Club?'

'What about Wednesbury Old Athletic?'

'Too far to go after our shifts. Anyone local?'

The discussion continued. Birmingham Clerks FC (later Calthorpe FC) had been started by two Scots – J. Campbell Orr and John Carson – but they and the other teams were considered a bit too strong as first opposition for the chapel team. If the Aston boys got completely hammered, who would bother turning up next time? Nods of agreement went around the circle. And so it was decided that the men from Villa Cross would play their first match against Aston Brook St Mary's rugby team where the first half was played under rugby rules and the second under association 'Sheffield' rules (see Chapter 10). The score at half-time was 0-0. In the second half, Jack scored the winner. More importantly, the 15 chapel players were hungry for more.

The next winter, the new Aston Villa Football Club found more opposition and played both at Aston Hall and in the Lower Grounds Meadow.

Then, in the winter of 1876, it was Villa's turn to receive a Scottish import – George B. Ramsay – with his sparkling ball control that was born and bred in Glasgow. George had just got a job as a clerk and was eager to carry on his favourite pastime in this new town. His work done for the day, he made his way to the patch of land where he had heard there was a practice game. Heavy leather boots swinging from their laces, he approached the group. 'From Scotland?' they asked. 'Sure, you can give it a go.'

The Aston Villa Wesleyan Chapel, whose cricket players formed a football team as a winter activity. Image by permission of the Library of Birmingham WK-A7-18.

The Aston boys were completely outplayed by Ramsay's dribbling style. However bruised their egos were, by the end of the practice game it was clear: this guy had to be on their team before any of the other Birmingham clubs found out. With several slaps on the back and pumping handshakes, Ramsay was immediately signed up and even elected captain. It was also Ramsay who would discover some grazing land by

Wellington Road and managed to rent it from the butcher who owned it for £5 per year. There they would stay for the next 21 years, changing their kit in a blacksmith's shed opposite and using the Old Crown and Cushion coaching house as their headquarters. This itself seems an odd choice of name for a Birmingham pub given their anti-royal past and the fact that Oliver Cromwell had the ancient crown and all other monarchy items melted down after the Civil War. But this was no time to dwell on ancient troubles. The Scottish and the English were brothers now. Pints were finished and weary legs carried the players home with happy hearts.

The early Scottish influence continued at Aston Villa when another impressive player, Archie Hunter, came to Birmingham from Ayr in 1878. Initially he wanted to train with Calthorpe but he could not find their ground. Luckily, a colleague told him about Ramsay's Villa and he joined them instead. Later, in 1890, James Cowan would arrive from Third Lanark (one of the original Scottish league clubs) and Ramsay also persuaded him to sign.

Team photograph of Aston Villa during the 1879/80 season. With permission of Aston Villa Football Club.

By the 1880s, the Swann family had returned to Wheeler Street in Aston, this time in a 'back-to-back' court dwelling and now including five young children. Wheeler Street was in an area of new development and attempted to provide individual working-class houses with parlours and several bedrooms, although some smaller housing remained which was all that Samuel and Elizabeth could afford. Many of their neighbours were jewellers and goldsmiths and so it made good business sense to rent a smaller set of rooms in order to live among the right people.

The newer houses – with the luxury of one per family – in Birmingham and the surrounding areas improved living conditions following the Public Health Act of 1875. Downstairs there was a kitchen and a front parlour, and upstairs two bedrooms, known as 'two up, two down'. A privy (small shed with a toilet) was in the back yard. There was mains water but heating was still from fires and a brick heated in the oven could be used to warm the beds at night. 'It will still be a few years before we can afford to live in something like this,' the Swanns thought as they walked past, 'but we will.'

Illustration of a typical layout of back-to-back housing. Each dwelling had a single room on the ground floor and one or two bedrooms above, accessed via a small staircase. Image: David Thorton/The Thoresby Society, the Leeds Historical Society.

No more than half an hour's walk away at the Wellington Road ground, Aston Villa were having a decent season in the winter of 1881/82 , reaching the fourth round of the FA Cup. Scotsman Archie Hunter was in fine form but Villa were outplayed in their friendly against Queen's Park from Glasgow. Howard Vaughton and Albert Brown became the first Villa players to gain international caps for England against Ireland in Belfast. Not to be outdone by their team-mate Hunter, they went and scored nine goals between them in a 13-0 victory.

Samuel would have heard all the football news in the local pub, although he lived close enough to watch the home games. Vaughton was a notoriously dangerous inside-left for Villa throughout the decade, picking up a cup winners' medal before his retirement through injury in 1888. Only Steve Bloomer of Derby County equalled Vaughton's record of five goals in one international. Samuel would have also known of Vaughton's successful silversmith's business (still in existence today), which was commissioned to make a new FA Cup trophy when the original was stolen while in holders Villa's care in 1895.

Like their local footballing hero, all three of Samuel's sons (my great-great-uncles) were firmly established in the jewellery trade: Alfred and Wilfred making gold and silver chains, and 13-year-old Walter as a jewellery apprentice. Boys were given apprenticeships around this age and earned four shillings on average. This would increase annually until they were 21, working 11-hour days. It might seem strange for the family to not live in the Jewellery Quarter itself. In fact, the area was a community of workshops and there were no jewellery 'shops' until the late 1970s when the economic recession prompted some of the manufacturers to open their doors to retail customers. This is a far cry from the trendy outlets and microbreweries of today. Instead, the

Swanns made their livings nestled alongside a whole range of neighbouring trades – including Aston's non-professional football players.

Lozells Wood was the common wasteland of Aston manor in the Middle Ages where local peasants had the right to pasture their livestock. In the 19th century, it was gradually being taken over for housing as the town of Birmingham swelled in size and officially became a city in 1889. Just as green fields were eaten up by workers needing a place to live, so too were the same spaces lusted after by local cricketers and footballers. In 1893, the Wellington Road football ground and stand was the latest victim to the building of two new roads of housing. Where would they play if every patch of land was built upon? So it was that, by the turn of the century – 250 years on from when Sir Thomas Holte was developing his beloved Aston Hall estate, and defended it from the rage of the local rebels – the footballers took a lease on part of Aston Lower Grounds. Almost as if an act of vengeance or defiance against the town planners, the club later drained the ornamental Dovehouse

An early sketch of the new 'Witton Road Ground', that would come to be known as Villa Park. Aston Villa beat Liverpool 3-1 in their league match on 30 October 1897. With permission of Aston Villa Football Club.

Pool to build their permanent stadium, Villa Park. And yet it was an internal battle that the local community could not possibly win on all fronts if it wanted public green spaces, higher-quality sports venues, and safe housing for working families.

The Swann family were also moving onwards and upwards, this time to the new Wheeler Street estate laid out by the Birmingham Freehold Land Society that wanted to improve the standard of working-class housing. By the grand age of 57 Samuel had finally taken a significant step up in life, moving just a few hundred metres to the other end of Wheeler Street where it meets Witton Road. There are two anonymous family photos that are believed to be Samuel and Elizabeth Swann in their later years. They are dressed in their finest clothes, possibly borrowed for the occasion, and posing in such a way as to portray every inch the status that they aspired.

Representing the changing fortunes of many families of the time, when Elizabeth passed away, Samuel went to live down the road again with their eldest daughter and her family. His other daughter, Amy (my great-grandmother), had married a jeweller called John and was living in leafy Selly Park with its grander houses to the south of the city (see Chapter 8). They would always be close by, however, especially on a Saturday afternoon as it was John who took his son (my grandfather) to Villa Park as soon as he was old enough.

In contrast to the long journeys south or north made by some of the footballers, the trade migration by these ordinary workers seems comparatively small. And yet there can be many understandings of the phrase 'to come a long way': to move county or country; to be able to live in a house that is all your own; to see a sport change from casual park entertainment to clubs with members and a sense of identity.

Family photos, believed to be of Samuel and Elizabeth Swann. The photographer was Hudson & Co. (formerly Sunderland and Hudson) who had a studio in the Great Weston Arcade.

If one belief united them all, it was that, if you worked hard enough and stuck together, there was a possibility that things could get better.

Chapter 5

Precious objects and professional attitudes

West Bromwich and Birmingham
(1840–1900)

1800s	George Clemson and Caroline Incley	Richard Tipper and Ann Austins
	Thomas Clemson And **Harriet Tipper** (and Arthur Jones)	
	George and Thomas Clemson	Ada, Austin and Arthur Jones

FOR CENTURIES, skills and employment opportunities were passed from father to son, and from mother to daughter. It was no different with my own family: coal miners produced coalminers; ironworkers produced puddlers and other metal labourers. And yet sometimes, one or more children would forge a different path. Where ancestors may have made rough pots and horseshoes, the descendants were crafting more intricate jewellery. This was the tide of change embraced in the Industrial Revolution: thinking differently; trying new methods. It was also the case in sport: new clothing and footwear; new approaches to training and playing. Of course, not everyone could expect revolutionary change in their lifetime. For some, the lack of money or education would keep them relatively still, with the world spinning around them. Even so, the protective power of association – particularly through trade unions and player unions – would be critical to survival and progress.

Tracing this side of the family led me down many mysterious alleys. I was often convinced I had found ancestors and had begun writing their story when new evidence caused me to stop, go back, cut the link, and start all over again. It turns out that there were a lot more relatives in Staffordshire and Warwickshire in the 19th century than we previously thought, including several who emigrated to America. The search through official records also raised a difficult truth about life at the time: that many did not have access to basic education and decent living conditions, and, even if they did, modern medicine was still waiting for the big breakthroughs of scientific research and technological development.

George and Caroline (née Incley) were married in West Bromwich, but Caroline was from a tiny hamlet called Little Aston in the Staffordshire countryside. The main manor house passed through the possession of various wealthy gentlemen while the Incley family lived nearby, until a lease was granted to a society for the 'Treatment and Cure of Inebriety'. Using the local stately home to cure wealthy drunks is quite an amusing idea knowing that Caroline later fell in love with a man who made malt, which was used for beer and whisky. Today, the area is better known for its footballers' mansions and residents have included managers Graham Taylor and Roy Hodgson; goalkeepers Peter Schmeichel and Mark Bosnich; and players Ugo Ehiogu, Andy Gray, Mark Kinsella, and Gabriel Agbonlahor.

Staffordshire had a national reputation for its pottery, innovating new methods to produce all kinds of table and decorative wares. A massive display of worker protest against sudden wage cuts led to a General Strike and the Pottery Riot of 1842. Although the uprising was quashed, the Miners' Association of Great Britain and Ireland was created soon after which would play its own powerful role in history.

George's family name, Clemson, does not relate to any particular trade. At some point in history, a male ancestor would have had a father called Clem and become known as 'son of Clem' or 'Clem's son'. The name Clem has a Latin origin to mean merciful or mild. 'Clement' is also an English word to describe mild weather or a person who shows forgiveness or compassion. While it is nice to think of ancestors as being kind, it seems that they also had the ideal personality to work for other people: to work hard and not to complain about it. Perhaps this is why there are no trade union leaders in the family that we know of, although there are several sports captains.

West Bromwich was the connecting point of many branches of the vast canal network that was built in the 18th century and snaked all the way into Birmingham, carrying coal. Coal deposits had been discovered in this area as early as 1315 and it became known as the Black Country. Coal was in high demand for anything a blacksmith could make and later for domestic heating. This demand ensured that West Bromwich grew rapidly and supported spring, gun, and nail manufacturing.

The West Bromwich Strollers football club was

A small Staffordshire-type ceramic mug from the 1860s featuring a colour scene of three children playing football and the inscription 'Foot-Ball'. Part of the National Football Museum collection.

founded in 1878 by workers from Salter's Spring Works, famous for their typewriters among other things. They were renamed West Bromwich Albion in 1880 and would become part of the new Football League when it was first created. Their first match was in November 1878: a 0-0 draw in a 12-a-side game against workers from Hudson's, a local soap factory. One story is that the 'Strollers' name came about allegedly because there were no footballs on sale in West Bromwich, so a walk to nearby Wednesbury was necessary in order to buy one. Other historians think this unlikely and that the name was used by several teams who had no football ground of their own, therefore content to 'stroll' to anywhere suitable to play.

Three decades later, a photograph by Albert Wilkes[9] (the son of a West Brom footballer of the same name) captured the West Bromwich Albion players out for a 'training walk'. Nothing to do with their original Strollers name, it was actually an official part of their regime. On Monday the players were free to do whatever they pleased. Training began on Tuesday with players reporting at 10am for a good walk in the country. 'They probably cover five or six miles, and do it at a fair pace,' wrote William Bassett in his 1905 *Book of Football*. 'There is no racing, but also there is no sauntering about.'

Although a far cry from the club physiotherapists and set-piece coaches of today, football clubs soon began to realise that they could no longer rely on the imagination of whomever was club captain that season to magic a team into an athletic army. Identifying new talent and encouraging

9   Albert Wilkes was a successful war photographer in the 1940s, working on *Desert Victory*, a propaganda film which documented the struggle between Rommel and Montgomery in North Africa (the real-life action involving my great-uncle William Cunningham; see Chapter 10). Wilkes also covered the D-Day landings in Normandy and followed the troops into Belgium and the Netherlands (a similar route to my grandfather, Thomas; see Chapter 11).

*Members of the West Bromwich Albion team out for a training walk, 1900.
Image: Chronicle.*

transfers was also not limited to players as other staff became
in demand.

Nearby club Aston Villa lured Joe Grierson from
Middlesbrough Ironopolis – the name being a clear indication
of that town's industrial strength, which also played a major
role in the building of the Sydney Harbour Bridge. Grierson
was in charge for six league titles and four FA Cup wins.
'The job of the team trainer was, for many years, simply
one of getting the players fit by organising their running,
exercises and weight training,' writes historian Simon Page.
'Tactics and skills were left to the players themselves and if
anyone directed the football coaching sessions it would be a
committee member or the captain.'[10]

Nevertheless, Grierson did influence the style of play. He
organised sessions for the different types of players – backs,
midfielders, forwards – so that they could focus on their
particular roles, and even pioneered specialist training for
goalkeepers. He devised mid-season training camps which
included dribbling and sprinting races, and even made the

---

10   Page, Simon, *Pinnacle of the Perry Barr Pets: The Men and Matches Behind
     Villa's Double* (Sheffield: Juma, 1997).

players take a Turkish bath followed by a dip in the Irish Sea at Blackpool before they played Preston North End.

Whether to indicate the dangers of the sport, the intensity for which it should be admired, or just out of pure gossip, newspapers printed short accounts of football injuries. In just the first few months of 1880 the *Birmingham Post* described two separate cases of broken legs, that Alfred Bibby of Warrington died from concussion after a collision, and that another player – a railway clerk from Stirling – also died from injuries.

Both medicine and sport were undergoing significant change in the 19th century in terms of their regulation, their codes of practice, and the concept of being a 'professional'. However, they were not necessarily mutually beneficial and no clear sense of 'sports medicine' for the benefit of the athlete existed, although some research was carried out on sportsmen. Part of this was a clash of society's ideals of the 'gentleman' (mostly the doctors) with a new sense of manliness (the sportsmen), which kept them apart.[11] Exceptions to the rule were men like Daniel Grey. He was born in Scotland and qualified at Glasgow University before moving to Wales to open a medical practice. He played for Wales against Scotland and was a founder member of the Welsh Football Association. Even after he stopped playing and became a spectator, he was often called upon to look after injured players.

If a player could manage a whole career without it being cut short by injury, they did not retire in luxury and with millions in the bank. John 'Baldy' Reynolds (sometimes known as Jack Reynolds) was born in Blackburn in 1869 and grew up in Ireland, winning the Irish Cup with Ulster

---

11 See Mike Cronin (2007), 'Not Taking the Medicine: Sportsmen and Doctors in Late Nineteenth-Century Britain', *Journal of Sport History*, Vol. 34, No. 1, pp. 23-35.

in 1887 before playing for West Bromwich. When he moved to Aston Villa, his first game was against West Bromwich where he scored the winning goal. In a reverse of the trend to move south, he later went north to sign for Celtic in Glasgow, meaning that he played for Irish, English and Scottish cup-winning teams. Having followed his playing days by coaching both at home and abroad, he had no early retirement but ended up working for a coalmine near Sheffield until his death at only 48 years of age.

The 1890 FA Cup Final between Sheffield Wednesday and Blackburn Rovers, painted by William Heysham Overend (1851–98) and titled The Football Match. *The goalkeeper appears like a muscular Renaissance statue, whilst the players around fall and shoulder barge each other at risk of injury.*

Returning to the very ordinary folk of Birmingham, George and Caroline had survived the cholera epidemic of 1831 to have three daughters and three sons who made it beyond infancy, at a time when many did not. In the 1860s the family was living in a courtyard around the back of New John Street West, in the centre of the industrial town. The youngest son was Thomas (my great-great-grandfather), who was still just a small lad and not yet old enough for paid work. His older brother William, 14, was a gun barrel filer and his sister Sarah, 12, was already working as a house servant. Thomas would have filled his days wandering into the open doorways of the neighbours, or getting under his mother's feet as she tried to earn a few extra pennies as a laundress. 'Heavens, Thomas, can you not sit still for two minutes?' Caroline would likely sigh. Drying clean sheets and undergarments in the smoky air of the courtyard, that also housed workshops and the shared latrines, was an insurmountable challenge and the rest of the family would be home from work soon enough.

George worked as a maltster his entire life. A malt house or 'maltings' was where the skilled maltster would soak cereal grain in water and then spread it and dry it on a large floor at a certain temperature to allow the precious little particles to develop (germinate) to the perfect point. The barley was then heated in a kiln to the desired colour and stored to develop the flavour. To avoid fraud, there were several regulations dictating precisely when and for how long the maltster could perform each stage of the process and tax officers visited to weigh the grain. Official procedures became so complex and so hindered technological advancement that an Association of Maltsters of the United Kingdom was set up to challenge the authorities and George would almost certainly have become a member. With workers fighting for their own rights for centuries, trade unions only became legal by an Act of Parliament in 1871, paving the way for many more in the future, including organisations such as the Professional Footballers' Association.

The malt that George created would have been used by one of Birmingham's breweries. Brewing was originally a standard everyday domestic activity because people needed something safe to drink. Cleaner water from Wales would not be brought to Birmingham until the end of the 19th century.

In medieval times, it was the monasteries that were the biggest brewers. Commercial brewing then moved to inns and taverns in the 16th century where the licences were strictly controlled by magistrates. Fast forward more than 200 years and the Beer Act of 1830 created a new type of 'public house', where any rate-paying householder could apply for a licence to sell (and brew) beer on the premises. Huge premises sprang up designed by dedicated architects. Birmingham built its own history of big breweries, of which Ansell's is one of the most well-known. Like George Clemson, Joseph Ansell was also a maltster and hop merchant. Later he moved into the brewing business with his two sons and within a short time they had established a massive empire including a modern brewery, nine maltings, rolling stock, horses, and 96 freehold and leasehold public houses.

An illustration of Ansell's Brewery in Aston, which appeared in the Brewers' Journal *on 15 September 1900. Image courtesy of Brewery History Society.*

In the 19th century there was a close relationship between football and the brewing industry. Teams got changed in local public houses as they played on pitches close by, including Sunderland who played on a field owned by the Blue House Inn. Supporters and club management alike met in pubs. Pubs also created their own football teams and entered local leagues. Inevitably, players were becoming more familiar faces in the street. The time they spent in the pub began to be judged alongside their performance on the pitch. Archie Hunter, a Scottish player for Aston Villa, was eager to quash the rumours at the time:

> 'I deny that footballers on such occasions go beyond proper limits. On the contrary, they are very moderate indeed in this way. The fact is they are obliged to be, or they would be no good ... Any recklessness in drinking and smoking would soon tell upon a player, and you wouldn't see him playing very long.'[12]

Villa's committee even rented a room at a coffee house in Aston High Street and tried to get the players to socialise there instead.

Down in London, the owner of the Thames Ironworks demanded that all players in their company football team not drink alcohol or smoke. Their committee were less worried about the performance of the players but more about them not being able to work. To enforce the ban, fines were handed out to anyone caught. Players were insured against loss of wages but if they were injured, they had to be home by 8pm, in other words not down the pub. In 1900, the team changed its name to West Ham United and their early nickname was 'The Teetotallers'.

Harriet Tipper – Thomas's future wife – was born in West Bromwich and had four sisters and a brother. Her family moved home several times: gradually north from

---

12 See Bernard Gallagher, editor (1997) *Triumphs of the Football Field: Narrated by Archie Hunter (The Famous Villa Captain)*, new edition, Sports Projects Ltd.

Cheltenham and Worcester, and then into Birmingham where Harriet grew up in similar crowded 'back to back' courtyard dwellings, built as a very cheap form of housing for the poorer working class. At number six Court 29 in Livery Street were Harriet, her parents, five siblings, and a boarder, all in the same few rooms. In fact, there were hundreds living side by side as Livery Street ran from the Jewellery Quarter, along the railway line, and all the way to Colmore Row in the city centre.

By the time she was 19, Harriet had taken the bold move as a young, unmarried woman to move out of her family home. She lodged in New Summer Street, which was just north of the city centre, sandwiched between the Jewellery and Gun quarters. To give a sense of the booming trade, there were 400 jewellers registered at the start of the 19th century and nearly 30,000 at the start of the next. The Jewellery Quarter has produced the PFA and FIFA World Player of the Year trophies, Lonsdale boxing champion

St Paul's Church, standing in St Paul's Square in the Jewellery Quarter. It dates from the 18th century and the spire was added in 1822. Image: Darren Haywood/Birmingham Fest.

belts, and the Wimbledon tennis trophies. The first football referee's whistle was also made there. Martin, Hall & Co. made the 'little tin idol' – the original FA Cup trophy – which was stolen from a shop window in 1895 after it was won by Aston Villa and never seen again.

Harriet was working as a military ornament maker and she would have met Thomas some years earlier when her sister, Rosa, married William, Thomas's older brother. It is not known who initiated the match, but if Harriet had the courage and independence to live among the thousands of independent tradesmen of Birmingham then it is safe to assume that once she had made up her mind about something, she would make sure that it happened. As soon as they were old enough, they married in St Paul's Church. They moved into Mary Ann Street, just around the corner from the pretty Georgian square where the church sits and where the Birmingham City University School of Jewellery is today.[13]

On the marriage certificate, Thomas listed his profession as 'Jeweller', marking his move away from both his father's malt work and the guns and metal tool trading of his brothers. It was not abnormal for Birmingham workers to switch metal trades – buttons, nails, gun parts, buckles – as demand went up and down. 'I'll teach you,' Harriet may have offered with a twinkle in her eye, meaning that they could work side by side in the early years of their courtship.

It was relatively easy to set up work as a jeweller. One needed a small bench, leather apron, a few tools, some copper and zinc, and some cash for other materials. Many worked from their own homes or rented the spare space above the

---

13 True to the history of Birmingham tradespeople producing national sporting trophies, students from the Birmingham City University School of Jewellery designed the medals for the Commonwealth Games in 2022.

wash house in the back-to-back courtyard. A week's output was then passed on to a middleman who sold the items on to shopkeepers. It meant that thousands of young people could be entrepreneurial enough to work independently and earn a decent enough wage without being highly educated, and that Birmingham could boast good-quality, handmade goods.

Thomas and Harriet's 1873 marriage certificate, showing the difference in writing ability.

Thomas, his brothers, and at least one of his sisters seem to have been taught to read and write. This was a good decade before attending school became compulsory, which suggests that his parents were conscious of their children receiving at least a basic education before, or alongside, learning a trade. His marriage certificate is signed in clear, cursive handwriting, indicating that he kept up his literacy skills. This is in stark contrast to Harriet Tipper who is unable to sign the certificate with anything but an 'X'.

It is curious that Harriet could not write at all, given that the 1861 census describes the young Tipper children as being 'scholars'. Although this is what census recorders would write next to the name for children attending school on a daily basis or receiving instruction at home, it is widely believed that this was not strictly followed by parents – especially those who needed the extra income. Particularly after the 1870 Education Act, parents may have been tempted to state 'scholar' in order to hide that their children were working part-time or full-time. More schools were opening to accommodate the swelling numbers of pupils but, before that, the only chance to learn might have been at Sunday school.

The Bagnall family – owners of three ironworks in West Bromwich – started an evening school for boys employed by them. Classes began at 7pm, giving the children (although they were already considered adults) an hour's break after their day shift had ended. They were taught reading, writing and arithmetic, along with some general knowledge. The Bagnalls encouraged attendance with small gifts and preferential treatment when it came to playing for the works' cricket teams. However, the attention on boys' education meant that girls often went without. West Bromwich would soon be rewarded for taking care of its young people and their earning and playing potential. In the 1880s it was one of the first places to boast a football club that had turned professional, won the FA Cup, and become one of the founding members of the English Football League.

Making school compulsory in 1880 would mean that, by the end of the century, most young people could read at least a little and that included Saturday's football match and other sports reports and lists of results. Right from the earliest days of local competitions and FA Cup matches, reports appeared in newspapers across the country. Typically, these were only a few lines: the names of the clubs; the fact that one or both teams gave a 'spirited display'; and the final score. They did not necessarily appear in dedicated sports columns but could be found on general news pages, before or after some criminal case or an advertisement for household goods. Members of the public would also write letters to the newspapers to complain about juveniles playing football in the streets or parks and disturbing local residents.

The development of the railways meant an even quicker spread of journalists, sports news, and newspapers, which could support the emergence of a more widespread fan base and the idea of a bigger sporting world out there than just the team around the corner. This does not mean that socioeconomic class differences in fan bases were irrelevant or completely ignored. William McGregor – the owner of a Birmingham draper's shop and one of the founders of the Football League – described who he thought actually attended football matches:

'My business premises are situated in a thoroughfare, which ... cuts through some of the worst slums in Birmingham. The inhabitants of these courts do not patronise football. The game is principally supported by the middle classes and the working man, and the latter are more particular in regard to the wearing of clean collars, than they were 25 years ago. When I first came to Birmingham, the lower classes ... were much more slovenly in their habits than they are today, and football has undoubtedly brightened them appreciably.'[14]

It is not clear if he is trying to make football fans sound more respectable than they actually were, for the benefit of his own aspirational venture as a club committee member and eventual chairman. Certainly, the fact that the club owners sealed off matches to paying customers created a division in society between those workers who could afford the time and admission ticket (and be trusted to be let in the ground) and those who could not. Other reports from England and Scotland in the 1880s and 1890s confirm, with some surprise, that cup ties were attended by factory workers, church ministers, and upper-class gentlemen alike. This

---

14   Quoted in *The Roots of Football Hooliganism* by Eric Dunning, Patrick J. Murphy, and John Williams (Taylor and Francis, 2014).

societal mix was welcome, fair, dangerous, or disgusting, depending on one's point of view.

The Football League originally insisted on a minimum admission charge in order to prevent price competition between clubs. This meant that devoted loyalty to a single team was not necessarily embedded in the culture. Fans were known to switch support between neighbouring clubs according to who was currently performing better and who the opposition was. The standard price was one shilling. A carpenter might earn 25 shillings a week but rent, food and fuel for him and his family could easily use up all of that. There would not be much spare for 'luxuries' such as football matches.

The minimum admission price would later rise to 1s 9d by 1950, but fans had more disposable income then and attendances kept increasing. The improved railway network was essential in getting both players and fans to away games and Bordesley (for St Andrew's) and Aston stations had already been operational from the mid-1850s. However, with increased availability of cars and television in the mid-20th century, attendances would eventually decrease and prices to watch the match in person would go up again, unfortunately pricing out some of the poorer fans completely.

While city authorities focused on improving living conditions for the working classes, football clubs were still sensitive to the plight of some local people and charity matches and donations were a regular occurrence. In 1880 there was a special match played by Burslem (later Port Vale) to raise funds after an explosion at a Sheffield colliery. Aston Villa donated to a memorial statue fund and Small Heath Alliance (later Birmingham City) donated the proceeds of one of their matches to the Birmingham and Midland Hospital for Women. Such charitable acts were not restricted to the full-time players. In 1887, a match was played between Mitchell's St George FC and a team of 'Actors of the

GRAND FOOTBALL MATCH.

CRESCENT V. SEAFIELD,
AT PLANTATION PARK, PARKHOUSE,
ON SATURDAY, the 8th MARCH.
Kick-off at 3.45 p.m.

Admission, 3d ; Ladies Free—the proceeds to be
given to the Poor of the district.

By kind permission of the Captain and Officers,
the Band of the 4th A.V.A. will be in attendance.

A charity match held in Ayrshire, Scotland, announced in the Ardrossan and Saltcoats Herald, *1 March 1879. The admission was three pence, and free for ladies, with proceeds going to 'the Poor of the district'. Image: Ardrossan Football Clubs.*

Prince of Wales Theatre' with the proceeds donated to the Birmingham Ear and Throat Hospital.

Tracing the family through the last decades of the 19th century, the records for Thomas suddenly ended. A copy of his death certificate confirmed that he died of 'phthisis' – an old word for tuberculosis – in 1879. Tuberculosis is infectious, causes terrible coughing, and killed about a quarter of the adult population in Europe in the 19th century. It was associated with the cramped living conditions of the lower class and it was not until after the Second World War that the vaccine, which had been developed some decades earlier, became widely accepted and used. This, of course, was too late for Thomas. He died in their small courtyard dwelling in Barr Street on 19 April, three weeks after the season ended with Old Etonians beating Clapham Rovers in the FA Cup Final – teams of London gentlemen from wealthy families who had been educated and practised their football at prestigious schools. On his death certificate, under Signature of Informant, was 'X' – the mark of Harriet Clemson who could not read the terrible piece of paper that the registrar presented her with.

If one thing could be said for the cramped streets of houses, it was that family were never very far away. Parents, grandparents, and in-laws were often just next door, down the road, or round the corner. Harriet's two sons, Thomas junior and George (my great-grandfather), were sent to stay with their grandparents (Harriet's parents), Richard and Ann Tipper. While Birmingham authorities celebrated their first steam trams and public supply of electricity, Harriet was once again navigating life without the support of a man and his income. She had greater social status than a spinster; in other words, she had been married. But she was no longer a wife herself. No longer fulfilling the Victorian ideal of running a household and being dutiful to a husband.

In 1883 Harriet married Arthur Jones, a brass worker. Neither Arthur nor Harriet were able to sign their name on the register, marking it with an 'X' (as did one of the witnesses). Their certificate shows them as both living in Great Hampton Street, a main thoroughfare of the Jewellery Quarter. They may have been neighbours or they may have been already 'living in sin'. Often, marriage certificates would list the address where they *intended* to live together, which was more respectable. A girl, Ada, was born after Thomas (Harriet's first husband) died, and before Harriet married Arthur. There may have been another potential father on the scene, or she was an early celebration of their new union, which was also very common at the time.

The marriage took place at Bishop Ryder parish church, which was built by public subscription in a densely packed working-class area of Birmingham. Now the site of Aston University, it was erected to commemorate the Bishop of Lichfield, himself involved in religious and educational provision for the working classes. Considering this, it seems ironic that neither Arthur nor Harriet, standing under its vaulted roofs and high church tower, had a good enough education to be able to write their own names. Even if beyond the help of the authorities, the family members all remained close and looking out for each other. Later, the marriage of Louisa Tipper (Harriet's sister) would be witnessed by Arthur Jones and Rosina, the niece of Thomas Clemson (Harriet's first husband). Harriet returned the favour a few years later by signing Rosina's own marriage certificate – with an 'X'.

Arthur and Harriet moved to live in Grosvenor Street West, on the west side of the city centre, between Broad Street and the canal. They were self-employed as 'japanners' and probably working as a partnership.

Back in the 16th century, beautiful glossy objects had begun to arrive from India, China and Japan and quickly became popular and fashionable items to display in the homes of the wealthy, particularly when serving tea to house guests. Tea was brought to Britain in the early 17th century by the East India Company and, although it was drunk by all classes, it became a social event for the wealthier people with time on their hands (usually attributed to the Duchess of Bedford who sought a small meal between lunch and dinner). The supply of genuine products was limited, particularly as the lacquering process used the sap of a native tree. British workshops, including those in Birmingham and Wolverhampton, devised new painting and varnishing techniques to imitate the style, thus 'japanning' grew as a skill and trade of lacquering tin to create a high-gloss finish.

Having created numerous intricate ornaments for unknown military men, Harriet was now turning her hand to stylish objects for fashionable ladies, whom she was also never likely to meet. Without being too sentimental, it is quite the contrast to imagine educated citizens of Harriet's age wearing or using and admiring her handiwork when she could neither read nor write herself, and certainly would not

A japanned tea tray with a view of St Martin's Church from the Bull Ring, Birmingham, 1815–35. Image: Birmingham Museums Trust, licensed under CC0. Harriet would have covered metal trays and boxes with black lacquer so that she or other artists could paint scenes or motifs in gold and coloured paints.

have had the luxury of afternoon tea. Of course, it should not be assumed that she was unhappy. She had a job, a husband, and probably no end of friendly neighbours. She did not know life any other way. She had three older children, all working in the brass trade, and two young ones.

Then, just like Harriet's first husband, Arthur disappears from the records.

At the start of the new century, in her late 40s, Harriet was still living in Grosvenor Street West and still working from home to support herself as a japanner. However, gone is any possibility of these small, creative trades being passed down in the family as her children switched to serve mass production in the city. Daughter Ada, aged 19, became a capstan lathe worker, performing the same operation over and over again on a factory line to produce metal components. Her brother Austin, 18, similarly worked as a steel tube driller and would later shift to making bedsteads.

It would be the youngest, Arthur, who would embrace new technology the most, becoming a fitter at an electrical works. As much as they were precious people to Harriet, they would be just another employee among hundreds and thousands of others to the factory floor managers and the business owners.

In the new football industry and mass production of fixtures, the hotly debated status of professionalism meant that more money was changing hands but change was yet to be reflected in all aspects of the game. Clubs still did not have any medical obligations towards their precious players, even though staff were recognising the benefit and various ways of keeping their players fit and healthy. Compensation for injury was only just beginning to formalise. It would not be until 1906 that the Workmen Compensation Act would be extended to all classes of workers and include professional footballers. It would also be some decades before medical and other specific training staff would take the step up beyond being merely another volunteer. As with the factories, even though health was starting to be monitored, the wellbeing of athletes was left to be dealt with in the home.[15]

Harriet – ever the constant in this story – stayed in Grosvenor Street West for many more years, even when hundreds of others were leaving for the suburbs. She kept her own family close and helped them throughout her life, including taking in her young grandson (John, my great uncle) as a lodger when times were hard. And, also never changing in other ways, Harriet could not sign her name on the 1911 census record. 'I am 60 years old and I've survived well enough without,' she would have protested. She left an 'X' instead.

---

15 See Neil Carter (2007), 'Metatarsals and Magic Sponges: English Football and the Development of Sports Medicine', *Journal of Sport History*, Vol. 34, No. 1, pp. 53-73

Chapter 6

Fighting for a better life

Herefordshire, Walsall, and
Warwickshire (1850–1900)

1800s	John and Catherine Hornsby	Mary Dubberley	Frederick and Elizabeth Holmes	John Heppell
	Edmund Hornsby and Emily Dubberley		John Holmes and Frances Heppell	
	Arthur Hornsby And Sarah Ann Holmes			

AS INDUSTRY continued to expand, more and more men and women gave up their lives in small villages to enter the towns and cities, although the nation still relied on farming and other rural crafts. Even the grain to make the malt to make the beer for post-match pints had to be cultivated somewhere. Many folks stayed in the countryside and still had to fight just as hard to make a living, perhaps more so as they were dependent on the hours of daylight, the weather, and the success of their crops.

Life in the second half of the 19th century certainly seemed like a constant battle for some of my ancestors: to find their way alone in a new place, to get money, and even literally to fight with fists and guns. They came up against the authorities on more than one occasion. Perhaps they deserved what punishment they got for their immoral behaviour, or perhaps they deserve more sympathy for trying to survive in difficult circumstances. Equally, football clubs jostled for position and argued for fair treatment. Unfortunately, the reputation of the working-class man and the football supporter (or both) went before him: violent and not to be trusted.

My great-great-grandfather, Arthur, was born in 1852 in Eardisland, Herefordshire, and was the eldest of nine children, although his youngest brother only survived for one year. Eardisland was, and still is, a small village, five miles west of Leominster. Arthur would have grown up playing, and then working, in the acres of farmland and ancient apple and cider orchards. The River Arrow runs through it, overlooked by Tudor-style cottages with typical timber frames.

A photograph of Eardisland in 1906 showing a bridge over the River Arrow and the timber-framed cottages. Image: Copyright The Francis Frith Collection

Arthur's mother, Emily Dubberley, came from an extensive family of farm labourers, which included both the men and the women. The principal agricultural activities were cider making, hop growing, and the raising of cattle and sheep; mainly the local breeds of Hereford cattle and Ryeland sheep. Unless they lived on the farm and were employed permanently, farm workers were only paid for the work done. During harvest and in the summer when there was more daylight, working days could be 12 hours or more for children and adults; however, in the winter, days were shorter but there was less paid work available. If the weather turned, if the ground froze, or if there was no work for some other reason, they would receive no pay. If they were ill or injured and could not work, they were not paid. This meant that families would also have to be ready to migrate.

The extended Dubberley family can be traced back as far away as Stirling, Scotland, in the late 1700s, and to Ross-on-Wye, on the border with Wales, in the late 1600s. Arthur's father, Edmund, worked as a basket maker, like his father before him. Basket making or 'basketry' goes back

A basket maker in the 19th century. Image: Heritage Images. Arthur's father and grandfather would have sat on the ground to work, either in a barn or outside their cottages to catch passing trade.

not hundreds of years but as many as 12,000 and is a trade that is found in all parts of the world. It pre-dates pottery and was vitally important as the main way of storing and transporting all manner of food and other items, as well as hunting and fishing. The hard work started with collecting the willow (or hazel or ash) and stripping it ready to be worked with. This was all done by hand before the 20th century. There were then seven construction methods in basketry that one would need to be skilled in – looping, knotting, plaiting, coiling, weaving, twining, and assembly – though some weavers may have had their particular favoured style.

Edmund, also going by the name of Edward, was a character with a rather mysterious past. In 1847, when he was 18 years old, Edmund was sentenced to two months' imprisonment with hard labour. All he had done was stolen a pair of boots but it was news that the *Hereford Journal* and the *Hereford Times* wanted to print, probably to warn other gentlemen of this local criminal in their midst.

Two years before that, Edmund had been charged, but later acquitted, of stealing a promissory note (a legal document demonstrating money owed) from his employer. This seemingly minor event later came up as possible evidence in a murder investigation. A Welsh farm worker had been killed with an axe to the head in 1848 and the fugitive – another farm worker – was tracked by a police constable across the countryside. As the constable questioned more of the farmers and innkeepers, it came to light that the murder suspect had been giving various pieces of false information to the locals as part of his disguise. However, one thing he supposedly did boast about was that he had been in Hereford jail for the crime of stealing a 5s note but was later set free. Checking the prison records, the police constable then became very excited to find that there had been such a person. As a result, Edmund Hornsby then became a key suspect as he matched the witness's description. A reward of £100 was offered. Fortunately for Edmund, and his present and future family, the investigation turned in another direction: the real murderer was caught while trying to steal a cake to help fuel his escape.

Hereford Journal - Wednesday 29 November 1848

manifestations of national feelings.

THE LATE MURDER AT CWMGOODY, BRECON.— We last week stated the wilful murder of Thomas Edwards at the farm of Cwmgoody, three miles from Brecon, and that a fellow-labourer, Thos. Williams, who had absconded, was suspected of the crime. The unfortunate victim, it appears, was robbed of a suit of clothes and 30s. in money. Police-constable Wililam Jones has since been through Herefordshire in pursuit, but has found that the fugitive had given an entirely false account of himself, and was not known at Kingsland, of which place he said he was a native. A person of the name of Griffiths, answering the description, is said to have lived at Tillington Common. He had stated to one of the boys at Cwmgoody, that he had been in Hereford gaol about a 5l. note, and a person answering the description, but giving his name as Edward Hornsby, was in that prison in June, 1847, on the charge of stealing a 5l. note, but discharged on the bill being ignored. A man has been arrested by the police at Cardiff, on suspicion of being the party, and a constable has been sent down, who can identify him if he is the right person. Two persons have been detained at Hereford, and two at Merthyr, but have since been discharged, on being seen by persons who knew the man called Tom Williams.

A newspaper article describing the tricky investigation into the murder of a farmer in Wales. Edmund Hornsby was one of the suspects. By permission of the British Library.

Married life seems to have settled Edmund down to a quieter existence, or at least one that kept him out of the newspapers and court records books. The thing about the official accounts is that they do not document what happens behind closed doors or in a man's mind. Terribly, Edmund would later meet his end by drowning in the river. The inquest ruled 'suicide ... while temporarily insane'. This does not mean that he was experiencing mental health problems to the extent that he did not know what he was doing. Even though the law and medical opinion were changing in that period, suicide had long been considered both a sin and a crime. Such deaths could be officially linked to temporary insanity by a willing local doctor to prevent the deceased person's possessions being confiscated or to allow a proper religious burial to take place. Even though these punishments were not common by the late 19th century, it may still have been part of a community's culture to save the reputation of their own. Again, we do not know what really happened to him. Perhaps the guilt of his younger years caught up with him. Or perhaps someone else made it look like suicide to finally take their revenge.

Arthur (Edmund's eldest son) worked as a farm labourer in his teenage years. For all the imagining of an idyllic country childhood among the apple orchards of the West Country, it is not surprising that Arthur announced that he was going to make his way to Birmingham. As he would have reasoned to his family, 'We get paid so very little compared to folks in the big towns who can work year-round in the factories. And, begging your pardon mother, I'm sick of the same meal every night of bread and potatoes.'

Sometime in the early 1870s, Arthur turned up in Latimer Street South, Birmingham. He could have managed it by hitching a ride in a cart to Kidderminster or Worcester and then jumping in the third-class carriage of a steam train, or hiding in a luggage truck to avoid the fare. Latimer Street was less than one mile south of New Street Station in the centre of this huge town and so Arthur did not wander too far. It was a long line of three-storey, red-brick homes that also boasted four licensed public houses, six beer houses, and at least one off-licence of some kind. To young Arthur, a country lad barely 20 years of age, it must have seemed like heaven.

Soon after arriving, Arthur met Sarah Ann Holmes, whom he married at St Barnabas' Church in 1876. It seems that Arthur was illiterate, marking the certificate with an 'X' as did his witness, whereas Sarah Ann was able to write her own name in the register (as did her witness). It is difficult to guess how they met, even though they lived only one mile apart. It could have been completely by chance or a social meeting of friends of friends. They did have some things in common that might have sparked an attraction. Sarah Ann was also a new arrival to Birmingham. Like Arthur, she had grown up in a large family with nine siblings in a tiny village outside of the industrial town. As a single woman, it was a brave but understandable choice to leave behind the small cottage that was her childhood home.

Sarah Ann's immediate family were from Pelsall, north of Walsall, which is itself north of Birmingham in Staffordshire. Her village was less centred on agricultural work and more on the mining of coal deposits that had been discovered there. In 1872, tragedy had struck the town when the Pelsall Hall Colliery flooded, killing 22 miners. Her father, originally from the ancient market town of Holt on the border with Wales, was employed in the ironworks. All four brothers, and another who had left home, were also puddlers at the ironworks. Puddling was a strenuous job with the heat and fumes of converting pig iron to wrought iron causing short life expectancy.

As an outdoor activity during their precious Saturday afternoons off work, Sarah Ann's siblings would have to wait another 20 years before their village football club was founded. It would be named Pelsall Villa – nicknamed the Villains – and they would play in black and red. Meanwhile, the founding of both Walsall Town (1877) and Walsall Swifts (1879) created some healthy local rivalry. This would continue for nearly ten years until a merger to create Walsall

Engraving of men using a 19th-century puddling furnace in an ironworks. Huge blocks (pigs) were added to a furnace and the molten iron was stirred with a rod (raddle). Immense strength was needed to lift the ball of puddled iron back out and for bashing with a steam 'shingling hammer' to force out small pieces of slag as sparks. This created a lump of iron with fewer impurities and ready to put through a rolling mill. Image: duncan1890

Town Swifts (later today's Walsall) suddenly happened in 1888. How could either club possibly agree to such a thing? The motive was simple on-field tactics. Walsall needed their best local players available for the Birmingham Charity Cup Final against Aston Villa. There was no rule against this happening and, once the dust had settled and the local supporters caught a sniff of possible victory, they embraced it.

It is said that over 500 Walsall Town Swifts fans travelled to Perry Barr for the big final. Despite the best efforts of both sides it was still all square after extra time. The replay was scheduled for Small Heath or Perry Barr (in Birmingham again) and Walsall were not happy. It was not as bad as the mill workers from Darwen having to repeatedly travel from Lancashire to London for their FA Cup matches (see Chapter 9) but the point was still argued that Walsall should be allowed to play at home given that Aston Villa had just done so. It was not accepted and Walsall were outraged by the injustice of the situation. In protest, Walsall withdrew from the competition and the trophy went to Aston Villa.

To add insult to injury, Walsall were not among the 12 founder members of the Football League in 1888. However, the same year, they beat Burnley – one of the selected 12 – which may or may not have made them feel better. It still meant more years of battling in 'friendly' local fixtures without what they felt was justice and recognition. Fortunately, by the time the Football League Second Division was created in 1892, Walsall were definitely in, alongside Small Heath (now Birmingham City), Sheffield United, Darwen, Grimsby, Ardwick (later renamed Manchester City), Burton Swifts, Northwich Victoria, Bootle, Lincoln, Crewe and Burslem Port Vale.

The Walsall team in 1893. Image with permission of Walsall Football Club.

During the 1880s, for all that Arthur and Sarah had aspired to by coming to the industrial heartland, life was seemingly just as difficult as it had been in the countryside. There had certainly been happy times with the birth of their first three children: Evangeline, Albert and Arthur. Unfortunately, Arthur senior, like his father before him, was about to feel the full force of the law, for possible reasons of desperation or malice or both.

During the winter of 1880, there was heavy snow and a severe frost. It had started unseasonably early in October in some parts of the country and there seemed no end in sight to the cold. On 25 December, Arthur stole seven fowls from his master along with fellow employee Henry Smith.

Henry had been caught and arrested that same day but somehow Arthur had returned home to wish his family a merry Christmas. Perhaps he had confessed to Sarah that evening or perhaps he had managed to hide his concern, playing with the children or bravely heading for a drink at the nearest public house. The next day was a Sunday, and a day of rest, but that would not have stopped Arthur peering through the frosted window panes or listening out for a heavy knock at the door. On Monday he heard nothing. 'Perhaps Henry kept his mouth shut and took the blame,' he would have said to himself, feeling half relieved, half guilty. On Tuesday, his time was up. The police found him and took him into custody.

Tried in front of a magistrate, they were both sentenced to 12 months of hard labour. Under the Prisons Act of 1865, prisons were to be a deterrent providing 'hard labour, hard fare and hard board'. Depending on the prison, the labour could include small tasks requiring a little skill: net making, weaving, or sewing sacks. More physical work included breaking stones, stepping up on a treadmill in six-hour shifts, or turning a crank alone in a cell. The work often had little purpose except to be so bad and painfully repetitive that a prisoner would think twice about reoffending.

Illustrations of a solitary cell crank and a prison treadmill. Images from Mayhew & Binny's The Criminal Prisons of London and Scenes of Prison Life, *published in 1862.*

Such petty crimes were also reported in the Birmingham press, which would add to a person's local reputation over time as well as the general entertainment of the readers. It may be hopeful to think that Arthur was undertaking some kind of Robin Hood mission for his poor family and friends on Christmas Day. What owner would miss a few chickens when there were so many hungry mouths to feed? Other prisoners on the same page of the court report were also found guilty of stealing a small number of necessary items: a wash tub, boots, pickles, and coal. There are also mentions of associated assault. One man who stole a scarf from another was sentenced to several years in prison. Arthur's sentence was luckily not so bad but it meant that he was absent from the family home for some time.

While Arthur was imprisoned, Sarah Ann looked after their three small children – aged three, two and nine months – in a few rooms in tiny Stoke Street, near the canal. She also took in a carpenter as a boarder to help cover the rent and George, Arthur's brother, who had also arrived from the countryside to work in a mill. It would have been cramped with eight families sharing the same rear courtyard washing and toilet facilities. However, as many previous residents have recalled, they 'had everything even though they had nothing'.

When Arthur returned, Sarah Ann gave birth to three more children: Lilian (my great-grandmother), Edward, and Emily. It seems, then, that things were looking up and Arthur was indeed something of a reformed character, also shaking off his father's traits. The Hornsbys moved out of the city centre to Hay Mills, across the canal from Tyseley station. It would have been a huge contrast for the six children and perhaps a reminder of happier days from Arthur and Sarah Ann's own childhoods. Red Hill Road was a long curving terrace of new workers' houses and there was also a new elementary school for the children. Arthur seemed to settle into an honest job as a wagoner and Sarah Ann supplemented the family income by working as a laundress.

Sadly, the peaceful existence did not last long and Arthur started getting into pub brawls. In January 1891 he was antagonised by a local man, William Cooper, known locally as 'Ironhead', who had served time in jail for assaulting a policeman and 'generally became very quarrelsome when he had taken a drop of beer' according to a news report. You have to question the wisdom in fighting a man with that name and reputation but who knows what was said between them in the dark drinking room. A muttered insult. The casual knocking over of a tankard of beer. Perhaps, after time in prison and working the physically demanding job of a wagoner, Arthur really did fancy his chances. They took the fight outside where Arthur struck his opponent to the ground, which was seemingly a fatal blow. Fortunately for Arthur, he had witnesses in his defence and 'Ironhead' lived

ICHABOD.—Arthur Hornsby, of 3, Red Hill Road, Hay Mills, wagoner, was charged with violently assaulting William Cooper, of Ward's lodging-house, Belmont Row, labourer. Mr. Tyler appeared for the prisoner.—Prosecutor and prisoner were in the Union Mill public-house, Holt Street, on Saturday night, when a quarrel took place between them. Being turned out of the house, they renewed the quarrel outside. Prisoner struck prosecutor, who fell and cut his head.—It was stated by some of the witnesses that prosecutor was very drunk, and was held up to be punched.—Police-sergeant Dowling (8 D) said he was told that a man had been killed in Holt Street, and he sent the ambulance down, but prosecutor had then gone to the hospital.—Mr. Tyler did not deny that the prisoner had struck prosecutor, but called witnesses to prove that the latter was the aggressor. It was shown that prosecutor commenced the quarrel in the public-house, but that prisoner struck the first blow outside.—Prosecutor, in cross-examination, had admitted that he generally became very quarrelsome when he had taken a drop of beer, that he had been to gaol for a month for assaulting a policeman, and that he was known as "Ironhead."—The magistrates thought that prosecutor had earned all he got, and they discharged the prisoner.

Birmingham Daily Post *article from 1891 describing the fight between Arthur Hornsby and the man known as 'Ironhead'. By permission of the British Library.*

to fight (or not) another day. The case was dismissed but the details were reported in several newspapers.

All of this could sound like a relatively harmless Saturday night and yet gang warfare and other isolated incidents were making the city streets a dangerous place to be, including the Navigation Street Riot of March 1875. This was where a mob of angry locals had tried to rescue a man who had been arrested on suspicion of burglary and it had ended in the death of one of the police officers.

Arguments between locals themselves were typically settled in the streets and police interference was not welcome. In fact, the involvement of the city authorities just added to the tension and potential violence.[16] Having said that, the actions of the government and political parties did not seem to help matters much. There was talk that senior officials had called the men of Birmingham 'ruffians' and did not care about their cause, which of course the men in parliament denied. In October 1883, when Arthur was recently out of prison, the Conservatives had held a meeting at Aston Lower Grounds, to show their support for a decision in the House of Lords. Unfortunately for the meeting organisers, they had chosen a prime spot that really belonged to the local people: where they enjoyed their free time and played their games of cricket and football. Representatives of the Liberals, feeling that most people in Birmingham would be against what the meeting was discussing, broke into the event by climbing over the walls and another riot ensued while they chased the speakers.

Football has been associated with violence as far back as the 13th century and in its early days could involve hundreds of players. Young men of rival villages and towns could use

---

16 Upton, Chris, *A History of Birmingham* (Andover: Phillimore and Co Ltd, 2011).

it to settle old feuds, personal arguments and land disputes. Equally, a jovial game to celebrate a feast day could be just as rough (see Chapter 2). From the 'folk-football' of Cnapan in Wales to Calcio Fiorentino in Italy, it had always belonged to the general populace before a more disciplined game with rules to support 'fair play' was supported by the British aristocracy.

Painting by Jan Van der Straet of a calcio (football) match in Piazza Santa Maria Novella in Florence in the 16th century.

Mostly with the exception of humans, much of the urban sport in the 19th century did end with something getting killed: cocks, bears, dogs, rats. Unusual human forms – very tall, short, hairy, or flexible, for example – and animals still formed part of the side shows at annual fairs but again, the complaints of disruption and drunken behaviour forced these events from the Bull Ring to outside the city centre. The Onion Fair was moved out to Aston, even though Aston Hall and Gardens was itself making a great effort to become a more refined place of leisure – theatre, aquarium, skating, cycling – for those who could afford the one guinea season ticket. In another attempt to prove its status as a cut above, it was at Aston Lower Grounds that only the second floodlit game of football took place – between teams from Birmingham and Nottingham – and this was before the sport even became organised into its leagues.

Unruly behaviour and vandalism by supporters happened in the early football games of the 19th century, of course, but they were not reported much by the newspapers. They were also not the problem of the referee, who was only concerned with what happened on the pitch. Nor were supporters the responsibility of the police, who were only concerned with what happened on the streets. One might consider those years to be relatively peaceful compared to the decades of 'hooliganism' that were to emerge 100 years or so later but there are some newspaper records that give an idea of what could happen. In 1885, the newspapers reported that spectators leaving a match attacked the players of Preston North End, who had just beaten Aston Villa in a friendly, this being when players had to make their own way home on public transport. On 10 January 1887 the *Birmingham Post* also reported that the conductors of trams to Perry Barr, where Aston Villa played, were 'subject to considerable annoyance by people attending the football matches there'.

One opinion was that violence surrounding football matches was usually the fault of the players setting a bad example. Anything that might kick off in the stands must be a direct result of seeing the behaviour on the pitch. In 1895, a news report noted that a referee had been suspended following a match in Dorset in which he had threatened the players with personal violence for not obeying his rulings. The report conceded, 'This is, indeed, a reversal of the usual order of things'; in other words, saying that the players are usually the violent ones. Some years later, in 1936, the FA also felt compelled to publish a memorandum regarding 'rough play' to the players.

The staff of a Birmingham Corporation Tramway depot, 1910, who would be familiar with boisterous football supporters. The trams behind are destined for Yardley, where the Hornsby family later lived. Some carry advertisements for Bird's Custard, a local product. Image courtesy of Judith M. Smith and David Smith.

Even away from the matches, in the 1880s 'football' as a word was being used publicly and in legal proceedings to mean doing something violently and also including a kicking action. A resident of Birmingham wrote in to the newspaper to describe how they had been walking home when they came across a game of street football, only to find that the players were using a small urchin (poor child, usually in rags) instead of a ball. In a village near Manchester, there were complaints about the graveyard being in a poor condition and local boys stealing bones. One resident had even found some children using a human skull to play a game of football. Back in Birmingham, a public complaint about a theatre concert compared the dangerous action onstage to a football or cricket match. In a court case, it was heard that a violent man had threatened to rip out the entrails of his victim and 'kick them about like a football'. In another case, a mob broke into a warehouse in London and reportedly used the enamel baths 'as footballs' until they were completely destroyed.

Despite the almost inevitable consequences of gathering large groups of excitable people together, clubs still did their best to maintain a community spirit. This went a little wrong for Everton FC when they advertised for 100 men to clear snow from the pitch prior to a match in 1886. Ten times the amount of people requested turned up and the club officials had to turn most of them away. The rejected volunteers were so upset that they started pelting the officials with snow and then tried to stop the other volunteers doing their job. The Liverpool police had to be called in to intervene. Almost 80 years later, press photographers captured Liverpool manager Bill Shankly helping young boys in scarves to clear the snow from the Anfield pitch with just rakes and brooms in December 1964.

Arthur was just 43 years of age when he died in 1897. Sarah Ann decided to stay in the quiet area of Yardley, the other side of the Coventry Road (which, in contrast, is now the A45 dual carriageway connecting Small Heath with the M42 motorway). She worked from home as a washerwoman to support herself and her three youngest children. They also took in a lodger, a bus conductor, to help with the rent.

With the Hornsby fighting spirit in him, her son, Arthur, joined the 3rd Battalion, Worcestershire Regiment, of the British Army. Dressed in his new khaki uniform and saying goodbye to his mother outside their tiny Birmingham house, he was already taking a brave leap bigger than those of most of his school friends. Between 1899 and 1902 the British Army was engaged in a colonial war – the Boer War – in South Africa, and Arthur was soon sent there to fight. The British wanted to unite their South African territories of Cape Colony and Natal with the Boer republics of the Orange Free State and the South African Republic, also known as the Transvaal. The Boers, the Afrikaans-speaking farmers, wanted to maintain their independence. Britain was motivated by the discovery of gold in the region and Birmingham's jewellers, among others, would have been eager to get their hands on as much of it as possible.

Although the army suffered many early defeats, thousands of men joined up, including from Canada and Australia, to be part of the adventure. The British had little respect for the land that they were invading and burnt farms and crops to punish and hold back their enemy, as well as keeping Boer families in concentration camps under terrible conditions. As many as 28,000 Boers died, 80 per cent of them children. In February 1902, towards the end of the campaign, there was fighting nearly every day. Arthur was badly wounded and died at Reitfontein Drift, South Africa. He was 22 years old. In an attempt to end the terrible hostilities, the two sides began negotiations for peace but the treaty took almost two months to agree before it was signed in May that year.

British soldiers under attack in South Africa. The painting is by Richard Caton Woodville (1856–1927) and shows the last surviving troops of the 17th Lancers near Modderfontein, September 1901. When the illustration was published in a magazine in 1902 it was with the title, 'All that was left of them'. Image courtesy of the Council of the National Army Museum, London.

Thousands of miles away, back in England, Arthur's brothers had taken up their father's trade of working with a horse and cart. Edward was employed by the railway while Albert worked for a brewery. They both lived with their families in the terraced streets of Small Heath, which was known at the time for the impressive new Birmingham football stadium, as well as the violent gangs referred to as Peaky Blinders (see Chapter 7). Lilian (my great-grandmother) also took this opportunity, like her mother, to seek out her independence, and yet she still lived in the same street as Edward and would also marry a carter. If they had read the newspapers, they would have known of the terrible losses to the British Army with the home press describing them as heroes and the Boers as the cruel enemy. Only Arthur and his fellow soldiers knew how they had been ordered to treat the African population and much of that truth died with him and the thousands of others in the sweltering heat of the medical tents, far away from home.

There is one final battle in the Hornsby story. Despite Sarah Ann probably begging him not to, her youngest son, Ernest, signed up to the army at the start of the Great War in 1914 for what he hoped would also be a thrilling adventure with his friends. He fought in the muddy trenches of France until he was wounded in a motorcycle accident while on duty between command posts and was returned home to his family in 1917. Initially it was thought that he was suffering from shell shock or a combination of this and a few lucky scrapes on his army bike. Closer inspection of his army medical records shows that he finally admitted to an army doctor that he had blacked out while on his bike and that this was the cause of the accident rather than the outcome. Furthermore, he then hinted that his father also suffered from such 'episodes' which may have been a case of undiagnosed epilepsy. Add to that a grandfather who died from suicide or some other health issues and the internal struggles of these men seem as difficult as the challenges they faced in the outside world.

For all the violence in these stories, and the malice, one can also sense the amount of frustration boiling over in people who desperately wanted something different out of life and struggled with the right course of action. Perhaps they truly believed what they were doing was honourable, or perhaps they were driven by an abandonment of morals and self-interest or amusement. As far as these labourers were concerned – and not forgetting the sports fans and players among them – if you wanted a better life, you had to go out there and slog it out.

Edward Hornsby, brother of Lily, with his wife Elizabeth. He and his brother, Albert, both worked as carters in Small Heath. Image: Christine Laughton.

Chapter 7

Gang violence, family welfare, and women's rights

Birmingham (1860–1940)

1800s	George and Caroline Clemson	Richard and Ann Tipper	Robert and Janet Charters	
	Thomas Clemson and Harriet Tipper (Jones)		Elizabeth Charters and John Perry	
	George Clemson And Frances Florence Perry			

BIRMINGHAM – like many towns in England – grew rapidly in the 19th century as more and more people, including my ancestors, came from the countryside and neighbouring towns for work and other opportunities. In 1801 there were around 70,000 people living in Birmingham. By 1851 there were more than 200,000, and by the end of the century there were more than 500,000. In the same time, the population of England and Wales had grown from eight million to 32 million. At the start of the century only 26 per cent of people lived in towns, whereas by the end only this many still lived in the countryside.

It was also an intense period of immigration from further afield. After the Irish potato famine, Irish families made up three per cent of the population in England and seven per cent in Scotland. Many stayed where they got off the boat in Liverpool but others trekked 100 miles south to Stafford and Birmingham. As working-class areas became overcrowded, tensions rose and immigrant communities could be harshly criticised, often based on stereotypes rather than real threat. Germans were the second-largest group of immigrants until Jewish individuals and families started to flee from persecution in Russia and eastern Europe towards the end of the century. However, emigration far exceeded new arrivals with around ten million leaving Britain for places such as the United States, Canada and Australia. The large towns, including their sports teams and arts entertainment venues, thus became melting pots of diverse trades and cultures.

Greens Village, where a number of Irish immigrants lived. Image: Birmingham & Warwickshire Archaeological Society WK/B11/1275.

My great-grandmother, Florence, was born in 1876 and spent her early years in the 'back-to-back' houses of the south-east side of Birmingham. In the early 1890s the Perry family – John, Elizabeth, and 14-year-old Florence – were living in Floodgate Street on the road side, the 'front', while there were other dwellings in a courtyard behind.

'Back-to-backs' were rows of terraced houses that backed on to a courtyard shared with other houses in the row and those to the sides and opposite. Typically, the building was divided into two and one family lived in the rooms facing the road, while another family had the 'back' rooms that faced into the courtyard. Ground floor rooms facing the street sometimes became shop fronts. Those with a room at the courtyard side could be multipurpose as a living room, kitchen and workshop, particular for 'cottage industries' such as jewellery making. The two rooms above – one on top of the other, connected by a narrow staircase – would be for the families to sleep in, typically with the parents and baby in one rooms and other numerous children or a lodger in the other. My grandfather (Chapter 11) recalled that all of his siblings – there were nine in total – slept in one bed.

In the courtyard would be communal 'brewhouses' for laundry and 'privies' for going to the toilet. Any remaining space would be for drying laundry or other activities if it was not raining, although the air would be thick with industrial smoke. Narrow alleyways gave access direct to the street. For the authorities, they were seen as a place of poverty whereas to many residents, they were an important place of community. Families continued to live there through the 1920s and 1930s, and the last ones moved out in the 1960s.

We had assumed for a long time that John Perry was Florence's biological father but the historical records tell a different and rather sad story. Florence's mother, Elizabeth Charters, was born in Liverpool to a couple who had migrated from Scotland, but her own mother seemingly died young. Elizabeth moved south with her father and aunt to start a new life in Coventry, following the same route

'Sketches in the Condemned Localities' was an ink print that accompanied an article printed in The Graphic *newspaper, 16 December 1876. It depicts inhabitants of John Street in central Birmingham. Image by permission of the Library of Birmingham WK/B11/2513-2517 (87/1975).*

that the many Irish and Scottish families were taking at the time. Her father then married another widow but she also died after they moved to Birmingham. Elizabeth was unmarried herself but fell pregnant. While it would have been quite normal for her father and community to cast her aside, Elizabeth was lucky to have been cared for at a time when women were not so easily independent without a husband and would have had little choice other than to go to an institution like the workhouse. Instead, Elizabeth was fortunate to be able to raise young Florence in her father's house and make some money as a laundress until she married John Perry, an iron worker, some ten years later.

This part of Birmingham where they lived, on the south-east side of the heart of the city centre, dates back to the seventh century. The area to the west of the river is known as Digbeth, while the section to the east, a little further away from the centre, is known as Deritend. The Old Crown – an inn for travellers and now a public house – is believed to be Birmingham's oldest non-religious building and has existed there since 1368.

View of Deritend *by the artist George Warren Blackham (1870–1910). The timber frame of the Old Crown is visible on the right. The similar building on the left, nearer the church, is the Golden Lion Inn, host to a protest meeting against local police brutality in 1839. Image: Birmingham Museums Trust, licensed under CC0.*

The Digbeth side was at the very heart of heavy industrialisation, which is clear from the occupations of the family's neighbours at the time: brass workers, wooden crate and packing case makers, and bedstead makers. Floodgate Street and its immediate surroundings were also made famous by the Bird's Custard factory, now a popular cultural centre. The story goes that Mr Bird was experimenting with a way to create eggless custard for his wife, who was allergic. One day it was accidentally served to friends who enjoyed the taste and the celebrated yellow powder later found huge commercial success.

Digbeth was a notorious area for gangs, notably the Allison Street, Milk Street, and Barn Street Gangs, as well as the Peaky Blinders who were a gang in Small Heath, although it is believed that the term was used to collectively describe many different gangs.

An advertisement for Bird's Custard that appeared in an 1889 issue of Farmer and Stockbreeder, *formerly the important* Scottish Farmer and Horticulturalist *publication. The text explains that it can help save on the cost of sugar because of its sweetness.*

The Allison Street gang has a long history, believed to go as far back as the Bull Ring Riot in the 1839. People known as Chartists had held meetings around the county, including in Birmingham. It led to

A pen and ink sketch by Richard Doyle, a young English boy, in August 1839. It shows London police attacking people attending a peaceful rally in the Bull Ring, Birmingham on 4 July that year. The police are wearing the typical top hat and double-buttoned, swallow-tailed uniform. Image: Library of Congress.

139

a petition requesting parliament to consider giving the working man the vote, and therefore more say in how the country was run. This was rejected and further meetings were banned. The people fought back against the police but also damaged properties, leading to many arrests, imprisonment, and even forced transportation such as to penal colonies in Australia.

While newspapers might play down public acts of violence by saying that they were the result of alcohol, there were clear political and religious motivations behind several incidents. A *Birmingham Journal* article on 18 July 1868 reported on the fatal outcome of one of 'those drunken quarrels, which, unfortunately, are only too common and frequent in Allison Street'. Incidentally, there is an Allison Street in an area of Glasgow that was also known for its ironworks, migration, deprivation, and community tension. Parallel to Allison Street in Birmingham is Park Street, where many Irish families lived. The Murphy Riots followed one of several meetings where the Protestant William Murphy gave a typical speech attacking the Pope, nuns and the Catholic Church. Local Irish workers threw stones and attacked the police in the streets. The next day, an English mob arrived at Park Street, breaking into homes and terrifying the Irish families inside. Such disturbances continued into the 1870s. After one fight, a green and black flag with a shamrock (three-leafed plant symbolic of Ireland) and skull and crossbones was found nailed to the railway viaduct in Allison Street.[17]

Milk Street, which runs parallel with Floodgate Street (where the Perrys lived), had their own gang with various enemies and targets, who would often be the occupants

---

17 Chinn, Carl, Peaky Blinders – *The Real Story of Birmingham's most notorious gangs* (London: Kings Road Publishing, 2019)

of a neighbouring street. Streets had fierce loyalties, particularly as several households would be from the same family.

The newspapers frequently reported attacks on both local residents and police officers, describing how the gang members used the buckle end of their belts as well as their fists. 'Slogging' gangs would purposefully meet in a particular street to fight en masse, and sometimes added stones, bricks, an axe or even a pistol to their weapons. Attacks were not limited to gangs fighting each other. They would also pick out vulnerable individuals. One account in the *Birmingham Mail* on 24 March 1890 describes how a local, George Eastwood, was seen ordering a non-alcoholic ginger beer in a pub. For this, he was chased through the dark streets by a gang. Fortunately he managed to climb over a school playground wall and then hide in a stranger's house, but he had already been beaten so badly that he suffered a fractured skull and ended up in hospital.

This is what Frances and her family would have grown up with, literally on their doorstep.

Gang members' mugshots detail minor offences including 'shop-breaking', 'bike theft' and acting under 'false pretences'. Image: West Midlands Police Museum.

A Watch Committee report raised the fact that the lack of recreation grounds made the streets the only place for youngsters to go after they had finished work, which was now at 6pm according to the Factory Act. They threw stones for amusement as much as they also played 'bandy', like shinty in Scotland and hurling in Ireland, with a small ball and sticks – items which were also convenient weapons.

The term 'peaky blinder' is believed to have numerous different origins. Some say that the gangs hid razor blades in their peaked caps. Historians think that this is unlikely, although the members did hide weapons about their persons and struck or slashed the heads and faces of victims, causing a significant amount of blood to pour down their faces, which would blind them. The peaks of the gang members' caps would have been useful in hiding their own faces. A local slang term, 'blinder', was also used to describe particularly striking individuals. Gang members were known to take pride in their personal appearance, swaggering down the road in bell-bottomed trousers and hob-nailed boots, with a colourful scarf and 'prison cropped' hair, except for a quiff in front which was grown long and plastered down the forehead. Some members' girlfriends were known to wear pretty dresses and pearls.

Gangs existed not just in Digbeth and Small Heath but also in the north of town, where George was staying with his grandparents after the death of his father. Up round the corner lived William 'Billy' Kimber, who features as a character in season one of the television series *Peaky Blinders*. In real life, he did grow up into an existence of thieving and pickpocketing, particularly at racecourses, and then, after the First World War, become a notorious leader of the Burmmagem (Birmingham) Boys. Gang members frequented boxing clubs as a place to let out their anger or congregated on wastelands away from the eyes of the law –

or on street corners under their noses – to engage in illegal gambling or simple games of chance that offended Sunday church congregations. The only betting that was legal at the time was on large horse-racing events.

A Birmingham bookmaker at the horse races, 1919. Image: Mac Joseph/ Bonnier Books.

It was only some 30 years later that betting on football became an official additional feature to the game. Birmingham man John Jervis Barnard was a fan of football who recognised the potential in betting on horses, where those who had laid down some money could claim their winnings from the 'pool' of money collected. He thought he could generate a decent income in the same way by taking a cut of bets placed on football games but he could not get his idea off the ground. He shared it with John Moores who took a coupon back to

Manchester. With the help of friends, Moores handed out his first coupons outside Old Trafford in 1923. It was not an instant success but, with perseverance, Moores eventually established a thriving business. It was called Littlewoods Pools, more commonly referred to as 'the pools', from the way the cash invested was pooled together to give back particular sums to the winners.[18]

The Littlewoods Pools employed thousands of football coupon checkers, mostly women, at its premises in Liverpool. Image: National Football Museum.

Back at the end of the 19th century, humanitarian efforts were made in Birmingham to counteract gangs recruiting new members from within the factories. The way that the authorities dealt with their gang 'problem' was to try and directly improve the living conditions of the poor so that they would hopefully feel more positive about the authorities and their general welfare, and less inclined to drink heavily or

---

18 Dudgeon, Piers, *Our Liverpool: Memories of Life in Disappearing Britain* (Headline Book Publishing, 2011)

protest and riot. The Birmingham Medical Mission was set up in Floodgate Street in 1875 (decades before the National Health Service) to provide for the poor. One resident recalls being taken there for dental treatment. He had to sit on a wooden bench and move along it as the next patient was called into the surgery, while clearly hearing cries and shouts from the other side of the door. Other missions, often led by preachers and doctors, sprung up to help families and children in particular. The Floodgate School also opened to further improve the education of the local children.

Birmingham's School Board publicly acknowledged the popularity of cricket and football and the beneficial effects that sport could have on young people; both their mental and their physical health. There was a statement in the local press highlighting the increasing demand for spaces to play and they raised their concerns that there was simply not the land available. Even the reputable King Edward's School placed a request in the advertisements column, describing how they were looking for a sports field, ideally near the Aston and Witton rail stations. As is now known, it was Aston Villa Football Club who succeeded in that respect, acquiring land from Aston Lower Grounds some 25 years later. How could small local schools and youth organisations compete with the growing adult thirst for organised sporting fixtures? Industry was eating up the yards and the roads – the playgrounds of the youth – even leading to the death of one lad who was so engrossed in a street game that he did not see the oncoming tram.

More direct interventions were necessary for those who could barely find food and did not have a roof over their heads. The workhouse – or 'poorhouse' as it was known in Scotland – was an institution that housed the poor but also encouraged them to work, which could be profitable for the institution. They also took in the sick and the

(Left) Weighing day at a Birmingham infant clinic (MS 4101). (Right) A Christmas appeal for the poor, led by the Medical Mission in Floodgate Street (MS 4038/3/1/2). Images by permission of the Library of Birmingham.

elderly. Aston Poor Law Union was formed in late 1836 and took over the workhouse that had existed in Erdington since the early 1700s. Their role was to look after the poor and destitute in the local area and they were particularly concerned about the living and working conditions of young children who were being apprenticed to coalmines. In the mid-19th century, they built an impressive new workhouse with accommodation blocks, an infirmary, and a chapel. It also included individual houses which allowed groups and families to live together in a sort of village, rather than always being split into men, women and children, although there were boys' and girls' homes.

Different to the way that the author Charles Dickens portrayed workhouses as hostile and cruel environments[19] – and many were – the Aston Union workhouse seems to have been a little more caring. For instance, from 1904, all children born in the workhouse had the address of 18 Erdington Road on their birth certificates to protect them from stigma in later life. It was at Aston Union workhouse that Florence's own grandfather spent his last days.

---

19 For example, in Charles Dickens's novels *Oliver Twist* and *Bleak House*

Aston Union workhouse and the new cottages. Image: Mary Evans/Peter Higginbotham Collection.

Just as the 19th century drew to a close, Florence met George Clemson (my great-grandfather), who was working in a metal tube mill. George was born in the spring of 1876 – the same year as Florence – right at that boom time when factories were starting to give Saturday afternoons off and the number of football clubs rose dramatically.

Like Florence, George had also grown up in a very small family unit compared to other families and in the Birmingham 'back-to-backs'. For a long time, it was just him and his older brother, Thomas, and they were both still young when their father died of tuberculosis (see Chapter 5). Their mother, Harriet, was then in a difficult situation with little income and another baby on the way. Fortunately, and despite the crowded and poor housing in the city, Harriet's parents were on hand to help out. Manchester Street is a tiny road just north of the centre and at the root of the main road to Aston and the north-east beyond. The area was heavily populated with courtyard housing and sandwiched between the busy tramway and the canal wharves.

While his grandfather Richard was a bricklayer, most of the men in the street worked in the brass trade, and it was here that George – aged just four years old – spent much of his time, along with his brother, uncles, aunt, grandmother Ann, and four lodgers. Just around the corner was Shillcock's shoe shop, which supplied football boots to the Aston Villa team. It was from here that the FA Cup would later be stolen, while on display in the window for a few days in 1895.

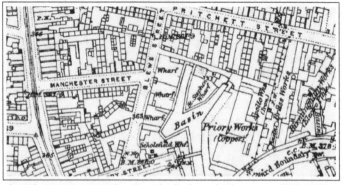

A 19th-century map showing the back-to-back courts of Manchester Street. Shillcock's boot and shoe shop faced the tramway lines around the corner. In the wharves to the rear, a variety of goods were loaded on and off the many canal boats in the basin. Image: from OS Map name 014/01, Map of Birmingham and its Environs, Southampton: Ordnance Survey, 1884-1891.

George and Florence were married early in 1899 and were staying in Floodgate Street with their two young sons at the home of Florence's parents. Living there would have certainly saved on rent, and Elizabeth could help with looking after the children. Both George and his father-in-law were melting iron in the great furnaces of the local mills and so they were gone for their long shifts each day.

If the people of Digbeth and Deritend were going through tough times, it was also a familiar struggle at Small

Heath's football ground that season. In January the ground was often a muddy and foggy swamp, although the matches still went ahead with mixed results. In one of their games, they lost their forward Jack Aston to a coughing fit, and later that month dismissed another player, Jack Leonard, for being drunk and disorderly, which he was later imprisoned for. Small Heath – later to become Birmingham City – were consistently in the top four of the Second Division but could not quite make it into the promotion spots. The club was also falling into debt and was forced to reduce player wages. This was not helped by a lack of trophies: Walsall knocked them out of both the FA Cup in the fifth round and the Birmingham Charity Cup in the semi-final, and Wolverhampton Wanderers beat them in both the Birmingham and Staffordshire cups. On a positive note, and in a show of goodwill to the community, the last match of the season was between the reserves and a Birmingham Police team to benefit the Association for Providing Boots and Clothing for Destitute Children.

There was certainly no let-up for the players, including in winter time. A few seasons earlier, in 1896, the Aston Villa team had departed Birmingham and toured up north, playing Hibernian, Celtic, Ayr United, and Newcastle United in just five days. They also played Liverpool on Christmas Day itself, attended by 25,000 supporters who were making the most of their rare extra day off work (it was a Friday that year). On Boxing Day, they played Wolverhampton Wanderers. It is incredible when compared to complaints of the current cramped Christmas schedule or adding European games to the Premier League calendar. Player emotional welfare also seems to have been less of a concern. In order to decide the starting line-up for the opening of the new season, Villa held a public training session, attended by thousands of supporters, in which the 'Probables' played the 'Improbables'. No code names. No 'colours' versus 'bibs'. It was clear who the favourites were. But anyone who plays team sports knows exactly how it goes. There's no softening the blow when you are listed on the other side in training to the club's strongest and most-established players.

At matches across the country, men and women, young and old, braved all weathers to watch their favourite teams at the end of the 19th century. They stood together on low, uncovered terraces backing on to ordinary working-class homes, as can be seen in very early film footage of a Blackburn Rovers v West Bromwich Albion game in 1892. A one-minute clip of Liverpool v Small Heath in 1901 shows enthusiastic supporters and a fire brigade. Another piece of footage of the crowd at Sheffield United v Bury in 1902 shows men mostly in rough shirts and flat caps, but with the occasional smartly dressed man in a dark suit and bowler hat, and the odd straw boater. Ladies were given free entry at some clubs although women's attendance at football matches, usually in the seated section, in England in the 1880s and 1890s made up only five to ten per cent of the total crowd.

The painting *Going to the Match* by L.S. Lowry gives an insight into matchday in the industrial towns. Although dated to the 1950s, it appears almost timeless. Not unlike today, there is a great sea of people drawn towards the local stadium and the long row of turnstile gates. Fans – men, women, old and young, and the occasional dog – troop down residential terraced streets while the factories in the background are still shooting out plumes of smoke from the morning shift.

Lowry also painted other industrial-town matches, including pitches without the stands and crowds huddled around the touchlines. Many of his paintings – not just about football – have since been bought by the Professional Footballers' Association. The former chief executive of the PFA, Gordon Taylor, who played for Bolton, Birmingham,

Going to the Match (formerly named Football Ground) by L.S. Lowry (1887-1976). It was bought by the Professional Footballers' Association in 1999 for £1.9 million, and then by The Lowry arts centre in 2022 for £7.8 million. Image © The Estate of L.S. Lowry. All Rights Reserved, DACS 2022.

and Blackburn, was a huge fan of the artist but bought them as an investment – as a kind of pension fund – for the organisation. In this way, support for the welfare of football players and their families was created via an artist who recognised and vividly expressed the close links between football and industrial society.

The early wooden terraces of football stadia were structurally perilous, especially as attendances increased. When Scotland played England in 1902, it had rained heavily the night before and the wooden terracing at the Ibrox stadium collapsed. More than 600 people were injured and 25 lost their lives having fallen 50 feet. Police allowed the game to continue as they feared a riot if it stopped, which would also hinder rescue attempts. Stadium architect Archibald Leitch, born in Glasgow in 1865 and a Rangers fan, was reputedly devastated but went on to design Stamford Bridge and Craven Cottage with terraces on more solid

An illustration of the disaster at Ibrox Park. Image © Illustrated London News Ltd / Mary Evans

banks of earth and concrete. He designed numerous other stadiums in his lifetime, including the much-loved Trinity Road stand at Villa Park that was itself replaced in 2000.

In fact, many stadia would remain unchanged throughout the 20th century. It was not until the Bradford City fire in 1985 and the Hillsborough disaster in 1989 that changes were widely recommended and became a requirement under new rules.[20] One might observe that, at both ends of the century, it took significant loss of life to initiate improvements to spectator conditions.

There were several women's football clubs by the end of the 19th century and one game in London was reported to have attracted 10,000 supporters, signifying its popularity. It was much further north that women's football was flourishing, despite the fact that medical professionals called for girls and women to be banned completely from playing. In Edinburgh, in May 1881, a team representing Scotland had beaten one from England 3-0. A report by the *Glasgow Herald* described the Scottish team as 'looking smart in blue jerseys, white knickerbockers, red belts and high heeled boots'.[21] This was perhaps an attempt by the journalist to be respectful; to indicate that these were not ruffians. However, it could also be understood as the newspaper downplaying their athleticism and objectifying the players as more of a fashion display.

In contrast, a few days later, it was reported that a women's game in Glasgow 'had to be abandoned when hundreds of men ran on to the pitch. The players escaped on a bus drawn by four grey horses amid chaotic scenes of vandalism and fighting between spectators and police.' Such

---

20 The 1990 Taylor Report recommended that all Football League stadiums become all-seater, but, in the end, this was only applied to the top two levels (now the Premier League and Championship). In 2021, Chelsea announced that Stamford Bridge would be trialling 'safe standing' areas (with both rails and seats) as part of ongoing research by the Sports Grounds Safety Authority.

21 See BBC News (online) 'The Honeyballers: Women who fought to play football', 26 September 2013.

a description could have hardly helped the women players to be taken seriously, nor supporters to be trusted, and they would need better backing than the odd journalist.

There are two points to make here which are as much about societal attitudes at the time as they are about how we look back from today and try to appreciate what life was really like and what really happened. First, the recording of events was not done from a broad perspective. For centuries it was limited to those who could read and write, and to those with the time and position of authority to do it. And so much of reported history comes from monks, clerks, military officers, wealthy travellers, and the odd respectable poet. What was accurate, including portraying people in society they had limited contact with, was up to them and the message they wanted to convey. The second point is that the gap between what men and women could and should do was not the same over time. In 19th-century Britain, the roles of men and women became much more sharply defined. Previous centuries saw wives and sisters lead armies into battle, or work with their fathers and brothers on the land or in the store. Then a definition of women being physically and intellectually inferior, yet morally superior, to men led to the Victorian ideal of women performing domestic duties – or refining their skills in art and music if they had servants – and raising dutiful and obedient children.

Women's participation in industry was a necessity for employers and working-class families alike, but participation in football was a choice against the 'ideal' and it troubled the delicate balance of society. It challenged the male journalists who had to write about it and the male doctors who were asked to comment. It was frowned upon by the British football associations, who did not see a place for women in a man's sport. The Council of the Football Association warned its members not to permit the playing of charitable matches by women.

The Birmingham Women's Suffrage Society had been formed as a committee of the National Society for Women's Suffrage some 50 years earlier in 1868. Eliza Sturge was secretary of the Birmingham society from 1871. She was the niece of Joseph Sturge, who had played an important role in the mid-19th century electoral reform movement, as well as the anti-slavery movement. Activist Mary Hutson founded the British Ladies' Football Club in 1894. She was middle class herself but persuaded Dumfries aristocrat Lady Florence Dixie to be the club's patron. Mary was also the team captain and played under the pseudonym Nettie Honeyball.

A painting by Glasgow artist Stuart Gibbs of the 1895 British Ladies football team. By permission of the artist.

With such a strong division of societal roles, a mother's ability to watch or play sport, or pursue any interests of her own, was even more limited with a large family. Activists highlighted this in their publications. However, they still felt the prevailing attitudes running against them. By 1907, Birmingham had a branch of the Women's Social and Political Union (WSPU) at Edgbaston. The WSPU had been formed in 1903 by Emmeline Pankhurst and her daughters Christabel and Sylvia and the Birmingham branch engaged in acts of militancy including arson and vandalism. While reports of violence at both men's and women's football matches would certainly not have aided women's participation in sport, it was clear that when it came to social and political campaigning, the women felt that aggressive acts were the only option in order to be listened to.

An illustration published on the cover of the magazine Votes for Women, *21 July 1911. It says 'A man works from sun to sun, a woman's work is never done' and shows men relaxing with a pint after work whilst a mother takes care of a large family at home. Image: The Women's Library, LSE Library.*

Whatever her desires for her own role in society, Florence was destined (or perhaps pre-destined) to stay home and become the mother of a large family. By 1911 they had their own house just off Grosvenor Street West in the centre of Birmingham but they had eight of their children living in it: George (11), Robert (ten), John (nine), Arthur (eight), Ada (seven), William (four), Florrie (two) and Susan (one), to be followed the next year by Thomas Richard (my grandfather).

In the mid-19th century, women bore more than six children on average, compared to three in the early 20th century. There are many possible reasons for this decline and no one reason could be claimed to be true for all families. Historians argue that there was not necessarily a change in financial incentives for working-class parents to have fewer children; they did not necessarily believe that they could 'save money'. Yes, children were more likely to attend school for a few more years and fertility decreased around the time that the authorities were more insistent on school attendance. However, teenage children might then usefully enter higher-paid employment and support their ageing parents.

What was happening at the time was an increase in the representation – through newspaper pictures and stories – of the ideal small family unit: two respectable parents and only a few children enjoying leisure time together in comfortable socioeconomic circumstances. Added to this was a greater social and religious acceptance of birth control, and the cultural expectation that parents – mothers in particular – should 'care' for their children better, as opposed to merely bringing them into existence. Nevertheless, if a woman wanted only a few children, it depended on both husband and wife to agree on these points. In other words, it depended on a (patriarchal) societal respect for what the female wanted from her life.[22]

Later, Scotland-born Marie Stopes gained fame as a scientist (palaeobotany) and women's rights campaigner and became the first female lecturer in her subject at the University of Manchester. In 1918, she published the books *Married Love* and *Wise Parenthood*, describing the benefits of contraception and avoiding excessive childbearing. She published a shorter pamphlet aimed at the lower classes

---

22 See Siân Pooley (2013), 'Parenthood, child-rearing and fertility in England, 1850–1914', *The History of the Family*, 18(1), pp.83-106

and less educated. While to contemporary society this may seem an obvious and morally 'good' thing to do, she was not without critics. Some said the methods of contraception she was willing to trial were dangerous. Some also did not like the fact that she was aligned with eugenics, which is the principle of controlling reproduction (for example with sterilisation) for more favourable qualities in a community's offspring. In *Radiant Motherhood*, she even wrote about the 'ever increasing stock of degenerate, feeble-minded and unbalanced who are now in our midst and who devastate social customs'.

The following years in Britain were characterised by further violence – the First World War (1914–18) – and further social and industrial reform. George did not join the army. He was already 38 when war broke out and both men and women were needed for military armaments work in the city. Despite the disapproval of the all-male football authorities, women's football became popular during the war, which was directly linked to the increase of female employment in heavy industry.

Before the war, almost half of women worked in domestic tasks and service (such as sewing, laundry, and house cleaning) and the factories were feared by respectable society as being rather rough. This changed when men were recruited overseas with an estimated two million female workers replacing them. Thus the communities around the workplace supported the growth of the game just like it had for men. One outcome was that a female team from England played a team from Ireland on Boxing Day 1917 in front of a crowd of 20,000 spectators.

In August 1917, a tournament had been launched for female munitions workers' teams, the Tyne Wear and Tees Alfred Wood Munition Girls Cup. Blyth Spartans defeated Bolckow Vaughan 5-0 in a replayed final tie at

Middlesbrough on 18 May 1918 in front of a crowd of 22,000. In the following season of 1918/19, the ladies of Palmer's shipyard in Jarrow defeated Christopher Brown's of Hartlepool 1-0 at St James' Park in Newcastle. More new teams also emerged in Scotland, including one from Beardmore's Forge in Parkhead, Glasgow, that played an unofficial match against an English side at Celtic Park on 2 March 1918.

The Blyth Spartans Munitions Ladies team with match officials. Image: Yvonne Crawford/blythspirit.wordpress.com.

The Carlisle Munitions Ladies team in 1918. Image: Sheila Angus/ blythspirit.wordpress.com.

In November 1918, the Great War was over and the surviving men started to return home. An Act of Parliament would eventually give the vote to all men over 21, as well as all women over the age of 30 who met minimum property qualifications, later extended to all over the age of 21 in 1928. However, women had to step aside and let the men have their jobs back. Likewise, the munitions teams did not have the same workplace backing, and certainly not the backing of the FA. This did not mean that jobs were readily available to all men and women who needed them. Economic output fell by 25 per cent and industrial exports ran at only 80 per cent of their prewar levels. In 1921, George was out of work himself, aged 45, as was his eldest son.

By the end of the 1930s, George and Florence had moved just up the road to Oozells Street North, another step closer to the industrial centre of Birmingham and its network of canals. George had found work laying electric cables, while Florence continued to keep house and my grandfather was the only one of their nine children still living at home. It was to become a precarious place to live at the time, surrounded by factories that were prime targets for bombing as the Second World War cast its shadow. In the same street, the Atlas Works lived up to its big name: a vast complex of buildings focused on the production of beds. Such factories were targets, regardless of what they made. Many factories converted some or all of their lines to support the war effort and therefore the enemy aircraft were keen to stop them, even though civilian houses lay just metres to either side. The same was true of allied bombing strategies abroad.

The works suffered serious bomb damage on the night of 5 November 1940. George and Frances emerged from their shelter the next day to find their street, and much of the city, in need of repair. As an electrics worker, George would have been in demand to get the city homes and factories up and

The eastern end of nearby New Street in April 1941 after bombing damage to the northern side. Image by permission of the Library of Birmingham LF 75.82.

The Atlas Works on Oozells Street, Bingley Hall, the Birmingham Canal and environs, Ladywood, 1938. Image: Historic England.

running once more. Small businesses were also at risk. Amid the fear and serious risks of daily life, there was one amusing story of a bomb hitting canal barges which had been loaded with prunes and other fruit. The cargo was projected on to the streets, creating a terrifying red and sticky mess for the neighbours to wake up to.

Both George and Frances, and all of their nine children, survived the war and managed to live long lives. It was then for my grandfather to continue his own journey of supporting football and fighting for survival (Chapter 11).

Chapter 8

Guns, gold, and a new Football League

Wolverhampton, Aston, and Birmingham (1850–1940)

1700s	Joseph and Ann Grainger	Joseph and Sarah Munn	Joseph and Elizabeth Smith	Thomas and Elizabeth Swann	
1800s	**James and Sarah Grainger**		Thomas Coton and **Elizabeth Smith**	James Swann and Mary Spencer	Thomas Cox and Ann Caldicott
	John Grainger And Elizabeth Coton (and John Chapman)			Samuel Swann and Elizabeth Cox	
	John Joseph Grainger And Amy Swann				

SHOWING OFF national talent on a world stage in the 19th century was not the kind of four-year cycle we are used to. The modern Olympic Games as an international event did not start until 1896 when it was first held in Athens. Having said this, there were what were called 'Olympic' games before this in different countries, including England, France and Sweden. These were sports festivals where people could compete in various events. They included standard athletics disciplines, as well as cricket and football, but also wheelbarrow races and cycling on penny farthings. The first football World Cup would not be until 1930 in Uruguay. England, Scotland, Wales and Ireland would not take part in the first three stagings of the World Cup, instead choosing to play against each other in their own British Home Championship, and against other countries in friendlies.

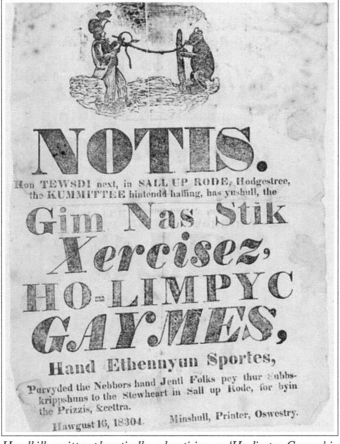

Handbill, written phonetically, advertising an 'Ho-limpyc Gaymes' in Oswestry, Shropshire, England, in 1834.

This kind of organised sport was rooted in the culture and outward-looking businesses of industrial society. While there was a clear appetite for festivals that could both celebrate the diversity of sport and make a show of the very best skill, the exact same was happening in trade.

The Great Exhibition of 1851 was a project led by Prince Albert, husband to Queen Victoria, and Henry Cole, council member of the Royal Society for the Encouragement of Arts, Manufacturers and Commerce. Much attention had been given to France's Industrial Exposition of 1844 and the men desired something similarly impressive that would be for all nations, not just Britain. An enormous glass and iron building was constructed, named the Crystal Palace, to house the 100,000 exhibits of pottery, porcelain, ironwork, furniture, perfumes, pianos, firearms, fabrics, steam hammers, hydraulic presses and even houses.

The Great Exhibition Hall in Hyde Park, London, named the 'Crystal Palace'. Image: Read & Co. Engravers & Printers, 1851.

James, my three-times great-grandfather, is included in the list of exhibitors at the Great Exhibition which was held in London's Hyde Park. Catalogue entry 278 states,

'J. Grainger of Wolverhampton, Staffordshire exhibited tube and bar action guns and rifle locks.' This was a trade that had been passed down from father to son, and would continue into the next generation.

While guns – or rather handheld cannons – existed in China as early as the tenth century, and were gradually used from the 14th century in Europe, 'rapid fire' guns as we understand them today were not developed until the 19th century. Birmingham was at the forefront of this innovation, in an area of the city centre known as the Gun Quarter. This started with the first recorded gunmaker in 1630. Birmingham-made muskets were used in the English Civil War; by William III and the British Army in the late 17th century; and even for the slave trade. In the 19th century the Gun Quarter shipped firearms to the Napoleonic Wars, Crimean War, and American Civil War.

It is likely that my ancestors had a more rural occupation before making guns. Wolverhampton is named after the Anglo-Saxon noblewoman Wulfrun, who owned much land in Staffordshire. The name literally means 'Wulfrun's high or main farm or enclosure' and so it is possible that the work there was predominantly agricultural. Grainger – or Granger – is a surname of English and French origin. It is an occupational name for a farm bailiff, who would oversee the collection of rent and taxes from the barns and storehouses of the lord of the manor. The Old French word *grangier* is derived from the Latin *granicarius*, a derivative of *granica*, meaning 'granary', and so it could also be that the family trade was traditionally looking after grain stores.

James spent most of his life in Wolverhampton and built up his own gunlock-making business successfully enough to employ three other men and one apprentice. This itself is an impressive early achievement in my family who were mostly working alone or for other people. The work would have required a good degree of skill with the hands and a sharpness of the eye. Precision was crucial in order to create a reliable product. The 'lock' of a firearm is the mechanism used to initiate firing. In the earliest guns, the charge was lit through a hole. Later, 'caps' (rather than loose powder) and metal cartridges could be ignited by striking them with a hammer and firing pin within the mechanism. Other people's lives literally depended on – or could be swiftly lost by – the effectiveness of the gunlock.

The lock of a single-barrel smoothbore percussion musket, 1859. Image: Collection of Auckland Museum Tamaki Paenga Hira, 1932 (515, W0600, 393782).

Six million people visited the Great Exhibition in 1851. The event was so successful that it even ran to profit and was able to fund new public buildings, such as those that are now the National History Museum and Albert Hall in London. The great glass structure of the Crystal Palace was dismantled and reconstructed in the Kent countryside, now part of Greater London. In 1861 an amateur football team started playing its matches there, and became one of the original founder members of the Football Association in 1863, reaching the semi-finals of the first FA Cup competition in 1871/72. Their existence was followed by the professional Crystal Palace Football Club from 1905 and the stadium was used for FA Cup finals, as well as other sports, from 1895 to 1914.

As the Great War escalated, the military authorities required the club to leave the premises in 1915, and so they moved to Selhurst Park. The original glass exhibition hall was later destroyed by fire in the 1930s although this area of London kept the same name, Crystal Palace.

A photograph of the 1905 FA Cup Final at the Crystal Palace stadium.

James and Sarah had eight children who, depending on their various young ages and skills, were either at school or employed at home, working to help their father be successful. Ten years after the Great Exhibition, the family had moved to Vyse Street, in the heart of Birmingham's Jewellery Quarter. Perhaps James felt that he could secure a better future and better social connections by living and working in the 'City of a Thousand Trades'. Their neighbours in Vyse Street were not just jewellers, but also schoolteachers, tea dealers, drapers, and many other professions. The houses had been built as part of extensive construction in the 1840s when buildings were also converted into workshops. With a reputation as a Great Exhibition trader, it was the place to be. Still pursuing work in the gun trade, James and Sarah also returned to London for a time – sharing a single residence in Chelsea with three other households – before returning to south-east Birmingham.

One of their sons, John (my great-great-grandfather) was a 'gun viewer' with the equally important role of assessing

Vyse Street homes doubling as jewellery workshops. Image: The Phyllis Nicklin collection / University of Birmingham.

each weapon's accuracy and construction. In 1869, he married Elizabeth Coton at the parish church in Edgbaston.

Elizabeth had grown up in the small back-to-back courts of Bordesley High Street with her shoemaker parents and surrounded by craftspeople of all types making paper boxes, pearl buttons, and iron bedsteads. By the time she was 13 her father had died and so her widowed mother took on the pawnbroker business with her eldest daughter in Duddeston-cum-Nechells. At the time, this was just a hamlet, far out of the industrial centre, towards Aston Park. Elizabeth's elder brother was a gunmaker, like the family she eventually married into, and perhaps this is how she met John.

The Cotons' business of broking – lending money with interest against an object of worth – was in demand. In Britain in the late 19th century and early 20th century, there were nearly as many pawnbrokers as public houses. The word 'pawn' comes from the Latin word *pignus*, meaning pledge, and the items being pawned to the broker are called pledges or pawns. The place was often known as the 'pledge shop'. An item is taken to the pawnbroker who lends an amount

A map of the east of Birmingham showing Duddeston and Nechells Green villages in 1834 before they were consumed by the spreading industrial town. Image: Ordnance Survey First Series, Sheet 62. CC BY-SA 4.0.

of money to the owner of the object. The item is held by the pawnbroker for a certain length of time. If the owner returns within the agreed time limit and pays back the money lent plus an agreed amount of interest, the item is returned. If the loan is not paid within the time period, the pawned item will be offered for sale by the pawnbroker.

When families were in need of cash to get through the week, they would take personal items to the local pawn shop and then get them back as soon as they could. Birmingham residents talk about their mothers pawning their wedding rings or cutlery, and even pawning their husband's suit on a Monday and collecting it on a Friday ready for church on a Sunday. Boyfriends and fiancés bought uncollected jewellery.

A typical pawnbroker's shop, re-created at the Black Country Museum, Dudley. Image: HelenTaylor15 (CC BY-SA 3.0).

After their wedding, John and Elizabeth moved into Oliver Street; the same road as the Cotons' pawnbroker business. They did well enough to employ a 14-year-old domestic servant and the next year they welcomed their first son, Albert Thomas. Unfortunately, little Albert only lived for one year. His death certificate describes how he gradually faded away over a period of four months (due to 'atrophy'). After bronchitis or pneumonia, this was a common cause of infant death in Birmingham at the time, particularly in undernourished children.

John continued his work as a gun viewer. Checking firearms was already an official practice under law and a busy profession in its own right within the city. The Birmingham Proof House was established by Act of Parliament in 1813 to ensure small arm user safety and, over 200 years later, it claims to remain at the forefront of international standards for the testing of firearms and ammunition.

A daughter, Florence, soon followed and then, in November 1873, John and Elizabeth welcomed their second son, John Joseph (my great-grandfather), into the world. For a long time it was the family story that Elizabeth died in childbirth and John, seemingly overcome with grief, committed suicide. Suicide attempts were reported in the notices section of the press with the details of the prisoners' reasoning and their sentence. Three such attempts were reported in the *Birmingham Daily Post* on 24 December 1873. By the 1870s, the medical diagnosis was more on the social factors and with less of an attitude of suicide being a criminal activity.[23] The attitude of the judicial authorities – or at least the journalists on their behalf – is that not all acts – for which the accused were sometimes 'very sorry' – could be taken as serious and permanent decisions. As the same paper noted in January 1874, it was common for a jury to return a verdict of 'temporary insanity' and that 'lads usually find some interest in life, even under disagreeable circumstances'. In 1886, a known Sutton Coldfield footballer took his own life having run into difficulty as a bank clerk. The *Birmingham Post* reported on 21 May 1886 that it was a sad loss to the footballing community.

After managing to acquire his death certificate, we now know that John died just before Christmas 1873, aged 32, having suffered from epilepsy for over a year. At the end of the 19th century, epilepsy was largely misunderstood and stigmatised. There were few employment prospects for people with the condition and many ended up in the workhouses or asylums. Epileptics, with their occasional seizures, were often associated with violence and criminal

---

23 See B.T. Gates (1980), 'Suicide and the Victorian physicians', *Journal of the history of behavioural sciences*, 16(2), pp164-74.

activity.[24] Potassium bromide was used to try and manage the seizures before more effective treatments were developed in the 20th century.

The mystery of what happened to his wife, Elizabeth, only came to light after several attempts to find her death and burial records in England. With nothing confirmed, the search was widened until it was discovered that she married a sergeant in the Royal Engineers in Roorkee, in the north of India, in 1880. How she got there and met her second husband, we do not know.

All we know of her son John Joseph's early life is that he was baptised a year after his birth in St Matthew's Church, Duddeston (east of the city centre). The record gives his address simply as Oliver Street, which is where his parents had lived and also where his maternal grandmother was living and working as the head of a pawnbroker's shop. John Joseph does not appear on the 1881 census when he was aged just seven years old. Neither his mother's brother or sister had taken him in and already had large young families of their own. His father had seven siblings and none of those had a young John Joseph living with them. It was not impossible to be missing from a census record: one could easily be away from home for some nights unexpectedly, or be working with no one at home to give an accurate record. John Joseph's older sister, Florence, was left to live with grandmother Coton at the pawnbroker's shop. Perhaps he had been taken to India, with his sister left behind, and returned with his mother and new stepfather in the mid-1800s.

Meanwhile, two miles away at Wellington Road, Aston Villa were having mixed successes in the FA Cup, put out in the early rounds – mostly by Midlands teams and once

---

24 Jack Gann (2016), 'A fit of mania: epilepsy, violence and murder in the Victorian', Leeds Trinity University Blog, 25 May 2016.

An extract from the 1881 census showing John Joseph's sister, Florence (Florie), living with Elizabeth Coton at the pawnbroker's shop in Oliver Street.

by Queen's Park of Glasgow – until 1887 finally brought silverware. They had to replay their tie with Wolverhampton Wanderers three times in the third round, and then narrowly beat Darwen in the sixth round before getting past Rangers in the semi-final and then winning 2-0 against West Bromwich Albion in the final. This was a glory season with the Birmingham Cup and Birmingham Charity Cup also added to the cabinet.

The Villa players were the pride of the city and almost too popular for their own good. The next season, thousands (various historical records put it at 27,000) trekked to Aston to watch the fifth-round tie against the ever-strong Preston North End team. Such was the desire to get a good view, police struggled to contain the crowds who spilled on to the pitch and turned it into a mud bath. Preston were 3-1 up and the Villa players agreed to a replay but the FA disqualified them for an unsuitable pitch. Their quest to defend the cup was cut short.

The players and supporters were not the only ones with big ideas. A Scottish man working in Birmingham, William McGregor, was hatching his plans for a football league. This seems like a perfectly acceptable concept, given that it has now been in existence for well over 100 years. However, one need only think of the brief attempt to create a European Super League in 2021 and the outrage that ensued to understand how, in the 1880s, many club owners and

An action shot from the 1887 FA Cup Final. Both teams wore striped shirts: Villa in claret and blue, and West Brom in blue and white.

The Aston Villa players of 1887 with the FA Cup: Frank Coulton, James Warner, Fred Dawson, Joe Simmonds, Albert Allen; Richmond Davis, Albert Brown, Archie Hunter, Howard Vaughton, Dennis Hodgetts; Harry Yates, John Burton.

players were worried about the elitist attitude of 12 clubs exclusively playing each other.

William McGregor – often called the 'father of the Football League' – had been born in 1847 in Braco, a small village north of Dunblane, Scotland. He had started out as a draper's apprentice with Richardson and Pearson in George Street, Perth, before joining his brother's drapery shop in Birmingham and then setting up his own in Aston. He had seen a football match back in Scotland between Ardoch locals and some stonemasons from Callander who were building a nearby mansion. When he arrived in Birmingham, he was initially a follower of Calthorpe Football Club, who had been set up by a fellow Scotsman, before becoming involved with Aston Villa who also had several Scots. With his business mind and entrepreneurial spirit – which Birmingham was not short of in the industrial age – McGregor quickly rose from being umpire, to club administrator, to being on the board of directors.

Portrait of William McGregor (1846–1911).

Many clubs, and not just in Birmingham, were frustrated with the ad hoc manner of finding opposition and arranging fixtures with suitable opposition outside of cup competitions. There was certainly nothing official to require home and away matches, nor any sense of progression from year to year. The cup competitions simply began again when the cricketing summer drew to a close.

After discussion with his friends, William McGregor invited who he considered to be leading clubs to a meeting in a hotel in London in March 1888 and then again in April in Manchester. His letter said:

Every year it is becoming more and more difficult for football clubs of any standing to meet their friendly engagements and even arrange friendly matches. The consequence is that at the last moment, through cup-tie interference, clubs are compelled to take on teams who will not attract the public.

I beg to tender the following suggestion as a means of getting over the difficulty: that ten or 12 of the most prominent clubs in England combine to arrange home-and-away fixtures each season …

… I am only writing to the following – Blackburn Rovers, Bolton Wanderers, Preston North End, West Bromwich Albion, and Aston Villa, and would like to hear what other clubs you would suggest.

After discussion, a resolution was passed and a new Football League of 12 clubs was formed. McGregor became its chairman and then president, continuing until 1892 at the same time as the Second Division was added.

RESULTS TO DATE.			
	Played.	Won.	Lost.	Drwn.
Accrington ...	2	0		1
Aston Villa ...	2	2	0	1
Blackburn Rovers...	1	0	0	1
Bolton Wanderers..	2	0		0
Burnley	2	1	1	0
Derby County ...	2	1	1	0
Everton	2	2	0	0
Notts County ...	1	0	1	0
Preston North End	2	2	0	0
Stoke.	2	0	2	0
West Brom. Albion	2	2	0	0
Wolverhampton W.	2	0	1	1

The Football League table from the first season published in Cricket and Football Field *on 15 September 1888. Since the points system had not yet been introduced, the teams were listed in alphabetical order.*

McGregor had many other grand ideas and opinions about football, including turning clubs into limited companies and setting up more junior teams as ways of scouting talent. His statement about the type of person that should be a football club director is particularly pertinent in today's context of billionaire owners and whether they really understand or love football: 'Directors cannot be remunerated for their services. The FA very rightly insists that the men who run football clubs shall do so as a matter of sentiment. [This] is wise because it brings into the work the right class of men – that is to say, men who love football for its own sake ... I can tell you candidly that the position of football director of a League club carries with it an amount of work which, if any man looked at it through business spectacles, would call for heavy remuneration. But it would be a bad day for football if you divorced the sportsman and substituted for him the guinea-pig, or the man who does not mind doing any work that he is well remunerated for.'[25]

Even with all of his football commitments, William McGregor still continued his drapery business while also being married with two children and regularly attending church in Wheeler Street, Aston. Whatever the young John Joseph Grainger knew of all this at the time, he probably could not imagine that his own son would eventually marry a family friend of the famous McGregors (see Chapter 10).

Although Aston Villa were among the leading teams in the Football League, by the early 1890s they had still not won it, as they might have expected or at least hoped to. Taking a business approach to the problem, Frederick Rinder was welcomed down from Liverpool and masterminded the club finances, later becoming chairman. At a tense meeting

---

25 William McGregor's statement on football directors, quoted in *The Pinnacle of the Perry Barr Pets: The Men and Matches Behind Villa's Double* by Simon Page (Juma, 1997).

at Barwick Street, Rinder accused the men currently in charge of the club of allowing it to get into a terrible financial state and accepting ill-discipline by the players. The entire committee was forced to resign and the Wellington Road gatemen threatened to sue. Rinder installed turnstiles at Perry Barr and the takings immediately rose from £75 to £250, which proved his point. However, some fans would still climb the water tower by the steam tram depot to avoid the sixpence entrance fee.

Club records document that the 1896/97 income was £11,000. Over a third went on players' wages. A further £621 7s 6d went on high win bonuses, which was criticised in the press, and £1,100 went on travelling, hotels, and training camps. The record profits were £1,300 thanks to Rinder's careful financial management.

Other innovations included areas for supporters to park their bicycles. Rinder registered the club as a private limited company and helped to negotiate the purchase of Aston Lower Grounds for a new stadium. He also challenged the Football Association for paying only a tenth of the gate money for the semi and final of the FA Cup in 1897, which led to a change in policy, although they still disputed it.

Rinder's impact was certainly felt on the pitch as well as off. In the 1890s Villa were FA Cup runners-up in 1892 against West Bromwich Albion, and winners in 1895 against West Brom and 1897 against Everton. They were also league champions in 1894, 1896, 1897, and 1899. In the 1920s the beautiful and innovative Trinity Road stand – the very best for players and supporters at the time – would go over budget. This time the shareholders would not approve of Rinder's management and would eventually force him to resign. His supposed parting words were to ring through the ages, 'Finance is important but one should never forget that we are not talking about a mere business. This is THE

Aston Villa Football Club and it deserves nothing short of the best.'

Aside from club income, travel and rail companies were noted to also be profiting from the interest in following football teams on the road. Messrs Cook and Son offered cheap packages and 1,000 of the 8,000 fans who travelled to see The Wednesday (later Sheffield Wednesday) in November were from Birmingham. On Christmas Eve 1896, the *Birmingham Daily Post* published the times of the trains on which the Aston Villa team themselves would be travelling to Liverpool and back for their game at Anfield. 'Follow your heroes' was even more literal in the days before players had their own flash cars and parking spots at the grounds.

Despite the obvious excitement of the Football League's early years, fate seemed to dictate that my great-grandfather would not be around to enjoy it. John Joseph's mother died soon after returning from India and it is likely that it was his new stepfather, the army sergeant, who encouraged him to follow in his own military footsteps.

There is a record of a John Joseph Grainger signing up to the army as a young boy of 16, listing his next of kin as Florence (his sister's name), and becoming a drummer who was posted to Egypt. Britain had invaded Egypt in 1882 and remained in occupation until the 1930s. Drummers beat time for military marches and would also have a bugle for sending communication signals and for sounding at ceremonies. John Joseph the soldier then returned home in October 1895 and was declared unfit for further active service, therefore able to take up a civilian job. One family possession that has long been a mystery is a small, tattered copy of a book from the Bible. Inside someone has written 'Grainger, Oct. 1895' and a reference to the Royal Victoria military hospital at Netley, Hampshire. If John Joseph had been injured in the army, it would explain the existence of the religious book and the time spent in hospital, although he never shared anything else from his military past with his family.

The vast Royal Victoria Hospital at Netley on the south coast of England was influenced by the work of Florence Nightingale. It opened in 1863 and rehabilitated wounded soldiers from overseas until after the Second World War. Image: Line engraving by T.A. Prior, 1857, after E. Duncan, from the Wellcome Collection (CC BY 4.0).

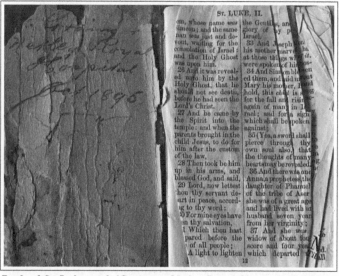

Book of St Luke with 'Grainger, Netley Royal Hospital, Oct 1895' written inside.

One thing that the army gifted John Joseph was a good education, which is noticeable from his elaborate signature on official documents that also suggests a creative hand. His army schooling would have then set him up for employment in civilian life and the chance of a better wage than he might have otherwise earned.

At the end of the 19th century, football players were also earning a decent wage with the lowest-paid member of the Aston Villa squad on 35s per week. However, they still considered that they needed more income in these emerging professional times of the new league. One player who tried to earn a bit extra on the side was James (Jas) Cowan, who was born in Jamestown, Scotland, and played for Vale of Leven's reserves. Apparently, his employer hated football and would have sacked him if he had found out that Jas was playing. Many Scottish players came south to Birmingham, although many also returned home in the late 1890s because the selectors for the international team were reluctant to pick players based in England. Warwick County club, based in Edgbaston, initially invited him down but George Ramsay got to Jas first.

Jas was a dominant physical presence on the pitch but quiet off it; that was until he had loosened up a bit and belted out traditional Scottish songs in the local pub. In 1895 Jas was playing for Villa but needed some extra cash. He faked a back injury to get time off and entered a famous race in Scotland: the Powderhall Sprint. The club were not wholly convinced and sent their doctor to accompany Cowan on his recovery trip home. This was a sticking point in Jas's cunning plan. 'Ach noo, Doc, tis a long train ride for nothing,' he reasoned, but the club insisted. Somehow, somewhere between Birmingham and Edinburgh, Jas managed to slip away from the doctor and enter the race under a false name. Three Villa players – Evans, Chatt and Athersmith – also put money on him. Jas won the race and the prize money but the press coverage revealed his escapade to the Villa committee who banned him for four matches as a punishment.

James 'Jas' Cowan, who played for Vale of Leven and Aston Villa. He also ran a pub in Aston High Street and was manager of Queens Park Rangers.

Sound finances and a nice stadium do not automatically gift a win on a Saturday afternoon. All football fans will know the agony of throwing away a 2-0 lead to the opposition, especially a local team, so carelessly in the last ten minutes. And so it is somewhat heartening – or maybe unsurprising – to read how such embarrassing defeats have happened through the ages. Even in Villa's great double triumph season of 1897, they gifted away a lead against West Bromwich Albion by barely playing any decent football in the second half. After seven games of the season, Villa were sitting mid-table due to the players' inconsistency and poor shooting, but as any supporter knows (although often forgets), the table in April can look very different to the one the previous October. Even halfway through that same season when at the top of the league, they still managed to lose to Burnley and Sunderland who were right at the bottom of the table. Such are the ups and downs of the game.

Another cause of public discussion and heightened emotions is the transfer of players to other clubs, which would have become more noticeable as the league created more regular fixtures against similar opposition, and also cast players of relegated clubs as rich pickings. Such transfers draw much speculation and focus on these players and can cause supporters to hurl abuse at the treacherous act, especially if that player has been part of the fabric of the original club for some time – and doubly so if they go to a local rival. Back in John Joseph's day, when Small Heath were relegated, Villa bought their star forward, Fred Wheldon. In return, Dennis Hodgetts left Villa after ten years to become Small Heath's captain. One can imagine the reaction of the fans, even without the echo chamber of modern social media.

From tragic beginnings, and nearly disappearing altogether, John Joseph's life was certainly on the up at the start of the new century. He was living as a lodger with a couple in Icknield Street, next to the Jewellery Quarter, and working as a gold ring maker.

Just ten years later he had worked his way up to jeweller's manager. He was also able to afford a large and comfortable home with six rooms in Selly Park for him and his new wife, Amy, and their baby daughter Gwendoline. Selly Park takes its name from the park and estate of Selly Hall, a Tudor-style, 19th-century red-brick stately home, which was sold to the Roman Catholic Church in 1864. Selly Park was developed in the parkland surrounding Selly Hall while the land to the west of Pershore Road was developed in the 19th century, with roomy plots and tree-lined streets aimed at the middle and upper classes.

As we know from the life of her father (Chapter 4), Amy Swann grew up in north Birmingham in a modest home. All of her brothers worked in the jewellery trade, as did many of their neighbours. Aged 18, Amy had also been working as a warehouse girl for a jeweller and so this is one of several possible ways in which she could have met John Joseph. They were married in 1908 and no doubt her family might have nodded among themselves and said, 'What a fine catch.'

John Joseph was 40 years old when war broke out in 1914 and he did not sign up to fight. Out of my four great-grandfathers, only James Johnson signed up, as did Peter, my great-granduncle (the experiences of their battalions, including the numerous games of football played in the army, are described in Chapters 9 and 10).

In England, the Football Association and the clubs in the Football League decided to play the matches scheduled in 1914 as they believed that the sport would be important in boosting the morale of players and supporters at home. Aston Villa, spurred on by targeted propaganda posters, had encouraged their players to enlist with the Middlesex Regiment's Football Battalion by offering to continue to pay half their wages to ensure that their families were provided for. The players were given strict military workouts by ex-army sergeant majors and were kitted out with special uniforms. Thirty Birmingham-made territorial rifles were ordered and plans were drawn up for a firing range to be built near the ground. The players – all fit young men in the public eye – really had little choice in the matter.

The Football League was then halted at the end of the 1914/15 season but some games did continue, raising money for good causes.

Research into the military archives suggests that there must have been an Aston Villa fan involved in the drawing up of the trench map for the Battle of Bazentin Ridge (14–17 July 1916, part of the Battle of the Somme in France). In a military map, there are two parallel trenches named 'Aston Trench' and 'Villa Trench'.[26]

Some professional footballers and staff found themselves trapped in Germany when war broke out. Steve Bloomer was an iron foundry worker before playing for Derby County and Middlesbrough and then going to coach Britannia Berlin 92 in 1914. He was arrested as a prisoner of war and detained

---

26 'Villa's unknown roles in the First World War revealed', (Aston Villa Football Club website, 1 November 2011).

In this 1914 recruiting poster, a line of British infantrymen fire at the enemy from a trench while an inset picture illustrates the German view of the British as just football players. It describes fighting in the army as the 'greater game' and suggests that this is more honourable than remaining a professional sportsman. Image: National Army Museum.

in the Ruhleben camp, six miles west of Berlin. Imprisoned there were also Sam Wolstenholme (Everton, Blackburn Rovers, Norwich City), Fred Pentland (Middlesbrough), John Cameron (Queen's Park, Everton, Tottenham Hotspur), and John Brearley (Everton, Tottenham Hotspur). Gradually, the camp formed its own society organisations with cricket, athletics, and a miniature football association, using names of their teams from back home. Some 1,000 prisoners were reported to have spectated. They even had an international match pitting an England XI (including Bloomer, Pentland, Wolstenholme, and Brearley) against a World XI captained by Cameron. After he finally made it back to England at the end of the war, Bloomer was widely quoted as saying, 'Myself and many others would not have survived without football.'[27]

Back in Britain, football was being used as part of rehabilitation, as it had been before the war. Film footage exists of sailors – some with crutches and only one leg – kicking a ball about with their nurse at Brooksby Hall in Leicestershire. The manor house was the home of David Beatty, 1st Earl Beatty. His wife, Lady Ethel Beatty, ran a naval convalescent hospital there, caring for the men who

A still image from film footage showing wounded sailors, officers, and Matron-Nurse Mortlock playing football at Brooksby Hall in Leicestershire, 1916. The film was produced by the War Office and The Topical Film Co. Ltd. The section is titled 'Lady Beatty's Sailor Guests.' Imperial War Museum NTB 277-2.

---

27 Brown, Paul, *The Ruhleben Football Association: How Steve Bloomer's Footballers Survived a First World War Prison Camp* (Goal Post, 2020)

served under her husband. The same military hospital in Netley where John Joseph recovered is also known to have allowed patients to play football.

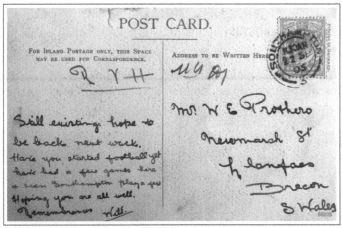

A postcard from a patient at the Royal Victoria military hospital in 1905, describing how they 'had a few games' of football. Image: Russell Masters/ Historic Southampton.

As an act of charity, Aston Villa voted to donate £50 to the War Fund and a percentage of all gates for the season. In a meeting, the players also agreed to contribute five per cent of their weekly earnings to the war effort. The minutes of the annual meeting of Aston Villa Football Club, held in June 1918, describe how:

'Mr Joseph Ansell, who presided, said it would be unthinkable to attempt to play football on the old lines during the war, but what football they had played had enabled them to purchase an Aston Villa ambulance for the use of the Red Cross, and it was one worthy of the standing of the club. The cost has been approximately £1,000. This point was followed by a round of applause.'

The 1919/20 season was the first full run of fixtures after the end of the war. Aston Villa started strongly and were FA Cup winners, also finishing ninth in the table, while West Bromwich Albion were league champions.

Despite the postwar economic depression and strain on industrial output, home-produced jewellery became increasingly more affordable and an item for mass consumption. The firms in Birmingham had to combine specialty and mass production as a strategy to both satisfy and create demand. Like his grandfather before him, John Joseph had to stay on the move to keep up with the pace

Amy and John Joseph Grainger in their later years.

of change in the industry. He took up work as a travelling watches and clocks salesman, representing a firm in London. This meant days on the road, going to his customers rather than having them come to him.

John Joseph, Amy, and their daughter, Gwendoline, moved to Bristol. It was there that my grandfather, Denis (Chapter 13), was born and the family enjoyed a very different life beside the sea before returning to the city of Birmingham and watching local football again in the 1930s. At the end of the decade, Aston Villa had just earned their way back into the First Division after a two-season spell in the Second Division, but play was to be suspended again in 1939 at the start of the Second World War before a new wartime league structure was drawn up.

By the time the Football League started up again later in the 1940s, John Joseph was in his 70s. He and Amy moved one final time to London, where their daughter was living – the first time that this branch of the family had been there since gunlock-maker James and Sarah in the 1870s – to spend their later years relaxing with their comfortable slippers and the newspapers.

Chapter 9

War horses and fair wages

Lancashire, Birmingham, and northern France (1870–1940)

		Edmund and Emily Hornsby	John and Frances Holmes
1800s			
	Robert Johnson	Arthur and Sarah Ann Hornsby	
1900s	**James Johnson and Lilian Hornsby**		

A FUNDAMENTAL unit of modern sport is the 'club', which is a tangible organisation of people and equipment, as well as a less tangible network of community relationships. In Britain from the 18th century onwards, the state stepped back from controlling such associations and private organised activities took their place. This is different to countries such as France and Germany where the ruling authorities were still involved, aligning modern sports with the objectives of the state, including maintaining the readiness of citizens for military action.[28] However, as was the case in the First World War, both amateur and professional athletes in Britain were

---

28 Stefan Szymanski (2008), 'A Theory of the Evolution of Modern Sport', *Journal of Sport History*, Vol. 35, No. 1 (Spring 2008), pp. 1-32.

encouraged to fight for their country. In addition, sport was considered an important part of both the military training and recuperation of these men (see Chapters 8 and 10).

In a similar cultural approach, owners of vast mills and factories understood the benefit of communal activity for the wellbeing and the sense of belonging – the cultural identity – of their employees. They expected loyalty and hard graft in return for supporting the existence of sports clubs. In other words, their perspective was that happier and fitter employees can lead to bigger profits over rival businesses. This was something that the textile mill owners in the north of England would have been very aware of.

James Morley Johnson, my great-grandfather, came from Manchester. He was – and still is – quite a mysterious character in terms of his background. James's year of birth varies slightly between different official documents. This is not so unusual as there were relatively few occasions to verify one's date of birth. It was often what you just said (or believed) yourself – to the mill owner when you wanted to start work; to the vicar when you wanted to marry; or to the army recruiting officer when you wanted to join up. The modern form of passport for international travel would not be issued until 1921 and driving licences would be first introduced with the Motor Car Act of 1903, but only as a way to identify vehicles and their drivers. Many people, especially in the working class, would have had no need for these documents.

At the time, society defined people by their financial status but folks also grouped themselves into communities: the church they worshipped in; the places they drank; the clubs and social organisations that they joined; the trades they chose. As work skills often passed from parent to children, what the father did for a living was also part of this identity and was recorded in official documents. James's marriage certificate stated that he was the son of Robert Johnson, a painter. In such records, including the census, this typically means painting the interior and exterior of houses, rather than landscapes and portraits. It was a skilled trade. A house painter would have to mix the various elements on site although, by the end of the 19th century, paints could be mixed in factories using horse and steam power.

At the time, Lancashire was famous for its textile mills, the majority of which were cotton mills. At the peak of its production, the county made up over half of England's exports and supplied the world with over 30 per cent of its cotton goods. Industrial development made a few people incredibly wealthy and also created a new 'middle' social class of business managers. These men and their families could afford to move out of the city centres to leafy suburbs and have their homes decorated by independent tradesmen such as Robert Johnson. As for the working class, writers and social commentators at the time tended to describe the bleak and filthy condition of their environment, whereas the workers themselves found some positives to living in Manchester and other towns: plentiful churches, societies, trade unions and other cultural activities.

A typical view of the Lancashire landscape in the late 19th century with new mill towns expanding into the surrounding fields and hills.

One activity in which men of all classes chose to invest – financially and physically – was football. In the north, the sport was almost entirely wrapped up in the lives and fortunes of the mill owners and workers. What is different today, of course, is that the investment of billions of pounds into certain top-flight clubs comes from a different country or continent and/or by wealthy businessmen who do not necessarily have previous experience of the game, and certainly not daily contact with the players and supporters. This is deemed acceptable if the team is winning consistently and preferably with silverware within a season or two. If it does not, then tensions mount and can have repercussions for years, as has been seen recently at several high-profile clubs. What has always been true – whether those rival clubs and the wider footballing community like it or not – is that money attracts talent.

The concept of needing investment and carefully building savings for resources had possibly not entered the

Darwen football team of 1879/80. Fergus Suter is at the front, lying on the ground.

minds of the football players from the schools of Eton (Old Etonians) and Harrow – they *were* the money. The financial cost of the team of mill workers from Darwen travelling back down to London twice for two replays of the 1879 FA Cup quarter-final might have simply not occurred to this wealthy opposition. As it turned out, in the original match, Darwen came back from 5-1 down to draw; the replay finished 2-2 and they then lost the second replay 6-2 having worked weeks of mill shifts in between and taken the overnight train back down to London again.

Darwen is a market town just south of Blackburn, on the road north from Manchester and Bolton. Football was not new in the 1870s. The mill workers had had lunchtime kickabouts for decades.[29] However, an official football and cricket club was created by a Mr J.C. Ashton and three sons of Orchard cotton mill owner Nathaniel Walsh, who had all been to Harrow School in London where football was played under their unique school rules. The chief difference to these 'old school' clubs was that the committee was made up of the businessmen and the players were the mill workers. This was also in contrast to many other emerging clubs across the country who were formed out of church groups, including Christ Church which later became Bolton Wanderers, or pub teams.

In the late 19th century several players moved down from Scotland to north and central England. They were especially welcome if they had mastered and shared with others the impressive short-passing game that could unravel the traditional run-with-the-ball-until-tackled tactics. In 1878, one such skilled player was Fergus Suter, as portrayed in the 2020 Netflix series *The English Game*. After transferring to

---

29 Sanders, Richard, *Beastly Fury: The Strange Birth of British Football* (Bantam, 2010)

Darwen from his Glasgow club, Partick, Suter stopped work as a stonemason, which fuelled rumours that he was being paid to play.

Local rivalries naturally existed and heightened the communities' sensitivities to the outcome of matches. In the 1890s Blackburn Rovers, financed by John Bootman of Hollin Bank Mill, complained that Burnley were illegally fielding Scottish players. Around the same time, Blackburn won a large textiles contract which brought more wealth to the town and increased the bitterness in Burnley. The cotton mills derby is still a hotly contested match to this day when it occurs.

Other funded clubs included Turton, established in 1871 by the Kay family who had a large amount of wealth built up in the flax-spinning industry. Blackburn Olympic were funded by Sydney Yates and his iron foundry wealth and became the first working-class team to win the FA Cup in 1883 (followed by Blackburn Rovers in 1884). The financial investment in the sport actually increased significantly after the 1878 textile strike, leading some to claim that the mill owners were deliberately trying to use football to distract the workers from revolution. Coming back to present-day, debates on investment, including the public outrage at an attempt in 2021 to create a European Super League, one can see the historical division between the needs and interests of the players and local community and the financial desires of the wealthy owners.

As more transport routes opened up, and people migrated for work and sometimes leisure, comparisons might be more frequently made about how others lived. The village, town, or area of the city that you lived or came from – your 'home' – was also part of your identity as well as your religious beliefs or trade. It is here that James's social status would have come into question. He does not appear clearly on early

The 1883 FA Cup Final between the Old Etonians and Blackburn Olympic was played at Kennington Oval. This illustration shows the teams' captains – Arthur Kinnaird and Albert Warburton - and venue, some match action, and the prize-giving ceremony.

housing or church records. In fact, it was said in my family, sometimes in a whisper, that James 'had gypsy blood'. Like other traveller and fairground families, Roma communities had no fixed address and this made them appear strange and not like the settled county clerks keeping the records.

Roma – or Romany – refers to people who originated in northern India but lived across Europe by the 15th century and are now worldwide. They are traditionally itinerant – meaning travelling from place to place – and speak some form of Romany language related to Sanskrit. They were known as 'gypsies' because the Europeans believed that they came from Egypt and were often persecuted. The French word *tsigane* and German word *zigeurner* for gypsy come from the Greek, meaning 'untouchable'. Because of their lack of obvious roots, Roma remained on the fringes of an industrial society that was measured on its tangible stuff: huge factories that workers belonged to; solid brick houses that they were registered under; churches and community buildings that they sat inside. Roma seemed different to other townspeople and were therefore believed to be untrustworthy, even automatically criminal.

Roma people had jobs that allowed them to travel: horse and other animal keepers and traders; musicians and entertainers. Unlike the indoor mill work of half a million Lancashire residents at the time, James's own profession was a 'horse keeper' and it was with that identity that he arrived in Birmingham sometime around the end of the 19th century. The area around Birmingham was farmland, right up to the factories and workshops of Small Heath, and so there was plenty of space for keeping animals and camping, if necessary. On the other side of the city, at Smethwick, was Black Patch Park, home to a large community of traveller families, until they were eventually evicted to make way for a new community park that was more suited to the genteel leisure ideals of society.

A travelling family with their horses and caravans in Norwich, 1897. Image: The Romany and Traveller Family History Society's Robert Dawson Romany Collection.

A family camped on the Black Patch to the west of Birmingham. Image by permission of the Library of Birmingham – LSH/Slides Collection Set 0062 Slide 0041 (19/2067).

Lilian 'Lily' Frances Hornsby was the daughter of Arthur Hornsby, himself already deceased and with a reputation for petty theft and violence, but from a wider family of agricultural labourers and horse and cart workers (see Chapter 6). In 1901, Lily was 18 and no longer living at home. Her mother, working as a laundress, and three youngest siblings were living on the outskirts of Birmingham and her brother, Arthur, was fighting in the Boer War in South Africa. Her sister, Eva, had married and was living on Cattell Road, metres from where the new St Andrew's football ground would soon be built, with her new husband and two boys. Lily was living with them as a lodger and working with her sister as a laundress, the female family trade.

It seems that Lily had managed to find a partner in James who was rather less troublesome and more law-abiding than her father. He was some 12 years older than her, and perhaps more sure of himself than the boys her own age. When they were courting, James had found work in furniture removals and Lilian continued as a laundress in a foundry. James would have needed to be physically fit for the job. Working with a horse and cart, though relatively slow-paced, was also potentially dangerous. Carters could be crushed under their carts while loading up if the horses were startled, or could even be attacked and looted on quieter rural roads. However, if he had grown up in a traveller community, James would have likely been more than capable of this independent work. References that he later got to support his army application describe him as 'honest and straightforward' and very knowledgeable about horses.

Horse-drawn carts carried people, food, milk, coal, and even fire engines and their crew. This is Powell's bakery cart in Coventry Road around the year 1900, near to where Lily Hornsby lived. Image: South Yardley Library.

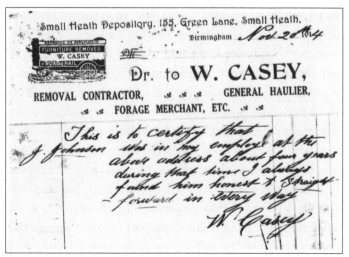

A reference from one of the men James worked for, praising his work with horses.

In 1904, James and Lily married in St Andrew's Church, when Lily was already heavily pregnant with their first child. The church gave its name to the St Andrew's football ground that was built on a former clay pit and hosted its first game two years later in 1906. It was a necessary venture for Small Heath, having outgrown their previous site on Muntz Street. Around 15,000 fans had been able to watch the club play under its new name of Birmingham FC and beat Sheffield United in September 1905. The new ground was built to accommodate 75,000 supporters in one impressive grandstand and one terrace; this being the days of thousands of fans standing up, pressed together, and even children sitting round the edge of the touchlines.

The years and football seasons passed, as they so quickly do. In 1911, James and Lilian were settled in Eversley Road, just a ten-minute walk from St Andrew's with their two children. Birmingham were having an average season, finishing 12th out of 20 teams playing in the Second Division in 1911/12, and suffered an early defeat in the first round

St Andrew's, the new home of Birmingham FC when the land was first acquired in 1905 (photograph by Sid Jackman) and on completion of the ground in 1906 (photograph by Percy Wynne). With the permission of Birmingham City Football Club.

of the FA Cup to Barnsley. They were not the only 'Blues' in the Second Division, however, sharing that nickname with the likes of Chelsea and Leicester City. Birmingham were greatly helped by their new signing of forward Jack Hall, who scored 21 goals in 37 appearances that season. When he retired in 1915, he stayed local – literally across the road – and became the landlord of the Small Heath Tavern until 1949.

In 1915, the Football League was suspended due to the war, which had not ended as quickly as everyone had expected. It was an opportune moment for the FA to regroup given the recent scandal in the First Division. Manchester United were struggling against relegation and, on Good Friday, were due to play Liverpool, who were comfortably mid-table. Manchester United won the match 2-0. Due to the gambling laws at the time, it was only permitted to gamble at race tracks – everything else was illegal – but a rumour forced the FA to investigate. They found that the match had been fixed to guarantee a United win and that their own players had betted on the result. Several players from both teams were banned for life for manipulating the outcome for financial benefit.

It is worth remembering that this was many decades before footballers were on lucrative contracts, able to afford several houses and cars. They may have been motivated into betting by their own low wages.[30] Another possible motivation was the fact that the war was clearly going on longer than expected and with a bleak outlook for the soldiers involved. More public pressure was being placed

Alexander 'Sandy' Turnbull was a Scottish player for both Manchester City and Manchester United. He was first suspended from playing in 1905 following City's pay malpractice and then banned in 1915 for his part in the Liverpool–Manchester United match-fixing. He was killed in action in France, 1917, and the ban was overturned in recognition of his service to his country.

---

30 See Graham Brooks and Anita Lavorgna, 'Lost Eden: The corruption of sport'. Chapter 6 in Lisa Kihl, *Corruption in sport: causes, consequences, and reform* (Abingdon: Routledge, 2018)

on footballers to sign up to the army. The players perhaps realised that they might soon die on the battlefield, as was the case with Sandy Turnbull, and were determined to provide for their families as best they could.

As has always been the case, the concept of an appropriate wage for a footballer at this time was argued by bearing in mind their relatively short-lived and precarious career. The weekly pay packet was, and is, also compared to what club owners are making at the gate. Nevertheless, at the turn of the century, the FA had passed a rule at its AGM that set the maximum wage of professional footballers playing in the Football League at £4 a week – double what a skilled tradesman received at this time. Some years previously, the Manchester United players had formed an Association Football Players' Union and persuaded counterparts from several other clubs, including Aston Villa and West Bromwich Albion, to join, but their negotiations with the FA were unsuccessful.

We do not know what James made of all of this. Perhaps he felt some allegiance to players in the north where he grew up. 'I've seen these mill workers and the shifts they put in 'fore them Football Association gents in London be out their beds,' he would have shrugged, gathering up the reins and clicking for his horse to move on. In any case, he was already far away in France. He had joined the British Army in November 1914. It was less than a month after his third child (my grandmother) was born and he was already 44 years of age.

It might seem strange for a father to take such a step. He was hardly young-blooded, nor the kind of naive 20-something that we imagine enlisting as some extension of school playing field games. In fact, he was very close to the army upper age limit of 45. There was no conscription in the first two years of the war which suggests that the two million men who volunteered early had genuine commitment to the national cause. On the other hand, in the big towns, working-class men were much less likely than middle- and upper-class men to express eagerness for going to war, and many urban workers staged anti-war demonstrations of their own. Whatever his own personal motive, James was, at least, mindful enough to add to his enlistment papers 'I agree to allow one-third of my pay to my wife and children,' which recruits had the option to do.

His service record was stamped by the recruiting officer at Suffolk Street. The Hippodrome Theatre had moved to the site of Curzon Hall in 1914 but this building was soon in dual use as an army recruiting station and it was here that James would have signed the army's Short Service Agreement. Boxing events were still staged at the old exhibition hall to raise funds for the upkeep of the Soldiers' and Sailors' Club in Newton Street. Thus sport, entertainment, and war found a shared home from the earliest days.

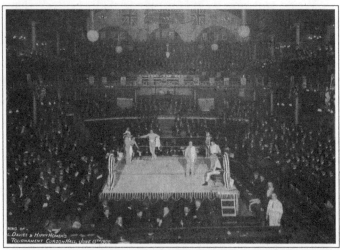

Curzon Hall on Suffolk Street was a sports and entertainment venue but was also used as an army recruiting office in the First World War. It is where James Johnson signed up for service in 1914. Image: Mary Evans/Pharcide.

James was part of the Horse Transport section of the 2nd New Army and his division supplied soldiers with food, equipment and ammunition. This type of work was almost identical to his previous occupation: moving belongings around the streets of Birmingham with a horse and cart. The rural landscape and the opportunity to be on the move might have also been a welcome return to his former traveller family roots. However, he would still have had to have proven himself capable of the work to avoid the 'get a move on, old man' taunts from his superior officers who could have been half his age.

James spent the first two months as part of the Expeditionary Force training in England before going to France in January 1915. He was given the role of horsed transport (HT) driver. HT companies consisted of five officers and 185 other ranks, and they had at their disposal one motor car, seven bicycles, three carts, 22 general service wagons, and 13 riding and 104 draught horses. A driver in the Army Service Corps was on the lowest pay grade of 1s and 6d per day in 1914 – less than £5 in today's money.

There are many reports of the heavy rain that fell during those winter months, already creating the muddy and close-range setting that we are familiar with in images, novels, and cinematic reconstructions of the battlefields. It was also the winter of the famous Christmas Truce, where British and German troops were reported to stop firing, sing songs together, and meet in no man's land to exchange gifts and play games of football.

Even with the water-filled shell holes covering the land, the Army Service Corps continued to move all kinds of resources from the ports on the north coast, where it was collected in base depots. From there, the supplies were moved by train to regulating stations, and then to the local supply depot. For the final leg they would be moved by

Horses carrying ammunition through mud and water in a bombed-out village on the Western Front, around 1917. Image courtesy of the Council of the National Army Museum, London.

horse, mule or motor transport to the staff of front-line units. Thousands of horses were requisitioned from owners across England for these tasks, although many families begged to keep theirs. Owners had to prove that their horse was essential for transport or agricultural work in order to keep it and some succeeded, though many did not.

Horses required a great deal of care and food – ten times as much as a single soldier – and this also had to be rationed. The Blue Cross produced *The Drivers' and Gunners' Handbook to Management and Care of Horses and Harness* for soldiers. Thousands of horses perished during the First World War, including when boats were torpedoed.

In 1917, James was stationed at No. 3 Home Depot in Rouen, north-east France. Rouen was used as a supply base by the British Army and Commonwealth forces and was the site of numerous hospitals. It also had other resources such as field bakeries, exclusively for soldier rations. Even with the increased use of tanks, horses were better in the mud

Stables of the East Kent Regiment. Image courtesy of the Council of the National Army Museum, London.

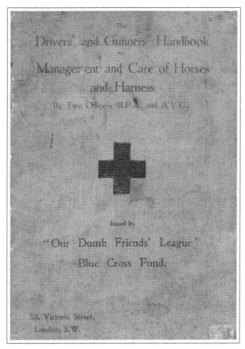

A printed booklet, produced by Our Dumb Friends League (Blue Cross Fund) during World War One (1914–18) to provide vital information for soldiers working with artillery, ambulance and supply horses. Image courtesy of the Council of the National Army Museum, London.

than other vehicles and they continued to pull heavy guns, as well as carrying explosives and wounded soldiers to and from the front line.

The soldiers in charge of these horses also had to support their superior officers when they competed in army sports days of racing, jumping and point-to-point, as if they were still back at home. There were cash prizes to be won, not that there was much to spend the money on in a countryside obliterated by war.

Army Service Corps with horses and carts in 1917. Image: Imperial War Museum Q 4831.

After four years of war, James was demobilised in 1919 and was awarded the 1914/15 Star and the Victory Medal. He had not been 'home' in a very long time, if he even thought of one place as where he belonged. Nevertheless, Birmingham was where his wife and children were, and he was determined to be with them once more.

By the time he returned, Small Heath had become a fully developed urban area compared to the farmland that had still existed up to the start of the 20th century. The Birmingham Small Arms factory had supplied thousands of rifles to the war and then started to focus on cars and motorcycles, the future of transport. It continued to produce rifles, however, later making it a prime target in the 1940 bombings. Small Heath also boasted impressive public baths and a library, numerous schools, and churches. The terraced streets were also attracting many Irish immigrant families who further changed the cultural character of the area.

Despite such changes, the canals were still in use to transport coal and refuse, with the boats often pulled by horses instead of burning fuel. Very few people owned motorised vehicles, so good horse keepers were still required in society. Horses also continued to pull the carts to deliver milk, bread, and laundry. Having been reunited with his family, James was employed by the Birmingham Corporation to be a stables foreman, his reputation no doubt boosted by his services in the war. Corporation horses fulfilled various public tasks, such as road cleaning and salvage collection. His role required looking after the daily work of the horses and staff, giving duties to grooms and stable boys. He would have also had to work with a vet if any of the horses needed medical attention. No longer under the strict hierarchy of the army, and no longer under enemy fire, it must have seemed like a new world of opportunity. And yet the hard work still needed to be done at a time when the financial and emotional cost of war put untold strains on its workers.

James and his pals were equally relieved to find that Birmingham FC was also on the up. The club came top in the Second Division in 1921, earning promotion to the First Division. It was also in a good financial state and able to buy the freehold to its beloved St Andrew's ground. Of course, the highest attendances by far the next season were for the local derby games against West Bromwich Albion

Handsworth Dairy horses and carts lined up for delivery in the 1920s. Image courtesy of Handsworth Historical Society 7/2473.

(both of which were lost), and Aston Villa (an away draw and home win). The Blues' top goalscorer, Joe Bradford, was coming into his own. He had been to Villa for a trial but Birmingham were the only club who were prepared to pay his travel expenses and so he signed a professional contract with them instead and was heartily welcomed into the rival community.

Living so close to St Andrew's, the Johnsons were surrounded by the pre- and post-match atmosphere that would seep into every Small Heath home and public house every Saturday. British Pathé film footage from 1920 shows the Birmingham players running out for their home match against Coventry. The supporters in the crowd are mostly male with younger boys at the front, all of them in jackets and most with flat caps. A few men appear to be in army uniform and there are one or two women, also in coats and hats. As they are all standing, the crowd seems to constantly sway like a school of fish, trying to get a good view. When the players emerge, the supporters mostly stare in wonderment with only a few fans clapping or offering an encouraging shout.

Oral accounts of supporting football in the first part of the 20th century, printed in *Kicking and Screaming: An*

Oral History of Football in England by R.P. Taylor and A. Ward, bring the scene to life, with noticeable similarities and differences to today.

The Rev. Peter Smith said, 'There was only one match and that was it, and in those days people walked or went on the bus … We marched shoulder to shoulder to and from, especially when it was a big crowd. It was a thing people did together … Well it's a religion, isn't it? … It's a drawing together of people with a common interest, a common devotion, you might say, a degree of commitment to something that people think is important.'

Dr Sydney Woodhouse reflected, 'We went as boys and … they were a pretty rough crowd at St Andrew's but they were an orderly crowd. They weren't a boozing, shouting crowd. They were mostly cloth cap and on the poorer side … Large crowds of working men.'

Meanwhile, Alec Lodge revealed, 'Everybody smoked, of course, and … the big attraction for my mother was when it became dusk. There were no floodlights, of course, and it became dusk about four o'clock in the winter, and she used to watch all the men lighting their cigarettes and pipes. It was just like a monstrous Christmas tree.'

Joe Bradford who signed for Birmingham FC in 1920 and played for England, with his dog. Image: Colorsport.

The idea of singing at a football match was catching on and it was at the 1927 FA Cup Final that an organised sing-along, or community singing, as it was known, first took place. Song sheets were printed in the newspapers for supporters to take to Wembley, including the hymn 'Abide With Me'. Where soldiers had sung 'It's a Long Way to Tipperary' on their many wartime marches in faraway places, they were now filling the stadium with the same song in one voice. The *Hull Daily Mail*'s report on the match noted the impact of the singing on the event: 'This community singing is something new and strange in our national life. It is still only in its infancy, but the stadium revealed its stupendous power to unite and unify us and to ennoble us with high emotions.'

In the early 20th century, clubs began developing their own chants and songs, which became an expression of their collective identity. Beyond football, chanting and singing is an ancient folk tradition known around the world and throughout the ages. 'The Wild Rover' can be found in written documents going back to the 16th century and is largely associated with Ireland, but was probably known by Atlantic fishermen and other communities before that. It is sung with enthusiasm as a drinking song, although it also refers to avoiding alcohol (see Chapter 10). Today, the chorus 'And it's no, nay, never' is used by many fans to sing, 'And it's [name of football club], [repeat name] FC. They're by far the best team the world has ever seen.'

A good number of songs came from theatre and music hall entertainment. Records state that, as early as the 1890s, Sheffield United fans were singing 'Rowdy Dowdy Boys', a popular music hall song. Not specific to any particular club, 'Kick-kick-kick-kick-kick-it' was adapted from 'Chick-chicken' in the 1920s. 'Keep the forwards scoring' is derived from 'Keep the Home-Fires Burning', a music hall song popular during the First World War. The American song 'I'm Forever Blowing Bubbles' was often played by marching bands at matches. The boy in the Pears soap advertisements looked like player Billy 'Bubbles' Murray and so West Ham United fans adopted it.

Later on, after the Second World War, the musical theatre hit *Carousel* premiered on Broadway and in the West End. The track 'You'll Never Walk Alone', sung as one of the characters dies at the end of act one, was already popular when the cast recording was sold to the public. It was later recorded by Gerry and the Pacemakers and is now deeply embedded in Liverpool FC culture. In 1953, another recording hit the charts: the Obernkirchen Children's Choir from Germany performing the 19th-century song 'The Happy Wanderer' at a music competition in Wales. It seems an unlikely choice for a crowd of football fans but the catchy chorus 'Val-de-riiiiii, val-de-raaaa' made it a favourite of Wolverhampton Wanderers. Songs were also purposefully written for clubs, including 'On the Ball, City' for Norwich in 1902.

Just as religious texts can be set to different hymn tunes, sports fans and club communities have proven themselves highly adept at singing one song to the tune of another. Rather than praising a higher spiritual being, these adapted lyrics purposefully antagonise the opposition or a local rival. 'Sleigh bells ring' from the 1934 song 'Winter Wonderland' became 'Buuurminghum, are ya list'nin'?' and was sung by Aston Villa fans. West Bromwich Albion's 'Is this the way to hammer Villa?' comes from the 1971 song 'The Way to Amarillo'. 'Go West' by The Village People in 1979 became 'One-nil to the Ar-se-nal', although it is also broadly 'Stand up if you hate [insert name of opposition/ rival]' – in the case of Birmingham City, this would be 'Villa'.

Even highly religious songs have not escaped modifications: 'Simple Gifts', the tune of the Shakers, a

Christian sect from the 18th century and also known as 'Lord of the Dance', is still heard in the Midlands with the lyrics 'Fight, fight, wherever you may be; We are the boys of the Black Country', sung by Wolverhampton Wanderers.

For those who could not get to club games in the late 1920s there was the new BBC radio commentary, although this also required a radio device, which not everyone had. In order to aid the commentary, *Radio Times* published a diagram with the pitch divided into eight parts.

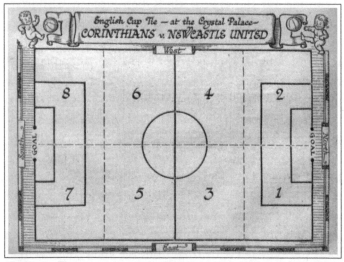

The Radio Times *match grid for The Corinthians v Newcastle United in 1927. The text explains that 'a running commentary of the match will be broadcast … reporting the to-and-fro of the game … [from a] sound-proof observation hut.' Image: Radio Times Issue 174 (Southern) 28 Jan 1927/ Immediate Media Co.*

Within the stadium, it was also impossible to know what was happening in other matches unless there was some way of hearing or seeing a public announcement. Some youngsters performed errands for their local clubs in order to overcome this issue, as one reported in *Kicking and Screaming*:

They had a big wooden screen up for the scoreboard. When I got a little bit older, I used to be a runner to the Empire Pictures to telephone for the half-time scores. There were no other telephones, you see. I used to come back with the scores and they put them up on the scoreboard.

Match reports were sent back to newspaper desks by carrier pigeons, with the scores and any essential details written on pieces of paper and attached to their legs so that they could be included in the evening and Sunday issues.

By the late 1930s, James and Lily were living in Lakey Lane, in the Hall Green district, a good hour on the bus from the bustling streets of Small Heath. They lived among builders, librarians, and mechanics; a community of tradespeople. Even when he was nearly 70, James was still working as a 'general labourer', according to the National Register, with Lily performing 'unpaid domestic duties' like the majority of her married female neighbours.

From a life on the move, it might seem either strange or comforting for James to settle in the suburbs in his later years, saying 'good morning' to neighbours over the fence in front of their identical homes. His world was rapidly changing. Horse-drawn carts and carriages were fading from use to be replaced by motorised vehicles, and James's own son worked as a maker of motorcycle parts. Hall Green's residents would also not escape the next war (see Chapter 12) when the enemy aircraft would seek out nearby factory targets. It would be another huge test of resilience and community spirit for Birmingham and its hard-working, football-loving citizens.

Chapter 10

Scotland's steel and playing football in Flanders Fields

Monklands and Glasgow, Scotland;
Flanders, Belgium; Sheffield, England;
North Africa (1850–1945)

1800s	Walker Cunningham	**Peter Cunningham** and Jean McGhie		Archibald Russell and Helen McLeod
		Robert Cunningham and Jessie Buchanan	**William Cunningham** and Mary Scott	Cornelius Russell and Marion Henry
1900s			**Peter Nisbet Cunningham**	**James Scott Cunningham and Helen McLeod Russell**
			William Cunningham Marion Cunningham Nisbet Cunningham	

THE CONTINUED growth of the iron and steel industry, the improvement in education and health provision, and the development of structured football leagues was following the same pattern in Scotland as in England.

Scotland sent many men to fight in the Boer and two world wars, and also traded with both continental Europe and the West Indies. This meant that Edinburgh's Forth and Glasgow's Clyde rivers became principal shipping channels. Families who were skilled in metalwork migrated there, as well as overseas, and new ironworks were starting to be built and flourished in the southern areas. These families were not just sources of labour; they needed shops and schools, places of worship, and sports clubs. They aspired to have a better life than their forefathers, and yet they lost a great many promising sons to global conflict.

The area of Lanarkshire known as Monklands was, back in the 12th century, exactly that: large expanses of land cultivated by monks who worked as successful sheep farmers and wool exporters, as well as gathering lead and coal from the ground. The earliest ironworks was actually in the Highlands, in the north of Scotland next to lochs and vast woodlands as a source of timber to create the wood charcoal for the furnaces. So great was the number of trees being cut down that laws were passed to forbid and restrict it. It was not until later in the 18th century and early in the 19th that coke (from coal) was more widely used. The invention of Henry Cort's puddling furnace in 1784, and the completion of the Monkland Canal in 1790 that created a fast and easy link-up to Glasgow, finally and firmly established the iron industry in this southern area.

Peter Cunningham, my three-times great-grandfather, started out his adult life as a labourer and a lodger with another family, having left his parents and siblings near Edinburgh (see Chapter 2). He lived in a village called Langloan, now a suburb of Coatbridge, south-east of Glasgow, and worked as an engineer; something that would carry through the family for generations. The village was well-known for its ironworks which opened in 1841 and

Peter, like most of the village, would have likely served it at one time. He married Jean McGhie from Dumfriesshire in January 1848 and they had an incredible 13 children in 24 years, while Peter worked his way up to being an engine fitter foreman.

The winter sport of choice in the early and mid-19th century in Lanarkshire was curling. The first recognised clubs were created in Scotland, although it officially dates back to at least the 16th century (with a challenge by an enthusiastic monk) and features in the winter landscape paintings of Flemish artist Bruegel. Well ahead of football associations, the Royal Caledonian Curling Club was founded in 1838 and created the official rules of the sport. Curling is the game of sliding polished stones with handles across ice towards a target. Points are scored for being nearest the target and the stones can be guided on their way only by sweeping the ice with brushes or brooms. A large painting of curlers from the nearby New Monkland Curling Club in the 1850s celebrates its popularity and the diverse occupations of the men who took part: bankers, bakers, merchants, and

The Curlers at Rawyards *by John Levack (1823–74). Levack's painting of 1857 shows a curling match in progress on a pond at Rawyards on the eastern outskirts of Airdrie. The painting depicts a selection of mainly middle-class local people and dignitaries, including Patrick Rankin and Provost James Thomson Rankin of Auchengray, and Gavin Black and Robert Graham of Rawyards. Image: North Lanarkshire Council/CultureNL.*

farmers. Women with food baskets and bottles of drink for sustenance, and children, look across the frozen pond with fascination.

Curling was taken to Canada by merchants and soldiers, although they had to play with iron stones due to a lack of Scottish granite rock. One of Peter's six sons, Robert, emigrated to the Ontario province of Canada. Between 1815 and 1870 over 170,000 Scots emigrated to Canada, often settling in Quebec and Ontario, including the aptly named Lanark County. They came from all over Scotland – Highlanders and Lowlanders – and were farmers, teachers, merchants, clergymen, and servants. They were also metal workers and the Canadian city of Hamilton, which had close trade links with Glasgow, acquired the nickname 'Steel City' or 'the Birmingham of Canada'. Robert, however, was a clergyman. He married Jessie Buchanan, whose parents were also from Scotland, and was pastor of a Baptist church in a small Canadian countryside settlement.

Another son, William (my great-great-grandfather), stayed in Lanarkshire and lived in Old Monkland with his many other siblings. By the age of 16 he was a clerk in the railway controller's office. The Caledonian Railway was designed to be the main line railway from Glasgow and Edinburgh to Carlisle, making long-distance connections with the English railway network. It was built over the previous horse-drawn coal railways to avoid the cost of new construction. Many ironworks were founded next to the Caledonian line in the Coatbridge area, as well as numerous pits, helping to boost the industry. Walker Cunningham (William's uncle and Peter's brother) had already taken his engine-fitting skills over to the United States, which was a month-long journey by steamship, to Indiana where the new railroads were also enabling industry to boom after the American Civil War.

William married Mary Scott and transferred from the railway to be a cashier clerk in the other dominant industry: the iron and steel works. Not content with this simple employment, he worked his way up and up over the years until, eventually, he became director of the Etna Iron and Steel Works Company Ltd of Motherwell. With so many new firms springing up like in England, the area was described as the 'Staffordshire of Scotland'. Thomas Miller eventually ran the Motherwell Bridge and Engineering Company Ltd, which was a competitor. He recalled his experience as a child:

> In the distance were the lochs of Woodend and Lochend, but from the town there came a continual roar from the mass of heavy machinery; this and the pounding of many steam hammers engaged on the shingling process seemed to make even the very ground vibrate under one's feet. A pall of dense black smoke from the chimneys of the puddling furnaces of the malleable ironworks blanketed the main centre of the town like a smoke screen in a naval action, and darkened the day. Later, the red glow from the surrounding blast furnaces illuminated the sky at night.[31]

Steel production on a large scale was relatively new. It was found to be incredibly versatile and was made from pig iron and scrap. Most firms acquired the new equipment necessary and added 'and steel' to their ironworks titles and advertisements. The first major steel bridge was the famous Forth Bridge, north of Edinburgh, built in 1890, while the Sydney Harbour Bridge in Australia would be built later in

---

31 From *The Monkland Tradition* by T.R. Miller (T. Nelson, 1958).

steel by a company from Middlesbrough. In the early part of the 20th century several firms would get together to create the Scottish Iron and Steel Co. Ltd. Many feared this would become a monopoly – rather like the criticism of the new Football League – but in time would prove to create financial stability and support overseas trade. Etna Iron and Steel, under the direction of William Cunningham, would boldly decide to remain independent, along with three other firms. This could have put them in a weak position, reliant on home manufacturers for supply. However, Etna would also take the positive practical step of introducing electric power to compensate for the loss of iron puddling steam power. They were apparently the first to do so and the electric motor was rumoured to have come from a wartime German submarine.

An advertisement for the Etna Iron and Steel Company from 1912. Image: Grace's Guide to British Industrial History.

Back in the 19th century, along with the growth in ironworks and the expansion of the railways, new football clubs – especially factory teams – were springing up everywhere, including Lanarkshire. The introduction of half days on Saturday for many trades gave the working-class citizens time for leisure pursuits. A swelling population in cities provided a captive audience for such simple entertainment, coupled with improved transport to get there and increased news coverage to inform them about it.

Queen's Park was officially formed at a committee meeting on 9 July 1867. Initially they played games within their own club, including one match featuring the 'Smokers' versus the 'Non-Smokers'. A year later, the player and secretary, Robert Gardner, received an invitation to a match by a team named Thistle. A young man of 21, he was not the typical older club secretary with years of business management but he took his football seriously and knew that this was an opportunity to set some official terms. Staring out of his window at the passing Glasgow traders and stroking his beard, he considered his reply. He had decided to accept, of course, but, picking up his pen, Gardner politely suggested that, for a game of 20 players a side, 'Two hours is quite long enough to play in weather such as the present.' He also wrote that the teams should change ends after the first hour 'so that boath parties may have the same change of wind and ground'. He finished by asking if Thistle would 'be so good enough to bring your ball with you in case of any breake down, and thus prevent interuptsion'.[32] The letter was signed, sent, and Queen's Park eventually won that match.

Similar to Williams McGregor's move in England on behalf of Aston Villa (see Chapter 8), it was Queen's Park who called the meeting in 1873 in order to propose a Challenge (later the Scottish) Cup and a Scottish Football Association. The other clubs were Clydesdale, Vale of Leven, Dumbreck,

---

32 See Kevin McCarra (1984) *Scottish football: a pictorial history from 1867 to the present day*, Third Eye Centre.

Third Lanark Rifle Volunteer Reserves, Eastern, Granville, and Rovers. The Scottish Football Association (SFA) was founded at a meeting of several clubs held at Dewar's Hotel in Glasgow in March 1873. Its members were predominantly against professionalism. They refused to select players for their international team who were either being paid, or who, perhaps a worse offence, were playing in England. Their hatred of professionalism went so far as to complain about the English centre-back, James Forrest, who was receiving £1 per week from Blackburn Rovers. They eventually conceded that the 1885 England v Scotland match could only go ahead if Forrest wore a different jersey to the rest of his team-mates, as if that might make a difference to the result. In the end Joe Lindsay had Scotland up 1-0 at half-time, but Charlie Bambridge levelled for the hosts after a double save from the Scottish goalkeeper, and the match finished 1-1.

Despite the adoption of association rules, the early games were not without confusion and suspicion. In 1873 Kilmarnock were still persistently using their hands and a goal was scored in 1876 when it was deflected off the umbrella of one of the on-pitch umpires, who were not moved to behind the sidelines until 1891.

In Motherwell, where my great-great-grandfather had his iron and steel company, football was dominated by Glencairn and their main rivals, Alpha of the Alpha Steam Crane and Engineering Works. The clubs eventually combined to form Motherwell Football Club, beating Hamilton Academical 3-2 in their debut fixture. As with all clubs relying on self-organised fixtures, competition was difficult to find and games would begin short of players, as they struggled to make kick-off or play at all due to a shift in the local ironworks.

With a different history to the other football clubs, Celtic was formed as a charitable institution devoted to helping the

The Motherwell team of 1886, comprising the best players from Glencairn and Alpha, who are pictured at the original ground Roman Road. The players are: William Sneddon, Tom Gray, Robert Sharp, James Murray, James Irvine, James Wilson, James Charteris, Tom Sharp, William Moodie, William Charteris and James Cassidy. Image courtesy of Motherwell Football Club/Keith Brown and Graham Barnstaple.

poor, particularly the Irish immigrants, in the East End of Glasgow. They became an instant success with a huge following, also attracting experienced players from other teams. As with the English teams, there was a demand for regular and reliable fixtures, but the various ways to go about it were still roundly criticised. A proposal of a qualification competition in order to enter the Scottish Cup was accused as being elitist. The Scottish Football League (SFL) was eventually established in 1890 comprising 11 teams: Abercorn, Cambuslang, Celtic, Cowlairs, Dumbarton, Glasgow Rangers, Heart of Midlothian, Renton, St Mirren, Third Lanark and Vale of Leven.

Shortly after this competition was formed, there was a heated debate at Motherwell's AGM of 1893, resulting in a vote in favour of turning professional. The SFA also conceded the same year. This resulted in an increase in gate prices with entry costing six pence (equivalent to around £8 today) and season tickets moving to 7s and 6p (equivalent to around £50 today). It also led to Motherwell joining nine other teams, including Hibernian and Partick Thistle, in the SFL's new second division at the start of the 1893/94 season.

Given that such fixtures would draw regular crowds that could be charged admission, the SFL announced new rules about professionalism to which *Scottish Sport* magazine responded in 1890, 'Our first and last objection to them is that they exist. The entire rules stink of finance – money making and money grabbing.' Scottish players were being lost to English clubs who had officially turned professional since 1885. Despite the Glasgow Charity Cup raising over £10,000 for various beneficiaries between 1877 and 1890, clubs were also raking in the cash. After various investigations and sanctions the SFA had to finally admit that professionalism was already widespread. This does not mean that all clubs were financially stable. Dundee nearly met with an early end and rumours of bankruptcy abounded. A telegram was sent summoning them to a bar. Representatives of the SFL

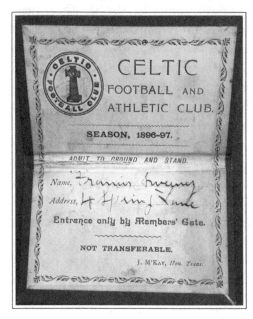

A season ticket for Celtic Football and Athletic Club for the 1896/97 season. It is made from folded card with the holder's handwritten name and address. Image: The Celtic Wiki.

offered to temporarily guarantee wages and expenses and the club was saved.

Bobby Templeton was a highly talented player, but he was one who was caught up in the persistent debate. Having left Celtic for Kilmarnock, he was being paid £4 per week and the club also paid for him to stay in the town's hotel. This was more than double the wage of the highest paid and skilled work in Glasgow sawmill at the time, who would fetch around £1 16s. Criticism about financial gain was extended to the successful businessmen who ran such clubs, including Willie Maley who managed Celtic from 1897 to 1940 and was also the owner of a sports outfitters and a restaurant.

Another significant and related cultural change in Lanarkshire was the growth of the Temperance Movement, which promoted religion and education, as well as sufficient wages for poorer people in order to fight against alcoholism. Wealthy industrialists took a lead in measures against alcohol for the benefit of their employees, and membership of temperance societies could come with insurance and pension benefits. Sashes and medals identified loyal participants, and handbooks guided organisers and speakers. Whole families were encouraged to sign up. Coffee houses and tea dances encouraged a different social scene to the local public house.

The Temperance Movement is also understood to have played a part in the split of Everton Football Club at Anfield in the 1890s. The club's president, John Houlding, was a brewer by trade and a Conservative councillor in his political life. He had bought new Anfield land and then wanted a large sum from the football club in order for them to use it. Committee member George Mahon was a chapel organist and others in the Temperance Movement were active in the Liberal Party. There was an inevitable clash of personalities and beliefs. Various disagreements continued and the famous club division in northern football duly followed with Everton moving to Goodison Road, and a newly registered club, called Liverpool, remaining at Anfield.

Like many religious Scots, William McGregor, one of the founders of the English Football League, was a teetotaller and a supporter of the Temperance Movement. He was also active in the Liberal Party, although his membership lapsed in 1882 because he spent so much time on football. He reportedly said that Scottish players who moved to England – in other words his own countrymen – needed to be supervised otherwise they would be out on the town. To be fair to the players, by the mid-1880s the sense of professionalism was such that they understood better what was required of a footballer. That is not to say that heavy drinking did not happen. After a tour to Scotland – which McGregor was in charge of – the Aston Villa players

Cartoons in 19th-entury newspapers and journals highlighted the negative consequences of drinking alcohol. Image: George Cruikshank (1792-1878).

227

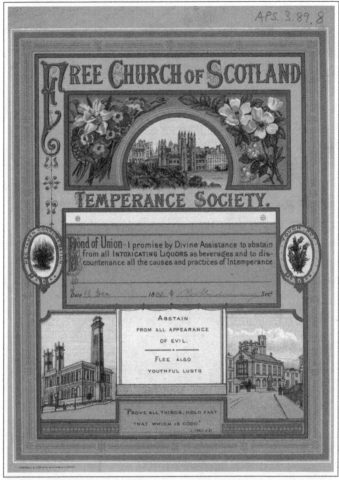

Members of the Temperance Movement signed pledges, and the certificate could be given by the local church. Image: Free Church of Scotland/National Library of Scotland.

were so out of shape that they lost their FA Cup tie against Blackburn Rovers 8-1.

James Scott Cunningham, son of William, was born in 1888 and followed the new family trade in the local iron and steel works as an assistant roller. Rolling is a metal-forming process in which young James would have been passing metal stock through one or more pairs of rolls in order to reduce the thickness and to make the thickness uniform, or to give it certain properties like shape or increased strength. Proving oneself on the factory floor also meant an opportunity to seem honest and hard-working in the eyes of colleagues and supervisors. And so it was that James was permitted to marry Helen McLeod Russell, who was the daughter of Cornelius, a clerk at the ironworks.

One of Helen's brothers, Robert, was another of my ancestors quick to sign up at the start of the war in 1914. He had been a chemist's apprentice at 18 and married at 22 but, in his early 30s, he was eager for service with the Gordon Highlanders and rushed up to the recruiting office at Aberdeen. Although being 5ft 7in and described as having a 'sallow' complexion (meaning pale or sickly looking), he was passed for training but in the end was considered 'not likely to become an efficient soldier'. This phrase was often written on army records in 1914 as the training – marching and gunmanship – served its purpose of making sure that men could cope with at least the basics and that there were no other health or learning difficulties that had not been identified at the recruiting office.

The verdict of Robert Russell's unsuccessful military training in 1914.

Helen's cousin, Archibald, had certainly broken the mould of the Russell coal and iron family trade. He was the only son of Thomas (Helen's uncle), a mining engineer with the Coltness Iron Co Ltd, and Janet Russell (née Stewart). Archie had done well at school and gone on to the University of Glasgow where he was a keen cricketer and graduated with a degree in medicine in April 1914 at the age of 24. Archie served as a surgeon with the Royal Navy, aboard HMS *Macedonia*, an armed merchant cruiser. On 16 May 1917 he was travelling home on leave aboard the merchant ship HMS *Highland Corrie*. Having not been home for some time, and thinking of his family and friends up near Glasgow, he waited with anticipation as the ship glided into the English Channel. Suddenly, the vessel was torpedoed and sunk by a German UB-40 submarine. Archie was killed along with four other crew.

(Left) Helen McLeod Russell as a young girl. (Right) Archibald McKerrow Russell was a trained surgeon in the navy, and a keen cricketer, and died in 1917 when his ship was torpedoed. Image: University of Glasgow Archives & Special Collections.

James Cunningham had a brother, Peter Nisbet (named after their grandfather), who had also signed up. Like Archie, Peter was a little different to his ancestors and siblings. He had won prizes for English and French at school. Instead of joining the local ironworks as a young lad, he too went up to Glasgow to study electrical engineering while also working as an apprentice at an electrical works. When war broke out, just months after passing his final examinations, he joined the 17th Battalion, the Highland Light Infantry. This had been formed by commanding officers purposefully targeting students within the Royal Technical College and other former students of Glasgow schools. The young lads – now suddenly men of the British Army – were gathered in their elegant college examination hall and taken off for training camp.

The 17th Highland Light Infantry – including many very young students and graduates – gathering at the Royal Engineering College in Glasgow before leaving for military training. Image from The Seventeenth Highland Light Infantry *by David J. Clark (1920).*

An extract from a diary of one of the students gives a hint as to their early experience and naivety:

> We watched and whispered. Some asked, who is that man with the loud voice shouting at us and giving us papers... We got the magic words, 'To camp at Gailes.' Then we were soldiers ... The crowd laughed and cheered us. Thus we left the city... for the last time.[33]

---

33   From *The Seventeenth Highland Light Infantry* by David J. Clark (1920).

In 1915, Peter and his battalion moved to the south of England for more training, which was probably the furthest that any of these Scottish men had been from home in their young lives. They played – and defeated – Bath City at football, as well as other battalions at rugby. Then, all of a sudden, the amateur games were over and they marched into France, right up to the front line in the frost of late November 1915. One week later they were knee-deep in trench water and rats, and the first of their number was killed. The following months were endless cycles of avoiding and returning fire, repairing trenches and communication lines, and venturing out into no man's land at night. Some offensives involved running out under the 'cover' of heavy explosives, attacking enemy trenches and taking prisoners.

One day in 1916, Peter could finally collapse down on to something resembling a normal bed after so long on the move. He was exhausted and relieved to have been retreated for recuperation. Listening from his bunk, he could hear some banter shared among the lads as they wondered how to spend this free time, if not already in the yard with a ball for a kickabout. In fact, the 'rest period' turned out to be more training in preparation for the Battle of the Somme. This infamous battle has since been widely criticised for poor leadership and planning, leading to tens of thousands of casualties. At the time Peter and his friends knew very little detail of what was coming, although they had already faced many horrors.

They moved back to the front line. Just days before the planned attack, Peter and his friends were suddenly ordered to stand down and await further orders. Soldiers in the fellow 16th Battalion had a game of football to relieve the agonising wait. Unfortunately a German shell landed between the makeshift goalposts, causing several casualties before the fighting had even begun. Then the order to advance came with more heavy shelling. Captain Wilfred Nevill of the East Surrey Regiment famously kicked a football into no man's land ahead of the troops. He and many of his men were killed instantly. Metres of land were won and lost, and over 450 of the 17th Highland Light Infantry were killed in a matter of days.

Peter had initially been registered as a private (the rank of ordinary soldier) but he was soon appointed as a lance corporal, which meant being in charge of a section in his battalion. He then rose to the rank of second lieutenant, giving him the status of a commissioned officer, which normally only takes place after specific training. The speed at which this happened was catalysed by the number of those officers above him being killed. The 17th Highland Light Infantry moved constantly around locations north of Amiens in north-east France. As if to lighten the mood, the military report details how, on Christmas Day 1916, 'B' Company beat a Headquarters team at football 4-0, which must have felt like some very minor payback for all the battle orders received. Resources were so stretched – or perhaps HQ were so offended by the result – that Christmas dinner was postponed to the 30th, although the Scots were permitted a concert to celebrate Hogmanay.

In 1917 there was finally some sense of real territorial advance among Peter's men, with continuous fighting punctuated by more games of football (6-1 win against the 121st Infantry and a draw against the 408th Regiment). Perhaps to make up for – or conceal – the reality of military combat, it was reported that the 17th played 'some of their keenest and most memorable games of soccer' while stationed at the village of Canizy. Finally, in the summer, they arrived in the Flanders region. Again, after surviving a German attack, a day of football and other sports was held and the records note that 'a good turnout of the British and Belgian nurses from La Panne Hospital brightened the gathering'.

In November 1917, the 17th marched towards the Passchendaele front line. At 1.55am on 2 December all four companies assembled for an attack, despite military intelligence that it was highly risky. The soldiers had faith in their superiors and believed that all seemed to be going to plan. Peter's breath would have risen in small clouds in the cold night air as he held position. Whatever his own personal doubts, he kept quiet; for his own sake as much

as those of his men. They trusted him and he would do his best to get them through this. It was dark in the dugout where they had paused. However, the moment that they moved forward they were exposed by the clear moonlight reflecting off the recent snowfall. The enemy were lying in wait and opened heavy machine gun fire in what has since been called the 'Moonlight Massacre'.

Peter Nisbet Cunningham (1892–1917) in uniform.

What happened next to Peter was reported back to his family by his battalion commander and featured in the local newspaper, 'He very gallantly "went" for a machine-gun which was holding up our advance, and in doing so met his death. We shall all miss him very much. He was a splendid officer and universally popular.' He was 25 years old.

Numerous professional footballers also joined the Highland Light Infantry. Some were so badly wounded that it meant an end to their playing careers, and some lost their lives.

In June 1915, Lieutenant Martin of the 8th Battalion, Highland Light Infantry, was injured by an exploding mine in front of the German trenches. He was heard pleading for water, unable to move. William Angus – a player for Celtic – volunteered to rescue the man who also came from Carluke (five miles from my family's home). At first the senior officers refused, calling it a suicidal mission, but Angus was determined. He crawled through no man's land and attached a rope to Martin but Angus was spotted and came under heavy fire. He signalled to the British troops to pull Martin to safety, running in another direction to draw the enemy fire away. Despite being hit several times, he made it back to the trenches but lost his left eye and part of his right foot. He was the first professional footballer to be awarded the Victoria Cross.

At the beginning of the 1914/15 football season, Heart of Midlothian had been Scotland's most successful team, winning eight games on the trot. A poem encouraged players and supporters to 'pack up your footballs and scarves of maroon'. Every member of the team joined the army but seven of them never returned.

In 1917, James's work in the iron and steel industry took him, Helen, and their young son Bill (William) from Scotland to Sheffield, England.

His employer, Vickers, was a famous British engineering conglomerate. In 1863 the company had moved to a new site in Sheffield on the River Don in Brightside and, by 1918, there were 16,000 workers employed there. It was a huge operation. It was during the two world wars that the business did particularly well, specialising in car and aircraft engines, as well as armour plates, battleship construction, and big guns. They suffered a little between the wars and merged

This souvenir postcard reminded supporters of their Heart of Midlothian Football Club players who were bravely serving overseas. Tom Gracie (1) and Duncan Currie (2) died in 1915, whilst Harry Wattie (3), Ernie Ellis (10) and James Speedie (11) were all killed on the same day: 1 July 1916. Image from the book Hearts At War 1914-1919 *by Tom Purdie (Amberley Publishing, 2014).*

many of the engineering and armaments assets with those of Armstrong Whitworth to become Vickers-Armstrongs in 1927 and eventually one of the largest engineering companies of the 20th century.

Of course, like the other cities in this journey, Sheffield was a key site in the development of both football and the iron and steel industry. It was Sheffield FC who had developed a code, or set of rules, during the 1860s, that was notably used by Aston Villa in their own first fixture. The Sheffield Football Association operated in parallel to the London-based Football Association until there was an agreement on one set of rules to take the game forward. The code included such concepts as throw-ins, corners, and free kicks. The rules developed as the game progressed and it would be a Scottish team, Renton FC, credited with scoring the first competitive penalty kick in 1891. The oldest officially recorded football match is believed to have occurred in Sheffield, despite the many accounts of village games elsewhere in Scotland and England through the centuries. In 1794, a game of mob football was played between Sheffield and Norton, a village in Derbyshire, that took place at Bents Green. The match lasted for three days.

James and Helen lived in Ecclesall, west of Sheffield, where their second child (my grandmother) was born. Also living nearby at the time was William McGregor, son of the Birmingham draper of the same name who had created the English Football League and served on the board of Aston Villa some 30 years before. The McGregor family were from Scotland and so it is unsurprising that they became good friends. They were also of a similar part of society: young manufacturing managers whose parents had worked their way up from the factory (or shop) floor.

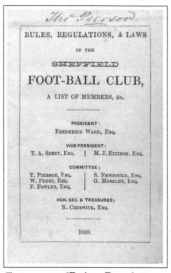

Front page of Rules, Regulations, & Laws of the Sheffield Foot-Ball Club *with a list of members, published in 1859. It is the only known surviving copy of the first printing of the first club's laws of football.*

William McGregor junior was in charge of clothing manufacturing and his father's work – probably more the football than the drapery shop – had left big shoes to fill. William would likely have told the Cunninghams all about his father's determination to set up a league in England where teams could play regular fixtures and pay their players a wage. James and Helen would have known about the growing popularity of professional football in Lanarkshire and would have been enthusiastic listeners, especially if an enterprising Scottish man had done so much to lead the English. William was known as 'Uncle Willy' to my grandmother, unaware as a toddler, but perhaps by then written in the stars, that her future husband would also be from an Aston family who loved football.

A family photograph taken in Ecclesall of James and Helen on deckchairs in the garden with baby Marion. On the right are son, Bill, with his cricket bat, and Helen's brother.

In the early 1920s the family returned home to Scotland, to Wishaw in Lanarkshire. The most likely origin of Wishaw's name comes from 'Wi', similar to via, and 'schaw' meaning wood. The old village of Coalness sprung up where a Roman road crossed the River Calder below Wishaw House. Travellers from the south had to go through extensive woodland to reach Coalness so the way became known as 'via schaw' or wi-shaw. An alternative theory is that the name came from a house or inn near Wincie's Well, an ancient site dedicated to the Catholic martyr St Winifrede. The house was used as a resting place for invalids visiting the well and became known as Wassail Ha or Wish Ha, a greeting to wish good health.

The town had developed from a weaving village planned out in 1794 – Wishawtoun – to become an industrial town in the 19th century with coalmining, iron, steel, smelting and distilling. After its period of boom, Wishaw would eventually lose its reputation when the iron and steel industry shut down in the 1990s with the closure of British Steel.

Rather like the local industry, football was also at the mercy of other forces. Motherwell had tried for years to be successful but could not keep the good players from leaving, including for England, since they did not have the financial status of other big clubs. Eventually they would manage to keep their emerging juniors together against all odds and they took the league title in 1932. This was rather an anomaly in the early history of Scottish football, similar to the 50 or so pairs of golden boots emerging from the coalminers of Glenbuck village (see Chapter 3). It does seem proof, however, that smaller clubs can still make it if they stick together, but only in the face of great financial adversity.

James and Helen were rather more into a smoother, heavier ball sport. Wishaw Bowling Club was established in 1860 and so could, if there was any need, boast a longer history than all of the surrounding football clubs. The sports are closely linked, however. Hampden Bowling Club (founded 1905) sits on the site of the original Hampden Park and the pavilion housed the original changing rooms for matches of Queen's Park and Scotland football teams. Bowls, cricket, and football were all popular in Glasgow and had to tussle it out with each other and the authorities for a piece of land. One cannot believe that they saw eye to eye on the state of the public ground. Imagine turning up at the bowling club to your favourite flat spot of park to roll the first jack on a Sunday after church only to find that the football players have completely destroyed the green the day before. Poor Queen's Park had numerous requests turned down themselves until they were finally granted their small patch; and only up until May on the condition that they erect fences to separate it from the rest of the park.[34]

A family photograph of the members of the Bowls Club and their immaculate green.

The first Hampden ground in Glasgow. Image from The History of The Queen's Park Football Club 1867–1917, *by Richard Robinson (published 1920).*

---

34 Robinson, Richard, *The History of The Queen's Park Football Club* 1867–1917 (1920)

During the 1930s, the family – James, Helen and their three children – was now doing well enough to spend their summers at the fashionable resort of North Berwick, 20 miles north-east of Edinburgh. Its sandy beaches and two golf courses attracted high society. The local newspaper regularly reported on the various lords and ladies who had arrived for the season. In 1929, they also announced that the England rugby team, who had taken part in an international match against Scotland one Saturday, were residing in the town 'along with a number of their supporters' and that 'several of the team engaged in games of golf over the West Links'. Similarly, in March 1939, following their league match at Easter Road against Ayr United, 'The Hibernian Football team ... took up residence in the Redcroft Hotel for the week-end prior to their Scottish Cup tie with Alloa.'[35]

Compared to the tales of early league footballers rushing from their factory shifts to play games in muddy meadows, this is more like the professional life of fixtures, hotel stays and team leisure time that we are familiar with today. As for my grandmother, she used to wistfully recall posing on – but not diving from – the high boards at the open-air pool, possibly to gain the attentions of a suitable boy, or professional sportsman.

Another recreation activity was to climb Scotland's many peaks and hike around the lochs. One popular destination was Loch Ness, near Inverness, which had caused much excitement with reported sightings of its mysterious monster. In 1933 the floodlights belonging to Caledonian FC were taken away in order to help illuminate the loch and aid the search. The lights never returned and the players would not benefit from a new system until 1959.

---

35 Jamieson, Bruce A., *North Berwick Between the Wars* (East Lothian Courier and East Lothian Council, 1996)

Photographs of the family enjoying the beach, swimming pool, and tennis courts at fashionable North Berwick. Suitably stylish hats, jackets, and dresses are worn by everyone.

War soon came again at the end of the decade and two of James's children enlisted: Bill into the army and Marion (my grandmother) into the Royal Air Force. Being only 16, Nisbet was too young to join up and so stayed in Scotland with his parents.

Lieutenant-Colonel William 'Bill' McGhie Cunningham served with the 11th Hussars. The regiment is known as 'Prince Albert's Own', but also by the nickname

242

'Cherrypickers'. This came from an incident during the Peninsular War, in which the 11th Hussars were attacked while raiding an orchard at San Martin de Trebejo in Spain. It is believed that the well-known football team, the Glenbuck Cherrypickers (see Chapter 3) used the same name because some of their men fought with the regiment in the Boer War. Another association of the term 'cherrypicking' is the process of sorting coal on a conveyor belt – equally appropriate for a Lanarkshire man.

Bill had his fair share of adventure in those years. The journey out to Africa seemed eventful enough, as described in a fellow soldier's memoirs: 'The heavy Atlantic swell increased, with every other boat in the convoy disappearing from sight each time we wallowed at the foot of a huge trough. It was like sitting on the floor of a deep valley surrounded by peaks, until the ship rose to the crest of the next huge wave. Then the whole convoy reappeared, before disappearing again as we slid to the bottom of the next trough.'[36]

Bill was awarded the Military Cross for his service in Egypt and Libya, fighting his way out of numerous difficult situations. The work certainly required creative minds. At one point the regiment resorted to building huge fake tanks out of wooden frames and camouflage net to fool the enemy surveillance photographers into thinking that they were up against a much bigger opposition.

Like his grandfather back in Scotland, Bill had the desire and determination to climb the ranks. At 4am on Christmas Day in 1940, he is recorded as leading a section of troops out on a mission and successfully returning unscathed.[37] By

---

36 Quoted in *Berlin or Bust* (Chester: Keith Osborne, 2000).
37 Clarke, Dudley, *The Eleventh at war, being the story of the XIth Hussars (Prince Albert's Own) through the years 1934–1945* (London: Michael Joseph, 1952).

1941 he was recommended for the staff of General (later Field Marshal) Alexander, leading operations in Tunisia and the capture of Italy before reaching Berlin in 1945. He was appointed lieutenant, Royal Victorian Order (LVO) and officer, Order of the British Empire (OBE). In 1946 he married Delia Holland-Hibbert who represented Great Britain in dressage and was equally adept at various water sports, having been a third officer in the Women's Royal Naval Service. She even taught her own children to surf waves in the 1950s; something that not many housewives could or would have done.

(Left) Young Bill with his siblings. (Right) A newspaper cutting found in my grandmother's possessions. Bill is in the background, behind General Montgomery who is talking with General Alexander and Prime Minister Winston Churchill on a visit to Egypt. This is a British Official Photograph (BM17540) that appeared in the Daily Telegraph *on 27 August 1942.*

Back in Scotland, James and Helen would have had to wait anxiously for news of their children, like all parents in the same wartime situation. Fortunately they survived and Helen and James spent their last years in Carluke, the small town in Lanarkshire producing many 20th-century soldiers and footballers alike, overlooking the River Clyde.

Chapter 11

A long way from St Andrew's

Birmingham, North Africa, France,
Belgium, Germany (1910–1950)

1800s	Thomas and Harriet Clemson	John and Elizabeth Perry	Robert Johnson	Arthur and Sarah Ann Hornsby
1900s	George Clemson and Florence Perry		James Johnson and Lilian Hornsby	
	Thomas Clemson and Irene Johnson			

THE FIRST half of the 20th century was dominated by war, taking millions of citizens to countries that they would never normally have visited, and leaving millions more families to fill the void and 'keep the home fires burning' as the old song goes. For the younger boys and girls, education was the standard daily existence, with schools now free for all and the leaving age rising to 14 after the First World War. Over the next decades manufacturing would expand, as would the size of some factories, with advances in machinery. However, Birmingham still had a vast number of small firms with fewer than 50 employees, especially in the jewellery and small firearms trades. This meant that those school leavers had a diverse range of trades open to them. And such it was also in sport, with professional clubs expanding alongside numerous new amateur clubs that existed in the working-class communities.

The Clemson family were living in the close community of Grosvenor Street West, just across the canal from the very centre of Birmingham. A lady named Mrs Walters lived in the same street and was reportedly well-known for acting as the local midwife, bringing many new screaming babies into the world. In October 1912 she would have hurried down the road to deliver Thomas, my grandfather, in one of the few small rooms shared by his six older brothers and sisters and his parents.

A creased family photograph of Thomas aged around three years old. He is sat on a donkey in the street, in front of a shop, led by a tradesman in a flat cap and white apron. There is a young girl looking on from a doorway behind.

His early life would have been much like his own parents': toddling about his own small world that was made up of the courtyard houses in the enclosed spaces behind the streets; being passed around various siblings and neighbours to 'please keep an eye on just for a bit, if you wouldn't mind, thanks'.

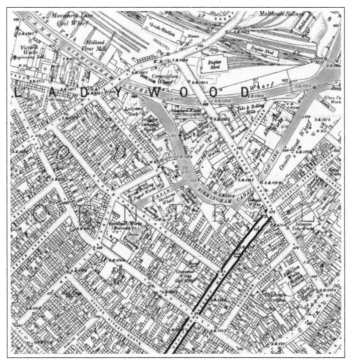

Map from the 1880s showing Grosvenor Street West (bold outline) in the area of Ladywood. It runs diagonally down from Oozells Street Wharf and the canal (shaded at the top of the image) and trainlines, which imported and exported Birmingham's many goods. The compact area surrounded by the canalways contained several metal tube works, which was a family trade. Image: Ordnance Survey 1884–91.

Thomas went to St Barnabas School, which was just around the corner from his own street. It opened in 1862 for both boys and girls and added an infants' school in 1880. St Barnabas also had a Sunday school, football teams, and a youth club.

The number of schools in Birmingham had increased in the 19th century with over 100 new schools created even before the Education Act of 1870. These schools had

A 20th-century photograph of the corner of Grosvenor Street West, showing the type of houses and shops that were there. It still remains mostly a residential street today, although with new accommodation blocks. Image: photobydjnorton.

limited funding, however, and needed to charge each pupil between 1d and 9d per week just to keep running, which not all families could easily afford. Despite this, Birmingham sat proudly ahead of other cities in improving and extending education and in encouraging attendance. For example, Oozells Street Board School opened in January 1878 for 800 pupils and remains in the city centre today as an impressive building of historical and architectural significance.

Town halls, hospitals, libraries, and railway stations were public buildings being treated to a more decorative form of architecture inspired by the pointed roofs and steeples of medieval churches – the 'gothic' style. Schools then followed as being worthy of elaborations, eventually paving the way for more imaginative football stadium designs, which was also necessitated by overcrowding (see Chapter 7). The designers believed that the schools should be a very different environment to the homes in which the pupils lived. The school buildings were characterised by red brick and terracotta, and with steep roofs supported by large arches of internally exposed ironwork. Boys and girls were segregated with separate entrances. The *Pall Mall Gazette* gave them worthy praise in 1894, stating:

'In Birmingham you may generally recognise a board school by its being the best building in the neighbourhood. In London it is almost vice versa. With lofty towers which serve the utilitarian purpose of giving excellent ventilation, gabled windows, warm red bricks and stained glass, the best Birmingham board schools have quite an artistic finish.'

In contrast, the catchment area was working class, with many back-to-back housing courtyards, hence the low fee of one penny a week (the minimum charge possible under the Act) which was later scrapped altogether. Schools linked to the Church of England, such as St Barnabas, continued to exist in their older buildings. Fortunately for the local families, the Education (Provision of Meals) Act of 1906 meant that breakfast, and later 'dinner', were served to those young students in need. The Birmingham City Education Committee also set up medical inspection and care. Classes covered reading, writing and arithmetic, as well as some physical exercise and sometimes Sunday school for religious instruction.

Thomas was a Birmingham FC (later renamed Birmingham City) fan. By the time he reached the senior classes, he and his friends would have been dominating the kickabout in the school yard, emulating their heroes: a miniature Johnny Crosbie (the Scotsman who had played for the talented Glenbuck Cherrypickers – see Chapter 3) picks up the ball at the imaginary halfway line, charges up the wing and passes to miniature Joe Bradford, the leading goalscorer of the time, who hoofs it hard against the high brick wall. A score. Arms go up in celebration. The schoolmaster appears,

(Left) The building of St Barnabas School. (Below) Two photos of Thomas, his siblings, classmates and their teachers around 1918–21.

ringing the bell, and the 'goalposts' – knitted jumpers – are snatched up from the floor where they have gathered yet another handful of dust.

Without any additional information from official records, and having never recorded it for future generations, it is difficult to know the details of Thomas's life story after leaving school. His older brother, Robert, wrote down some of his own early memories, which were very typical of many boys at that time. He used to get up at the crack of dawn and do a paper round before going to a nearby school for 'free breakfast – a round of bread, jam, a mug of cocoa' and then off to his own school, St Barnabas, for lessons. He writes how he and his siblings got their shoes from the police fund, and occasionally a pair of boots and trousers. At Christmas the *Birmingham Mail* newspaper fund gave them 'beef, Xmas pudding and veg'. Another way of supporting the family was to trade their own possessions on a regular basis:

'My dear mother was doing her washing at six o'clock on the Monday morning so as to get it dry early, then it was off to the pawn shop to pawn what they would take for a few shillings and fetch it on Saturday out of dad's wages.

'Drink could be had for free – if you knew how. When the public house on Grosvenor Street West cleaned out the on-site brewing vats, the local lads would run down with jugs, or anything else that would hold a bit of discarded beer.'

There were organised activities for children, to get them out of their immediate surroundings. Robert describes going 'up the cut' – a local expression for the canal – in a coal boat and being treated to a piece of chocolate, but being completely black with coal dust by the time he got home. Joseph Pentland, a printer and vice-chairman of the Birmingham School Board, had founded the Bull Ring Mission, which aimed to help slum children. Robert went on one of their annual outings. He describes how they 'met at the Old Rag Market, marched to New Street station, Mr Pentland leading with his shepherd's crook, and a train to Sutton Coldfield'. There they were given food and drink before journeying back to Birmingham, singing songs.

At the age of 13, Robert worked in Johnson's, the greengrocers. On Saturdays his job was to take the huge boxes of rabbits that arrived from the farms and skin them in the dark light of the cellar. 'I've done many a hundred,' he writes. By 14, he was then employed full-time at Chatwin's, the toolmaker. The hours were 6am to 6pm every day, and 6am to 12 noon on a Saturday. He recalls:

The busy factory floor of Barratt Shoe Ltd, Northampton, in 1935. All the men in this photograph seem to look like my grandfather: shirt sleeves rolled up and slicked down hair. Image: Mirrorpix.

'We boys had to work two lathes ... rough out on one, and finish on the other ... You had to work out what cog wheels you needed for the different type threads, [not] just moving a lever like the automatic lathes of today.'

While his account goes on with more details of hard work, army service, and volunteering, he finishes on a positive note, recognising how far he had come:

'I consider myself very fortunate having enjoyed good health, having had a wonderful wife ... and two good sons. Did I think years ago I should own my house and have a car to drive about in?'

Despite the continuing expansion, jobs were not always available and both his father and another brother were out of work at the start of the 1920s. Thomas (my grandfather), was working in the boot and shoe trade as a hand clicker. It is likely that he got a job as an apprentice and worked his way up to this role. It might not sound remarkable but he was the first in a long line not to work in either the metal or brewery trades. It is also ironic that he made shoes and yet he had to borrow football boots in order to be able to play at the weekend.

A boot and shoe clicker cuts the uppers for boots or shoes from a skin of leather or other material. Before the job was mechanised, the operator's hand-knife blade 'clicked' against the brass edge binding used to protect the board patterns which were laid over the skin. It was considered an elite skilled trade to maximise the number of uppers from one skin of leather, avoiding any thin and damaged areas, and incorporating the unseen lines of stretch and resistance which naturally occur in leather according to the style and construction of the particular shoe. Another major criterion is the need to colour-shade the respective parts of the shoe uppers which are cut as a pair, not only matching the colour variations but also considering the surface finish and grain texture.

Birmingham has long been known as the 'City of a Thousand Trades', but it was Northampton to the east that was the centre of the shoe industry. The nickname for Northampton Town Football Club is the 'Cobblers' and they have a shoe in the middle of the club badge, even though the first team was originally started by a group of school teachers. Back in 1911, Northampton had signed Walter Tull from Tottenham Hotspur who was the league's first black outfield player. He was born in Kent and his father's family came from Barbados. He played 110 games for Northampton, before dying in the second battle of the Somme in the First World War where he was Britain's first black army officer.

Walter Tull was not the first professional black player in the English Football League. This is believed to be Arthur Wharton who was born in Ghana (his father was half Grenadian and half Scottish, and his mother was half Scottish and half Fante). Arthur first trained as a missionary in Cannock, Staffordshire (north of Birmingham), before focusing on athletics. He was a world record holder for 100 yards sprint in the 1880s before playing as goalkeeper for Darlington, Preston North End, Rotherham Town, and Sheffield United.

The first black footballer in Scotland (alongside Robert Walker), and first black international player, was Andrew Watson. Andrew had been born in British Guyana to a wealthy Scottish sugar plantation owner and a local black Guyanese woman. His father brought him to be educated in Britain and he later went to Glasgow University, playing football for a local team. Thanks to his father's inheritance,

Arthur Wharton with Darlington Football Club, winners of the Cleveland Challenge Cup in 1887.

he set up a warehouse business and worked as an engineer, but was also able to spend a considerable amount of time enjoying football. He played for a number of teams in Scotland and England, was match secretary for Queen's Park in the 1880s – a position typically reserved for men of higher social status –, and captained a successful Scotland side on his debut in 1881

Even as a factory worker with long hours, there was still time for sports and recreation at the start of the 20th century. The concept of a 'weekend' had been pioneered by the middle classes in the 19th century and it depended on the 1850 Factory Act, the unions, or individual employers – or a combination – to eventually give workers that extra half a day on Saturdays. The impact can certainly be seen in football. In 1880 there were over 800 football teams in Birmingham, helped by engineers and textile factories closing at lunchtime. In contrast, in Liverpool, where dock workers had much weaker union representation, there were only two teams. In 1890, Sunderland drapers even made certain of and celebrated their half day by purposefully forming a football club.[38]

In addition to the professional game, the Birmingham and District Works Amateur Football Association was set up in 1905 with an aim to promote 'wholesome recreation … fostering friendship and promoting goodwill, by healthy rivalry … to assist in the social unity between employers and employed … and to help by recreation to fit men better for their daily task, and make them more contented workmen'.[39] Nearly 700 companies had registered up to the 1950s and

---

38 See Martin Daunton (2000) 'Playing and praying' in *The Cambridge Urban History of Britain*, Issue 3. Cambridge University Press, p. 751.

39 Adam Benkwitz and Gyozo Molnar (2017) 'The emergence and development of association football: influential sociocultural factors in Victorian Birmingham', *Soccer & Society*, 18:7, 1027-1044.

Birmingham & District Works A.F.A medals. Image: Mullocks Specialist Auctioneers & Valuers. The medals were made by Vaughton & Sons in the Jewellery Quarter. Howard Vaughton (born 1861) was the grandson of the company's founder and played for both Aston Villa and England with the record for the most goals scored by any one player in any England international game. Vaughton & Sons also manufactured the FA Cup and the 1908 Olympic medals.

included Bournville where Thomas's first son (my uncle) worked (see Chapter 12).

The 1920s had been an enjoyable decade for heading to St Andrew's to watch a match, although Birmingham FC tended to finish in the lower half of the First Division. During their first Christmas after promotion they had a double loss to West Bromwich Albion on 26 and 27 December 1921 with a home attendance of 44,505. At this time, it was customary for the same teams to play home and away on consecutive weekends. After an initial loss, this system gave little time for changing the approach but at least revenge could come quickly, if it came at all.

West Brom would be relegated to the Second Division before the two sides met again in the 1931 FA Cup Final. Yet again, they somehow managed to beat the Blues 2-1 and, to top it off, were promoted back to the First Division a month later. My grandfather – then aged 18 – would have

West Bromwich Albion players and supporters stepping off the train with the FA Cup. Image: J.A. Hampton/Stringer.

been bitterly disappointed. Birmingham's *Sports Argus* paper was printed on blue instead of its usual pink in recognition of the game.

The Duke of Gloucester (son of King George V), meeting the teams before kick-off. Image: Trinity Mirror/Mirrorpix.

257

The Birmingham FC team for the 1931 FA Cup Final. Image: Colorsport.

West Bromwich Albion captain Tommy Glidden savouring the 2-1 win before heading into the changing rooms. Image: Allsport Hulton/Archive.

When war was declared in 1939, Thomas, aged 27, was still working in the shoe trade and living with his parents, by this time in Oozells Street North. These days the road is filled with smart eateries, seven-storey offices, and commuter bicycle stands, whereas in Thomas's day it butted up against a maze of factories and workshops. The 1939/40 Football League season would begin but would be suspended to be replaced by regional wartime competitions, which would also be the same case in Germany and Italy, although Serie A managed to continue until 1943.

During the Second World War, the National Service (Armed Forces) Act imposed conscription on all males aged between 18 and 41. Those medically unfit were exempted, as were others in key industries and jobs such as baking, farming, medicine, and engineering. Conscientious objectors had to appear before a tribunal to argue their reasons for refusing to join up. If their cases were not dismissed, they were granted one of several categories of exemption, and were given non-combatant jobs.

Thomas was six years old when the previous war ended and so he may have heard stories from returning soldiers and their families in subsequent years. They may have told tales of unimaginable horrors. Or Thomas may have taken a more simplistic view from his schoolteachers, memorising dates and places of successful battles in his history lessons. Having only moved a few streets away from his birthplace and still living with his parents as a man of nearly 27, the potential for travel and new experiences must have been motivating for my grandfather and his friends.

A photograph of Thomas, smiling, in his army uniform.

A certain downside, however, would be to leave behind your girlfriend. So Thomas did what hundreds of thousands also did and married his sweetheart – also a shoe factory worker – in March 1940. The peak number of marriages at the start of this war is far greater than any year since.

Thomas joined the 40th Light Anti-Aircraft Regiment (LAA Rgt) within the Royal Artillery. At the beginning of 1939, the regular and Territorial Army strength of the Royal Artillery totalled about 105,000. In mid-1943 it reached its peak strength of some 700,000 men; about 26 per cent of the total British Army strength and about the same size as the Royal Navy. The 40th LAA Rgt were engaged in home defence, and then in North Africa and Sicily. They were then engaged in operations from the D-Day landings on the beaches in northern France, through Belgium, the Netherlands, and into Germany.

A 40mm Bofors anti-aircraft gun being dug in near a squadron of Crusader tanks, 29 October 1942. Image: Imperial War Museum E 18689.

Initially, up to 1941, Thomas and his regiment were based at Inverness, Scotland. They helped to defend vulnerable points during bombing raids, such as the port city of Aberdeen and the naval base at Invergordon. In 1942 they were selected to train for overseas action and formally joined the 51st (Highland) Infantry Division to sail on 16 June for the Middle East. This was the same setting where William McGhie Cunningham was fighting with the 11th Hussars (see Chapter 10), although the two men would have no family connection until my parents married some 30 years later.

Their first mission was to be part of the second Battle of El Alamein in Egypt. Here their goal was to force the opposition army to retreat until the moment that Tripoli, the coastal capital of Libya, and its port were taken by the Allied forces in 1943. From there, the 40th LAA Rgt were frequently deployed to protect the artillery further west in Tunisia. Anti-aircraft gunners like my grandfather were often engaged in short actions against fast, low-flying aircraft, who usually came suddenly out of the glaring sun.

Along with the 51st Highlanders, Thomas's regiment was designated for the invasion of Sicily (Operation Husky) on 10 July 1943. Their ships were attacked by U-boats and aircraft but were able to make it to shore and create a beach defence, even with technical difficulties and scarce ammunition. As more of the army brigades landed, the 40th LAA Rgt followed the action across the island where the opposition army was resisting hard. Finally, the enemy began withdrawing from Sicily on 11 August 1943. By November Thomas had now been in the heat of the Mediterranean for a year and a half, fighting along a coastline that was so far removed from the familiar streets of Birmingham. Tanned and weary, but probably in good spirits after a successful campaign, the regiment was suddenly recalled to Britain in the depths of winter.

In April 1944, large-scale training exercises involving many different regiments were taking place, which we now know to be the preparations for the invasion of Normandy. Extracts from the different regimental war diaries include long lists of resources which each regiment had to provide, including 'umpires' and 'senior umpires', in order to oversee the successful running of each exercise.

The word 'umpire' comes from an old French word, *nonper*, meaning 'not equal'. In other words, it was someone who did not have an allegiance to either of two people or

Bofors crew of 40th LAA Rgt on alert in Sicily, July 1943. The gunners are only wearing shorts, boots, and metal helmets in the heat of the Mediterranean summer. Image: Imperial War Museum NA 4715.

groups of people among whom there was a dispute to be sorted out. The word then became used in the Middle English language (spoken after the Norman invasion of 1066 until the 15th century). It was written as 'noumpere', or a variation of that, but over time 'a noumpere' was spread by hearing and speaking it, not reading and writing it. It became 'an oumpere' and, eventually, 'an umpire' in modern English.

Back in 1581, Richard Mulcaster, the master of a school in London, wrote about the benefits of playing 'Footeball' and other such games but advised that a 'Trayning Maister' should be present to judge the play with authority – but not get too involved – in order to avoid any serious injuries or other disputes among the pupils.[40] In the adult football of

40 The full text is titled *Positions wherin those primitive circumstances be examined, which are necessarie for the training up of children, either for skill in their booke, or health in their bodie.* It was written by Richard Mulcaster, who was 'master of the schoole erected in London anno. 1561. in the parish of Saint Laurence Powntneie, by the worshipfull companie of the merchaunt tailers of the said citie'. The work was printed in London by Thomas Vautrollier for Thomas Chare in 1581

the 1870s, the umpires were typically non-playing members of clubs and one from each side would hang about on the pitch. They would only discuss a matter if the players entered into a dispute and needed 'to refer to' these people. In 1891, the Football Association decided that a 'referee' would be the sole judge of fair play, without players appealing, and he could now award free kicks when he saw fit. Each club could still nominate an umpire to help the referee, but they were now banished to the side of the pitch. These assistants became known as 'linesmen' with flags to show their opinion. Neutral linesmen for important games were not introduced until the 1898/99 season, and referees also gave up their own club loyalties, creating their own Referees' Union in 1908.

Where sport recognised the value of umpires, the military had also developed its understanding of their role. In 1931, a published article on 'Military Umpiring' noted that the best results were obtained when umpires regularly held that role; when they were well-trained; and when they worked as a team themselves.[41] Today there are more than ten progressive levels of football refereeing, each with their own standards and training courses, although referees only turned professional themselves in 2001.

The 40th LAA Rgt landed in France in the days immediately following the start of the invasion on 6 June 1944 – 'D-Day'. They were initially defending ground troops from attacking aircraft and later moved on to support infantry on the ground with their guns. The regiment then moved north-east as the next target was to liberate Antwerp, a crucial port for supplies, in September 1944.

Antwerp and other Belgian towns had been subjected to bombing by the RAF while also being ruled by a German

---

41 Colonel C. G. S. Harvey D.S.O. (1931) 'Military Umpiring', *Royal United Services Institution Journal*, 76:503, 557-562

A 1903 cartoon by Tom Browne showing both football teams attacking the referee.

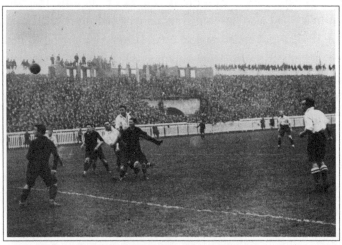

Royal Antwerp FC's brand new Bosuilstadion hosted an international match between Belgium and England in 1923. Image with permission of Royal Antwerp FC.

military government who charged high taxes for their war effort. Despite this dual hardship, club football matches had continued as a way of trying to uphold some sense of normality for the community as they also did in England. Royal Antwerp are the oldest club in Belgium, having been born out of their cricket club in 1887. They had been crowned Belgian First Division champions earlier in 1944, but they and other clubs decided to stop playing as a combination of British, American, Canadian and other Allied forces arrived. Thomas's regiment then moved north and east along the Belgium-Netherlands border. Today this is a popular area for holidaying and cycling by the lakes and canals. However, in October 1944 it was brutal countryside as they met heavy resistance by German soldiers. The vast network of waterways in the area provided the Germans with extra protection and so any crossing point became a prime target for both sides.

In September, men of the American 101st Airborne Division had parachuted just north of Eindhoven. The Americans fought to take control of the bridges over the canal at the towns of Best and Son. This was part of Operation Market Garden. Troops from the 15th Scottish Division arrived by land to support them but the bridges had been

Members of Entente Anversoise, a combination team of players from different clubs including Royal Antwerp. In 1944 they drew 2-2 against the British Forces, who fielded professional footballers. The British were apparently very disappointed, having beaten other Belgian clubs, and accepted a replay. This time the Belgium team won 4-2. Image: L. Van Cauwenbergh uit Deurne-Antwerpen.

destroyed and huge numbers of Highlanders were 'shot to pieces' in the following days, according to operation reports. At the start of October, Thomas's regiment arrived and immediately set up their huge guns to support and relieve the exhausted infantry. The massive amount of shooting is documented on a daily basis. Their regiment war diary also does not hide the fact that they shot directly at a house, a church, and a school where soldiers had sighted enemy movement.

On 22 October, Thomas moved north with his regiment to take over the defence of another bridge at Sint Oedenrode. It was here that he was wounded, along with two other gunners and their senior officer. Thankfully his injuries were not considered serious and he returned to duty as the regiment started to move north and fire, move north again and fire, almost on a daily basis. Turning sharp east, they headed for Nijmegen on the German border and were ordered to defend the area during winter. Then orders came again: frustratingly to not advance over the border but to move south in parallel with the Rhine until they had almost made three sides of a square in four months.

Operations in the Netherlands were taking a long time and it would not be until the spring of 1945 that Canadian and Allied forces could liberate further north. This was too late for AFC Ajax's first Jewish player, Eddy Hamel. Having moved from New York to Amsterdam, he played 125 league games before his retirement. He was arrested in 1942 with his wife and two sons, and all were killed in a gas chamber in Auschwitz concentration camp. One of Ajax's goalkeepers was allegedly arrested for resistance activities in 1943 but there are other reported instances of Ajax and other teams' fans collaborating with the occupying forces and shouting anti-Semitic slogans at Jewish players long before the Nazis arrived.

At the end of March 1945, it was finally time to cross the Rhine and it was done at night. Thomas and the other gunners fired shots across the water to guide the floating vehicles, and then provided cover from enemy aircraft. The regiment then crossed themselves and moved towards Dortmund – of the talented Bundesliga football team – constantly under attack.

BVB Borussia Dortmund had been founded in December 1909 and, like Thomas's Birmingham FC, it had been by a group of young men in a church-sponsored team. However, the original Trinity Youth football team played under the stern and unsympathetic eye of the local parish priest, Father Dewald. A meeting was held in a room of the local pub, Zum Wildschütz, to discuss forming a new club. The priest, thoroughly disgusted, apparently tried to break up the proceedings but he was blocked at the door. The new club continued to grow while Germany's political leadership shifted. Borussia Dortmund's president was replaced in the 1930s when he refused to join the Nazi Party. Despite this new management, some club members, who opposed the German regime, surreptitiously used the club's offices to produce anti-Nazi pamphlets. They were found out and were executed towards the end of the war.

Borussia Dortmund players of 1947/48 having rebuilt their club.

As if the club had not struggled enough, including near bankruptcy in the economic crash of 1929, the players and staff would later receive no sympathy from the British occupation authorities after the war. Clubs were swiftly dissolved in an attempt to distance all of the country's organisations from its political past. They had to close and restart under a new name. For all that the British Army – and the football players and supporters that filled its ranks – knew about the importance of sport, taking it away from any suffering community seems a cruel and unnecessary punishment. However, in the grief and exhaustion of postwar Europe, there seemed to be no impartial umpire to rule fair play on these matters.

Having made it north to Bremen, the 40th LAA Rgt formed part of the occupying forces and so Thomas did not make it back to Birmingham until 1946. He had left six years before as a local boot and shoe factory worker with a new wife and came home changed by so many unimaginable experiences.

In some ways Birmingham was also changing, but in some ways it remained very much the same. This may, or may not, have been comforting to those finally coming home.

The city had quite ambitious plans for rebuilding. Planners saw bomb sites as an ideal opportunity to get rid of unwanted buildings and also to build bigger roads for the increasing number of motorised vehicles. The government, however, clamped down on local authority spending and so Birmingham did not automatically get the glossy makeover it was expecting. Many of the poor-quality, working-class homes of the 19th century were still standing and still inhabited. Food and clothing were still rationed and only available to purchase along with a certain number of coupons allocated to each citizen. This would continue for some time and put a limit on any expectations of lavish meals or outfits.

Despite restrictions, Birmingham pressed ahead with its plans for five development areas around the outside of the city centre. For the first time, high-rise blocks of apartments went up and still with the aim of keeping a large number of people in the same place. This was despite a survey that indicated Brummies did not want to live in towers. People criticised the designers, feeling that priority was given to increased flows of traffic and ignoring the daily experience of humans. The 'housewife's dream' (as it was described) of the new Bull Ring shopping centre was also felt to be forcing people underground. Of course, there were benefits that the residents had not experienced before in their lives: a lift instead of stairs; water from taps inside the house; and their own private toilet. The trams were also on the way out, in favour of new buses. The last tram ran in 1953 and only recently have we seen tramways making a big comeback in Birmingham and other cities, and purposefully reducing individual car journeys.

Twelve-storey flats in the Nechells area described by an architect as 'mud pies'. Old 19th-century shops are still standing in the foreground. 1953. Image: Image: The Phyllis Nicklin collection / University of Birmingham.

The Reinstatement in Civil Employment Act of 1944 required companies to give former employees their old jobs back after they had left the armed services. Many chose not to accept these offers, feeling that they had had far greater responsibility in combat. Some who did return to old jobs quickly discovered that they were perhaps over-qualified with new knowledge and skills. Having worked in the shoe trade but then going on to man large warfare guns, Thomas decided upon the metal trade. He worked at W. Canning & Co., which had been founded as far back as 1795 and produced all kinds of equipment necessary for electroplating and polishing.

An advertisement for Cannings in 1954. Image from Grace's Guide to British Industrial History.

At his other 'home', the St Andrew's football ground, further changes had occurred since Thomas had been away. During the war, the National Fire Service had taken over the Main Stand. In a comedy of errors for a fire service, a small blaze started in a brazier. Apparently one of the firemen grabbed what he thought was a bucket of water but it was, in fact, petrol and the whole stand went up in flames, sadly also destroying over 60 years of club records. The Main Stand was rebuilt in the 1950s in time for Birmingham City to play Borussia Dortmund – where Thomas had been a decade earlier – and under new floodlights.

The coat of arms of the City of Birmingham County Borough Council, as depicted on the side of a Birmingham City Transport vehicle in the 1930s.

The Birmingham City FC club crest that was designed by local football fan Mike Wood in 1972. Image: Birmingham City Football Club.

The club had also been officially renamed Birmingham City in 1943. When the club changed their name from Small Heath to Birmingham in 1905, they had already started to use the city of Birmingham's coat of arms as its own, which was undoubtedly a bold move to state that they were the main club of Birmingham. Later, in the 1970s, the letters BCFC were used for a time on the playing shirts before the *Sports Argus* newspaper ran a competition to design a new badge. The winner was Birmingham fan Michael Wood, a conversion engineer with the West Midlands Gas Board. His design featured a globe on top of a football, with a ribbon wrapped around bearing the club's name and the original Small Heath foundation year, 1875.

After the war, manufacturers also upped their game in using football to promote their products. Supporters were faced with large signs on walls and pages in magazines. The message was simple: use this product and you will

Brylcreem advertisement featuring Denis Compton. Image: Retro AdArchives.

Bovril advertisement from the 1957 FA Cup Final programme.

automatically be more like your heroes. Players signed commercial deals and clubs accepted large advertisements in their matchday programmes for products that claimed to be just what the real supporter or player needed in their life. Denis Compton played both cricket for England and football for Arsenal. In *Kicking and Screaming*, he explained:

> I was approached [about Brylcreem] in 1947 by Beecham's and I must say I had a wonderfully close relationship with them ... I used it and it was on the posters and ... buses and all that sort of thing. The wind used to blow my hair all over the place and ... the crowd would say, 'Compo, where's your Brylcreem?'

Typical of so many returning soldiers, Thomas barely spoke of his wartime experiences until they returned to haunt him in his imagination much later in life. He enjoyed walking

A family photo of Thomas with his wife, dog, grandchildren and a small football, which became a typical weekend in Birmingham in later life.

the dog, playing a bit of kickabout with me and my brother in the back yard. With a good mind for maths that he was never able to fully use in his working life, he carefully worked out the best odds for the horse-racing and football results at the weekend. And, of course, he was always quick to wind my mother up when the Villa had not had a good Saturday and the Blues had done well.

Forever a 'Bluenose'.

Chapter 12

Entertainment, emigration, and keeping the home fires burning

Birmingham (1914–1960s)

1800s	Robert Johnson	Arthur and Sarah Ann Hornsby	Thomas and Harriet Clemson	John and Elizabeth Perry
1900s	James Johnson and Lilian Hornsby		George Clemson and Florence Perry	
	Irene Johnson and Thomas Clemson			

'I'M NOT a traitor to my class ... I'm just an extreme example of what a working man can achieve.'[42]

So says the main character in the hit television show *Peaky Blinders*. The fictional character of Thomas Shelby has grown up on the industrial streets of Small Heath, Birmingham. He has been away to war, and has returned to make the best he can for his family with grit and with knowledge of how society works above and below ground. In the statement, the character makes it clear that he is not turning his back on his roots; not totally escaping the

---

42 *Peaky Blinders*, series four episode four: 'Dangerous' (2017). Caryn Mandabach Productions, Tiger Aspect Productions, and BBC.

Birmingham of his youth. He is enjoying his own meagre success due to his own hard graft, and he shares it with his community, but he also accepts that not everyone is so fortunate. On another scale, he is also the voice of Small Heath, of Birmingham, and perhaps any industrial town or city at the time: work hard, diversify, be flexible, take opportunities, and you can make a life for yourself yet remain proud of where you came from.

My grandmother was born in Small Heath in 1914. The family were living in a typical red-brick terrace with a road wide enough for carts and horses. Irene – or Rene (pronounced 'Reenie') – was a later arrival after her ten-year-old brother and nine-year-old sister. Nonetheless, there were other children her age to play with down the road, such as the three Madden children whose father was killed in action in France.

Irene's own father, James, also signed up to the army at the start of the war (see Chapter 9). This was only one month after she was born and so she would not have known him, at least not properly, until he was demobilised five years later, in 1919. Thousands of families were put in a similar situation as men came forward to join the three city battalions that had been given much attention in the newspapers. Her mother, Lily, was left with three young children to look after and it was perhaps fortunate that there were not more.

Where they could, women and girls filled the spaces left by the men in the factories that were also converting to war work. In order to encourage this, over 100 nurseries were funded by two government departments, the Ministry of Munitions and the Board of Education, although mothers still had to pay a daily contribution. Small Heath Nursery, one of five established in Birmingham, opened on 1 November 1916 and accommodated 30 children.

When the British think of attacks from the air, we usually think of the bombings of the Blitz in the 1940s.

A photograph of a Birmingham nursery for the children of munitions workers, 1916. Image © Illustrated London News Ltd / Mary Evans.

Women and girls busy in the dangerous manufacture of hand grenades at Mills Munitions Works, Birmingham, 1915. Image by permision of the Library of Birmingham MS 4616/9.

This threat was also very real in the First World War and the city streets had to be kept dark with blackout curtains. A 1916 entry in the Moseley Road School log book notes that children were absent from school because of the Zeppelin raid which had passed over Birmingham during the night, later dropping bombs and killing 11 people in Walsall. Even once the war had ended, the flu outbreaks from 1918 to 1920 also took the lives of around 4,200 people in the city.

Requests for free breakfasts of cocoa and porridge that were provided by schools increased during the war, partly because of delays in families receiving their portion of soldier's wages from the government. In 1915, schools also provided meals at weekends and during half-term to prevent hunger. Sometimes the only hot meal a child would get was the one provided by their school. With food shortages and rationing, which continued until 1920, there were also fuel shortages. Some schools had to close early in winter because they did not have enough coal for the fire in the schoolroom.

Little Green Lane School was just around the corner from Irene's house and could accommodate over 1,000 of Small Heath's infants and junior pupils. Irene's education would have covered the 3Rs – reading, writing and arithmetic – but then focused more on sewing and other domestic duties as she got older. She left school at the age of 14, not staying on like some senior boys could, and then the world – or rather Birmingham – was her oyster.

Little Green Lane School. Image by permission of the Library of Birmingham S 118/6.

A girls' class at Little Green Lane School. Image by permission of the Library of Birmingham.

Adolescence was a recent concept developed by psychologists and leisure time for the working classes was becoming more established in the first part of the 20th century.[43] If you were a teenager in Birmingham, and you were not going to the football or visiting friends, then another escape from the daily routine of work and household chores was the theatre.

Irene loved going to the theatre. The Birmingham Hippodrome had been reopened at the start of the century as a variety theatre and welcomed acts from all over the world. A programme from 1931 lists comedians, a jazz singer, a 'paper tearer', and a dancing xylophone player, along with the Hippodrome Orchestra at the intermission. Irene also loved to hang around the stage door and collect autographs, even if she had not been to the performance that night. She had a healthy obsession with Fred Astaire and managed to get him to sign her autograph book while he was performing in London in 1933, before he returned to Hollywood for his next film.

---

43 Penny Tinkler (2003), 'Cause for concern: young women and leisure, 1930–50', *Women's History Review*, 12:2, pp.233-262.

The Alexander Theatre was another popular venue, of which there were many. It was no longer the variety theatre it had been but instead was host to ballet, operettas by the D'Oyly Carte Opera Company, and plays by its own Repertory Company. It reopened in 1935 with a new art deco auditorium and a production of the pantomime *Cinderella*. The Prince of Wales Theatre also hosted pantomimes but was completely destroyed by a direct hit in a bombing raid in 1941.

 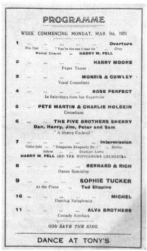

The Birmingham Hippodrome, built in 1899 by the Draysey brothers, and a programme from 1931. Images: Birmingham Hippodrome.

Entertainment was also enhanced by the arrival of 'talking pictures' in 1928. The first Odeon cinema in the country was built by Oscar Deutsch in Perry Barr, Birmingham, in 1930, and many others were to follow. In an exotic contrast to the red-brick houses and other public buildings, the exterior was painted white to look like North African domes and there were Moor-like scenes painted on the interior walls. The point of films was to fully enter another world and the building did its best to add to the escapism.

To fund all of these excursions, Irene needed money. She was still living at home but also needed to pay her own

Theatres, as well as performers and audiences, were at risk in both world wars. The Prince of Wales Theatre suffered a direct hit in 1941. Image: Trinity Mirror/Mirrorpix.

way in terms of food and clothes. In her position in society, it was expected that she would get a job immediately on leaving school.

In the 'City of a Thousand Trades', women and children had worked for long hours in dangerous conditions for decades. The Factory Act 1878 then restricted women to a maximum of 56 hours per week. With children staying at school longer, starting employment was then an important

The front of the Odeon cinema in Perry Barr. It is advertising the 1935 film King of the Damned *about an educated convict and prisoner who leads a group of other inmates in a rebellion against the cruel authority figures before one of their own gets executed.*

moment in the social, cultural and economic transition from girlhood to womanhood. It could be quite an abrupt individual change – leave school on Friday and start work on Monday morning – but could also signify a generational change where the daughter was suddenly living a different and more independent life to that which the mother had had in her own youth or had now.[44]

Birmingham trade covered the full spectrum in terms of the size of the enterprise: people's homes and back-yard workshops, right up to massive factory complexes. A century ago, there were several big factories in and around Birmingham. Fort Dunlop was the biggest in the 1920s. Demand for rubber tyres was increasing, both for commercial

---

44 Selina Todd (2004), 'Poverty and Aspiration: Young Women's Entry to Employment in Inter-war England'. *Twentieth Century British History*, 15, 119-142.

and private vehicles. It is still a well-known landmark today, seen from the M6 motorway, if one is not more focused on the nearby Villa Park. As well as its iconic factory site, the Dunlop Rubber Company built a sports pavilion as a memorial to its employees who had died in the First World War. Nearby, the Midlands Vinegar Company produced HP Sauce in Aston while Digbeth contained the Bird's Custard factory (now a well-known arts centre) as well as a Typhoo tea factory. The British Small Arms Company in Small Heath, where Irene grew up, produced motorcycles before and after the wars and firearms during them. Further out, the Cadbury family bought land and created a workers' village in Bournville to support their chocolate factory.

Factory production was not without conflict, despite some employers claiming to go the extra distance for their workers. In 1926, the same year that the Lucas factory in Tyseley signed a big contract with Austin motors, almost two million workers across the United Kingdom stopped as part of the General Strike. It was female activist Jessie Eden who convinced both male and female workers there to join the cause.

The massive Fort Dunlop when it was first operational in the 1920s. Note the scale of the site compared to the building that still remains today (top left) and also the expanse of fields and sports pitches.

Fort Dunlop sports pavilion.

Although it was not the centre of large-scale industry, making boots and shoes was a business that would always find customers and need workers in Birmingham (see also Chapter 11). I recall my grandmother telling me about how she and her fellow factory workers stitched individual parts of leather together – the uppers – to be passed on to the next department that would fix it to the sole of the shoe. One can imagine the music of her day would be the constant whirr of heavy-duty sewing machines. Perhaps this is why she was happy later in life, when babysitting me and my brother, to sit for hours humming along to the click-click of her knitting needles.

Owning watertight, comfortable footwear was still not something that everyone could afford in the early decades of the 20th century. Since 1889 the *Birmingham Mail* had been running a Christmas Tree Fund appeal that was used to distribute coal and toys, as well as footwear for poor children who would otherwise go without. By 1948 it had given out almost 500,000 boots and shoes to children in the city.

Having football boots was certainly a luxury beyond the imagination of many. However, children's boots did exist to the same design as adults', which did not change much from the 1890s to 1940s: a hand-made leather lace-up boot to above the ankles, with reinforced toe cap sometimes made of steel, and disc-shaped leather cleats attached to the bottom. These were heavy when first put on, but became significantly worse when wet and caked in mud. It was not until after the Second World War that boots became lighter and more flexible with changeable screw-in studs.

Shin pads were originally worn on the outside of socks. They were made out of leather, backed with cotton, and stuffed with animal hair for padding.

A football boot from the 1890s. Image: Leicester Museums and Galleries.

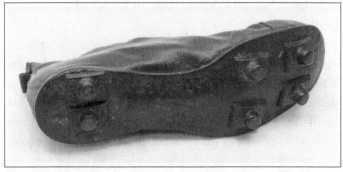

The underside and studs of a 1940s football boot. Image: The National Football Museum.

It was probably through work that Irene managed to catch the eye of Thomas (my grandfather), who was a hand clicker, carefully cutting the leather to take to the sewing

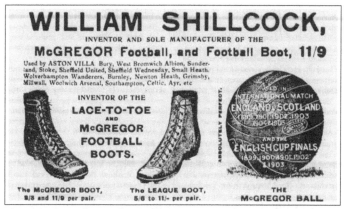

A 1905 advertisement for the League and McGregor boots, the latter named after William McGregor, founder of the Football League (see earlier chapters). It boasts a number of clubs endorsing the boots, including Small Heath and Aston Villa. The FA Cup was stolen from Mr Shillcock's shop window when he displayed it there on loan.

department. One wonders how many deliveries he had to make before asking this rather confident young girl out. Perhaps it was the other way around. Even once they had managed to confess their mutual interest, the onset of war in 1939 overshadowed their courtship and they were married in March 1940 in Birmingham before Thomas was posted to Scotland, North Africa, and then across Europe. Irene, then aged 26, stayed living with her parents in the suburbs.

Food (1940) and clothing (1941) rationing were introduced again, as they had been in the previous war. Residents were encouraged to grow their own vegetables in the garden or allotments. In November 1940, Birmingham suffered three nights of consecutive bombing. In this short time 800 people lost their lives, 2,345 people were injured and 20,000 civilians were made homeless. The bombing lasted for months and over 2,000 lives were lost. Because many homes did not have cellars, citizens were encouraged to go to public shelters. They could build Anderson shelters (a piece of curved iron over a hole in the ground) if they had a garden but these were damp and cold in the winter and often flooded. My grandmother told me that, instead, they often used to sit under the kitchen table and hope for the best.

Hall Green was a residential area and very different to the city centre and the streets around the main munitions factories. However, these homes were still under threat. There are many anecdotes from local residents who had to survive without water or gas and carrying water for cooking and bathing from a well in Robin Hood's Lane. On the night of 20 November 1940, a bomb landed on 20 Broomhall Lane, killing three young boys outright and destroying the house. One of them had an ear infection and the doctor had said not to go to a shelter, so the parents hid under the stairs. It is thought that the bomber wanted to hit the anti-aircraft gun set up on the Robin Hood golf course but missed their target. Irene and her parents lived just 50 metres around the corner.

Bomb damage to houses in Birmingham, 1941. Image: Balsall Heath History Society.

Factories needed to continue production, whatever the conditions, and so many workers would be on night shifts. In the day, if the buses or roads had been damaged, it meant a walk to work. The factory may also have been hit the night before and, if it was, all hands were needed to have the place up and running as soon as possible. Certainly, women were needed to fill the gaps in the production line left by men, even if they had families to shop and care for. Women's war work also brought those from different backgrounds together, which caused some concern. A personnel manager at a Birmingham engineering company wrote this entry in his diary in January 1942:

'See two more girls sent down from London. A striking blonde from a beauty parlour and a brunette from a gown shop, both in the West End. Capstan shop foreman afraid to put them on his machines; said they were too good a type. I was seriously concerned myself as our factory is an old shabby place and its sanitary arrangements of a very low standard ... Local factory class girls are used to them.'[45]

Factory girls race to be first served at the cafe for lunch, February 1942. Image: Trinity Mirror/Mirrorpix.

45 Mass Observation Archive, FR 1298, People in Production, June 1942, quoted in 'Women factory workers in Birmingham during the Second World War' by C. Price (charleneprice.wordpress.com, 2017).

Women with some free time, and the desire, also played football. This was even though the Football Association had banned women in 1921 from playing on Football League grounds, stating, 'The game of football is quite unsuitable for females and ought not to be encouraged.' Taking a different attitude, the government encouraged women to play football as the games boosted morale and reinforced the image that women were capable of jobs deemed only appropriate for men. The matches that women played in also raised money for war charities. In 1943 a team of electrical engineers, calling themselves Bright Sparks, took on a munitions workers' side dubbed Great Guns. The Women's Auxiliary Air Force and the Auxiliary Territorial Services also included football training and matches as part of their physical training and recreation programme.

Even when the war ended, life was the same for some time and Irene did her best as a single mother of my four-year-old uncle until her husband was able to return from Germany in 1946. My father was born two years later and Irene continued to live with her husband, her sons, and her parents in the same house in Hall Green. It must have been a strange time for many women in her situation: an absent husband returning with physical and mental scars; two boisterous young lads; two elderly parents. They were comfortable but certainly not financially wealthy. My father recalled that they had one pair of shorts and two shirts – one to wear and one to wash.

It was in the 1950s that life started to change. With the boys growing fast and with her husband now back in employment, they moved to Coney Green Drive. This was where Austin had their motor factory and had built vast housing estates for their employees in the early 20th century. It was also right next to the railway tracks into Longbridge Station, where my father could watch – or 'spot' (noting the time and number of) – the steam trains and diesel locomotives heading in and out of the city.

Coney Green Drive was built as part of the Austin Motor Company Village, a mix of prefabricated wooden bungalows and larger brick houses. In this picture even the trees – a mix of Laburnum, Maple, Rowan and Cedar –are new. Image: Austin Village Preservation Society.

Boy trainspotters in 1952. Image: Didcot Railway Centre.

Not only did my grandmother keep house for the man and two boys in her life, she also went out to work as a housekeeper for others who were living in slightly grander homes. 'Up at the Big House,' she used to say. Without a family car, it meant bus journeys morning and night. For the first half of the 20th century domestic service employed the largest numbers of women of any labour market sector in Britain. Historian Dr Lucy Delap writes, 'Predominantly female, these servants worked in other people's homes, where they did not only the dirty work but also formed deep attachments to those they worked for, and lived out their lives under the same roof as their employers.'[46] Even though magazine advertisements and household appliance manufacturers instructed women how to cope without servants, after the war there was still a quiet army of cleaners and childminders helping the upper-middle-class woman through her week.

The work ethic and opportunity to feel valued also extended to my father who used to help the local milkman on his rounds. Being a bright lad of 12 years old he also helped with the bookkeeping, although he couldn't work out why it did not quite add up on some occasions; yet to learn that adults might try to pocket some extra cash on the side.

My uncle worked and played his sport at Bournville. Back in the 19th century, the Cadbury family had been looking for somewhere to relocate their cocoa and chocolate factory. They acquired land about four miles south of Birmingham and named the area Bournville after the river Bourn and adding the French word for town, *ville*, to give it a more continental feel. Once the factory was established, they built a model village for the welfare of their workers, complete with parks, a fishing lake, a swimming pool, a theatre, and

---

46 Delap, Lucy, *Knowing Their Place: Domestic Service in Twentieth Century Britain* (Oxford University Press, 2011).

a running track. Schools, churches (the Cadbury family were Quakers), and other village meeting places completed the massive social project. My uncle recalls that there were 21 football pitches and three for rugby. The Northumberland turf was of the highest quality, the same used for the original Wembley Stadium, meaning that teams would train there before their FA Cup finals.

One of the many Bournville football teams in a goalmouth struggle. For the 80 acres of factory space, there were 120 acres of playing fields. Image: Cadbury Archive, Mondelez International.

Despite the large building programmes and initiatives by private companies, there was still a need for more housing. Large numbers of immigrants from Ireland, Pakistan, the West Indies and elsewhere came to Birmingham during the 1950s and 1960s. Many were skilled and found work with good salaries, which then encouraged their relatives and friends to join them. Unfortunately, council housing depended on them already being in the city for five years. In addition, there was little demand for unskilled labour and so some new immigrants found themselves without work and living in poor conditions.

Footballers were also arriving. Having escaped the Spanish Civil War, Emilio Aldecoa played for Wolverhampton Wanderers and Coventry in the 1940s. He won two league titles with Barcelona and had a spell as assistant manager of Birmingham City in the 1960s. Béla Oláh and Johnny Haasz both wanted to leave behind the Communist regime in Hungary in the 1950s. Oláh signed as an amateur for Northampton Town because the FA rules at the time stated that he could only play professionally once he had been in the country for two years. Haasz was less fortunate. He had been fighting in guerrilla activity against the Soviet occupying forces and was on the run, once having to hide in an occupied coffin in a graveyard. When he got to England, he found that the Hungarian FA had listed him as a deserter and banned him from playing any football, which FIFA upheld. He eventually made one first-team appearance for Swansea before playing with lower-league clubs.

There have been numerous other highly talented and high-profile players moving to Britain since, and many from difficult circumstances in their home countries. In the summer of 2021 the Football Moves People campaign attempted to educate and remind people that English culture, including football and other sports, has been richly developed by people travelling around the world and living in places other than their home towns or countries.

Emigration – moving abroad – was also part of the ordinary working person's vision for their future life. Perhaps without realising it, it was not only their trade skills that they were taking with them but also their way of socialising, exercising, entertaining, and undertaking weekly rituals. Some British football coaches went to work abroad in the first half of the 20th century, creating an intercultural exchange of ideas and knowledge about

Posters from the Migration Museum's 'Football Moves People' campaign, summer 2021. Image: Migration Museum/Wonderhood Studios.

football.[47] It was not always immediate, however. When Genoa Cricket and Football Club was formed in Italy in 1893, it was all-British, formed by Englishmen and Scotsmen. It was only when James Spensley, a doctor, arrived and actively encouraged other nationalities to join did Italians, Swiss and Austrians start to play. Others took on the same approach. Barcelona was founded in Spain by a Swiss accountant specifically for foreign players who had been prevented from joining other gymnastics clubs.

Much further away than Europe or America, it was Australia that was calling out for people to increase its population and boost its industry. The Assisted Passage Migration Scheme was created in 1945 with the promise of employment and affordable housing. Adult migrants were charged only £10 for the fare (equivalent to £441 in 2020), leading to the name 'Ten Pound Poms'. This is what my uncle, leaving behind the muddy football pitches of Bournville, took

---

47 Matthew Taylor (2010), 'Football's Engineers? British Football Coaches, Migration and Intercultural Transfer, c.1910–c.1950s', *Sport in History*, 30:1, pp.138-163.

advantage of. Unfortunately the idyllic conditions that were promised to him and his wife were not there for many new arrivals, who complained about the basic hostel conditions. My aunt recalls that stepping off the boat was also like going back in time ten or 20 years. This earned many new arrivals the nickname 'Whinging Poms' by the resident Australians, a term that is now used regularly in the media whenever England and Australia meet in sports fixtures.

Association football had enjoyed some brief popularity in Australia, even though the ball sport would eventually flourish in the forms of rugby union, rugby league, and Australian Rules football. On 11 August 1879 a letter from a member of Queen's Park FC to the *Melbourne Argus* proposed that association rules should be introduced as a more favourable alternative

An advertisement encouraging emigration to Australia, published by Australia House, the embassy in London. It led to the nickname 'Ten Pound Poms'. Image: National Library of Australia.

to the 'brute force' of rugby-style games 'in the colony'. The women's game also gathered momentum with 10,000 supporters attending a match in Brisbane in 1921. The Queensland Women's Ladies Soccer Football Association was formed shortly after, only for players to become nervous of public reaction following the English FA's decision that football was 'unsuitable' and they drifted away to other sports.

The various sports and other events available onboard a ship. The journey took around six weeks. Image: Immigration Museum, Victoria, Australia/ Barbara Alderton.

Back in England, Irene's second son (my father) was on a different path but no less exciting. After those long hours of counting the coins on milk rounds, watching the steam trains roll in and out of Birmingham, and playing school football and 'fives' (like squash but with leather gloves instead of a racquet), he was off on his own adventure to university. This was something that the family generations of ironworkers and horse keepers could not have dreamed of. However, he

My father's college football team.

My grandparents at my father's graduation. The chalk markings behind note a sporting victory over another college, which students are traditionally allowed to add to the old college walls.

stuck to his roots and remained a devoted Birmingham City fan all of his life. He did admit that a significant amount of time at university was spent playing and celebrating football rather than actually studying. But, at the end of that branch of the hard-working, brave-fighting, sport-loving family tree, who could deny a boy from Birmingham such pleasures?

Chapter 13

Peace, building a business, and forever Villa

Gloucestershire, Birmingham, Manchester (1918–1960s)

1800s	John Grainger and Elizabeth Coton	Samuel Swann and Elizabeth Cox	William Cunningham and Mary Scott	Cornelius Russell and Marion Henry
1900s	John Joseph Grainger and Amy Swann		James Cunningham and Helen Russell	
	Denis Grainger and Marion Cunningham			

FOR ALL the conflict between nations, as well as worker strikes, it would be understandable to imagine life for the average person in the first half of the 20th century to be all about fights and struggles. And, with the drama and intensity inside the cauldron of a football stadium, it is also easy to think of fans as being rather aggressive individuals, intent on hurling abuse and causing more harm than 'supporting' the club. But every person, every family, and every community are different. Sports enthusiasts appreciate and revel in the sense of competition; to strive to be the best version of themselves or better than others. This requires passion, dedication, and focus. But it is not necessarily the same as violence which intends to hurt or destroy. In the 20th century, war was not hidden away on a few battlefields; it affected everyone. Mental, physical and emotional scars were highly visible in all parts of society. People muttered 'never again'. Each time peace came, it was embraced as a chance for a fresh start and new dreams. And each time the Football League restarted, the supporters came back in their thousands.

My grandfather, Denis, was born at the end of August 1918, two months before the end of the First World War. Symbolising the coming new era, he was the first in a long line of men in his family not to be called John, Joseph or James. Denis's birth would have been a happy miracle surrounded by anxiety. The hospitals were full with both wounded soldiers and serious cases of Spanish flu, which killed one in ten in Bristol where the family was living and, worldwide, more than the total number of war casualties (of both armed forces and civilians).

Fortunately, Denis and his family moved from the city to Severn Beach, thus giving themselves a better chance of avoiding the deadly virus. Given their own start in Birmingham's crowded city housing, Denis's parents were making yet another move up in terms of living conditions. They were just minutes from the seaside promenade in a row of smart new bungalows created for this up-and-coming holiday resort. There was work, fresh air, and plenty of fun to be had. Mischief could also be made and little Denis was once reprimanded by the local police for trying to break into a beach hut. Putting on his most innocent face, he claimed to 'just be looking for a good hiding place' and managed to get off with a stern waggle of the policeman's finger.

It was four decades before the enormous bridge over to Wales was constructed, although a tunnel had existed since the 1880s. Severn Beach was known as the 'Blackpool of the West', with crowds arriving each weekend from London once the new railway station opened. It also meant that the family could more easily visit Birmingham every once in a while.

As England emerged from the war, the Football League was able to resume. The 1919/20 season brought more FA Cup success for Aston Villa, who beat Huddersfield Town 1-0 at Stamford Bridge, having beaten Chelsea in the semi-final. For all of the transfers from other clubs and canny imports from Scotland and Ireland, the sentiment 'he's one of our own' also rang true back in the day. Dickie York signed in 1919 and became a formidable outside-right. He had been born in Handsworth and grew up in the Lozells area of Aston, attending Icknield Street School (the same street where Denis's father had previously lived) and playing for the Birmingham Boys and England Schoolboys teams. Football also thrived outside of the cities and retained its connection to religious communities. The Bristol Church of England League was founded in 1910 with three divisions of amateur teams already keen to compete against other rural villages.

The new housing in Osborne Road, Severn Beach, on the south-west coast of England. Image: Pilning & Severn Beach Area History Group.

299

During the week, Denis attended Pilning School and was a good student, judging by his certificates. Aged ten he won a copy of the annual book *The Lucky Boys' Budget* as a prize for drawing, signed by the headmaster. With stories such as 'The Bridge Builders' and 'The Runaway', it encouraged boys to be enterprising but with a good moral compass.

Children's fiction was growing as its own genre and included daring adventures that required cunning, physical skill, resourcefulness, and bravery. Popular titles included *The Midnight Folk* by John Masefield and *Swallows and Amazons* by Arthur Ransome. The stories reinforced what would have been fine qualities of their fighting fathers but now could be admirably developed in peacetime by the sons. Boys' comics included the *Boy's Own Paper*, a mix of adventure stories, sport, puzzles and games. There was also *The Champion*, starring such characters as Rockfist Rogan (an RAF pilot and boxer) and Colwyn Dane (a detective). Other popular comics included *The Wizard* and *Hotspur*. *The Beano* and *The Dandy* were yet to make an appearance and were first published only in the late 1930s.

Much earlier, the *Boys' Realm Football Library* collection of short stories had been published between 1909 and 1915. It was so popular that it even organised its own youth football tournament.

The typical school leaving age was 14 and Denis's first job was in the motor trade for a local tyre company, working his way up in various positions. Just like his father before him, it was a journey of determination and grasping opportunities in order to climb the employment ladder. The few surviving family photos show a happy lad, clearly proud of his smart appearance but just as content to hang out with mates and chat about the latest football news.

By the end of the 1930s the family had moved back to Birmingham to live in Shenstone Valley Road, a long

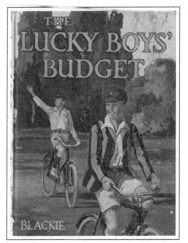

(Left) The Lucky Boys' Budget *collection of short stories, awarded to* Denis *as a school prize. (Right) A cover of the* Boys' Realm Football Library. *Image: ©The British Library*

Family photos of Denis as a young lad in his work clothes and hanging out with a friend by the beach in the 1930s.

suburban row of semi-detached houses. Each had small gardens both to the front and the rear, which signified another step up in fortune for the family. The area of Halesowen has its own long history, having been mentioned in the *Domesday Book* of 1086. It was known as 'Halas' until the manor was gifted by King Henry II to his sister, Emma, the wife of David Owen, Prince of Wales, in 1177. It then became known as 'Halas Owen'. Denis's father continued to travel for business while his mother kept house and his sister, Gwendoline, visited the sick in their homes. This was a decade before the creation of the National Health Service, for whom she later worked. Despite having to leave his friends behind, it was certainly easier for Denis to go to watch Aston Villa games with his father when he returned at weekends.

A black-and-white British Pathé newsreel from 1930 begins with the announcement 'Soccer again! With the "fade out" of cricket, thousands of football "fans" flock to all matches.' The word 'fan' is highlighted by the news editor, perhaps to indicate a still-emerging phenomenon. This word comes from either 'fancy' or 'fanatic', both 16th-century words indicating a particular hobby/interest or being passionate about something. In the newsreel, spectators are standing on the terraces, but also perched on the edges of walls and hanging over the white hoarding boards by the touchlines. Cries are heard from the anxious men in

18 February 1928: Police regulate the crowd at the touchline as great numbers of spectators crowd the pitch at Highbury in London for the cup tie battle between Arsenal and Aston Villa. Image: Davis/Stringer.

the crowd – 'Come on!' and 'Don't stand there!' – which have been typical shouts throughout footballing history. In contrast, the response to the goals seems rather more muted compared to today: a cheer, a round of applause, and some waving of hats. In other photographs, young boys in caps and shorts – even in winter with snow on the ground – are seen sat right up next to the touchline.

The wearing of scarves – hand-knitted in club colours – and rosettes gradually became more popular from the 1930s onwards and accompanied the jacket and tie that most men would own and wear to watch a match. A recent study found that replica kit for boys was sold from only the 1950s in order to 'dress like your heroes' but there was nothing on offer for adults. It was simply not part of the fan culture, nor was there any move to encourage it by the team strip suppliers. In fact, the wearing of club replica kit did not become popular until the 1990s and was begun by fans rather than marketing. It was initially only possible to purchase shirts in the team colours but without the badges, club names, and branding so that the same could be used for amateur teams.[48]

In 1936, Aston Villa were relegated to the Second Division for the first time in their history and Denis was mortified. The following season saw them finish in the middle of the table but they bounced back to the top in 1938 and also reached the semi-final of the FA Cup, losing 2-1 to Preston North End. Even in the Second Division their gates were regularly at 42,000 and a record 75,700 watched Villa beat Manchester City 3-2 in the FA Cup quarter-final, which greatly helped the financial health of the club. The thought of so many standing supporters packed in together is probably quite a terrifying one to many today. It was also

---

48 Christopher Stride, Nick Catley and Joe Headland (2020) 'Shirt tales: how adults adopted the replica football kit', *Sport in History*, 40:1, pp.106-146.

part of the culture to have a marching band at half-time – typically the Royal Warwickshire Regiment in Birmingham – and for the crowd to joyfully inhabit the pitch after the last match when promotion was secured.

In 1939, Aston Villa drew 1-1 with West Bromwich Albion in the Football League Jubilee Benefit Fund event which aimed to raise money in support of professional footballers' welfare. After this, only three games were played at the start of the new season before war was declared. The club closed down; the players commenced war work; the Trinity Road stand stored Air Raid Precautions materials; and the home dressing room housed a rifle regiment. The only games until 1945 were wartime competitions where players could guest for other clubs depending on where they were stationed with their war work or armed forces regiment.

Aston Villa lose to Everton at Villa Park in one of the last league games before war is declared. Birmingham Daily Gazette, *29 August 1939. Image: Mirrorpix / Reach Licensing*

Denis was not an official 'conscientious objector' but he was a pacifist and did not support the war. He had to sign up to the army, which was compulsory unless you had an official exemption, but managed to keep himself out of the direct line of fire. He was initially registered as a driver in the 48th (South Midland) Infantry Divisional Royal Army Service Corps, which was responsible for all land, coastal and lake transport; barracks administration; supply of food, water, fuel and domestic materials such as clothing, furniture and stationery; and the supply of technical and military equipment.

The 48th – without Denis – were initially involved in the early expedition to France in 1940 and the retreat at Dunkirk, before being based on home turf as a training unit for the remainder of the war. He was stationed in Scotland where a vast array of training took place as well as the protection of the coast and the building of new ports and transport links. Somehow his work took him to RAF Castle Kennedy near Stranraer on the west coast, across the sea from Belfast. It was here that he met a young radar operator, Marion (my grandmother).

Both Denis and Marion were members of the Peace Pledge Union (PPU), a non-governmental organisation which believes that war is a crime against humanity. A letter to the *Manchester Guardian*, and other newspapers, by Canon Sheppard of St Paul's Cathedral received over 130,000 positive responses and the PPU was born. Denis subscribed to the *Manchester Guardian* (now national newspaper *The Guardian*), which was traditionally liberal and supported slavery abolition and free trade in the 19th century. He and Marion both played their part to support the national war effort in the 1940s but in such a way that they could probably believe that they were helping and saving lives rather than actively destroying them. Having begun strongly, the PPU's campaign for peace did lose its initial support after 1940 and so the organisation then focused on matters such as food relief work and marching against the use of nuclear weapons.

After his posting to Scotland, and with the country still at war, Denis was transferred to the Army Pay Office in Manchester. The city and the surrounding area was a major centre of industry with many large firms concentrated in the Trafford Park area, making it an important target for German bombers. In March 1941, Manchester United's Old Trafford ground was hit by a bomb and put out of action until 1949. They temporarily shared Maine Road with Manchester City, paying £5,000 per season, plus a share of the entrance gate receipts. As a keen football fan, Denis took advantage of his army posting to watch United

Denis's own programmes for football matches featuring Aston Villa, Manchester City, and Manchester United throughout 1945. On many of them, he has noted changes to the line-up.

and City play, when not travelling down to watch the Villa. Marion sometimes went with him. In fact, the many match programmes that he saved in a box are the only record we have of his time there, which shows his priorities in life. Instead of the usual colourful booklets, these programmes were printed on single sheets of paper to save on resources during wartime restrictions.

The 1945/46 season was the last of the revised wartime structure before returning to its former setup.

A versatile player of the time was Harold 'Harry' Parkes. Before the war he was enjoying work as a tool setter and playing at weekends for the General Electric Company in the Birmingham Works League, as well as for local club Boldmere St Michaels. Harry was then catapulted into the limelight by being signed by Aston Villa as an amateur in 1939 and quickly joined the professional ranks.

Little did Villa know that they had not only brought in a highly talented full-back but also something of a clown who did his best to entertain both the players behind the scenes and the travelling fans.[49] In those days, players went to and from away matches on trains with the general population. After a good win the chatter and singing in the carriages would gradually die down as the last tankards of ale took effect (athlete nutrition also being very different compared to today). Just as everyone was nodding off, Harry would open one eye, sparkling with mischief, and shout out 'Tickets, please!' All the passengers would suddenly stir, scrambling in purses and pockets, only to find Harry in the corner seat, laughing hysterically.

Once, Harry slipped a stash of dining car cutlery into the bag of a journalist, who was then stopped at the station

---

49 Morris, Peter, Aston Villa: *The history of a great football club, 1874–1960* (Naldrett Press/Heinemann, 1960).

barrier and questioned by stern railway officials. Later, his team-mates were determined to get him back for all his pranks. Returning from another away game, they sent him onto the platform at a supposed long stop to 'please get some tea, old chap'. Harry was cheeky but good-natured and obliged. Just as he emerged from the cafe, steaming cups in hand, he was shocked to hear the guard's whistle and see the laughing faces of his pals at the carriage window as the train departed without him. Left behind with only a few

Villa player Harry Parkes in action in 1951 from the 'Football Stars In Action 1950s Series 2' card collection. Image: JF Sporting Collectibles.

notes in his wallet but a lot of hot tea, Harry finally got back
to Birmingham in the wee hours of the following morning.

Denis and Marion had married in 1944 but it was only
after the war had ended that they moved to Birmingham.
Denis was coming home, albeit in the southern suburb of
Northfield that was connected to the city centre by the
Birmingham Corporation Tramways and still ten miles
from his beloved Villa Park. He became a car tyres sales rep
at a good time when demand was increasing for motorised
vehicles.

In May 1946 there were still 338,000 German prisoners
in Britain, as well as Italians and other nationalities.
Hundreds of thousands of men, women and children had
come to Britain in a continuous stream in the 1940s, starting
with the arrival of the German and Italian prisoners of
war, and following with refugees and European Voluntary
Workers. There were hundreds of camps in the UK.
Prisoners were not immediately released as Britain needed
the labour; however, they were gradually permitted more
contact with local citizens, some even marrying and settling
in the country. Bert Trautmann was captured in Germany
and brought back to Camp 50 near Manchester. He played
in casual matches but his talent soon caught the attention of
some scouts. He signed for Manchester City and stayed for
15 years, even though some of the fans were against having
a German in the team so soon after the war.

In the summer of 1946, a petition was signed by
hundreds of church leaders and Members of Parliament to
try and speed up the repatriation process but it would still be
another year before the camps were closed and many could
return home. In the town of Accrington in Lancashire, home
to Accrington Stanley, the Rev. Howe of Oswaldtwistle
appealed to his congregation for books and games to occupy
the prisoners. He later accepted prisoners to his services,

even though this level of sharing of community life was not officially supported by the War Office. One resident recalls a friendship formed around football:

'We went out for walks together ... Franz was a keen footballer and so on occasions we watched Blackburn Rovers, and because [prisoners of war] were not at that time allowed on public transport we had to walk [five miles] there and back but it was still worth it for the obvious pleasure it gave.'[50]

Part of the Peace Pledge Union philosophy was to show respect and generosity to the many prisoners of war who had been put to work during their confinement. A statement issued by PPU headquarters in 1945 read:

WE OF THE PEACE PLEDGE UNION:
share the joy of families re-united;
join with all in thanksgiving that fighting in
    Europe has ceased;
rejoice with all that German and Italian military
    dictatorship is ended;
believe that violence and destruction are evil and
    that true victory comes not by force of arms;
and renew our pledge to work with all men of good
    will for justice and lasting peace.

As members of the PPU, Denis and Marion befriended two German soldiers who had been released and were living in Birmingham, waiting to go home. They invited them for lunch and tea, and took them to Villa Park to watch matches. Such was the mutual interest in football that Denis would include a copy of the weekly *Sports Argus* paper with his letters to Germany after the soldiers had returned home. They sent postcards and letters back. Denis, Marion and

---

50 Taylor, Pamela Howe, *Enemies Become Friends* (Book Guild, 1997).

their two daughters even went to visit one of them in Germany in the 1950s.

The *Sports Argus* was first printed in 1897 and, according to its masthead, was 'A Journal of All Manly Pastimes'. To a female sports enthusiast and athlete, the exclusivity of that line is almost laughable, although it is absolutely of its

The two German prisoners of war that my grandparents befriended, standing outside Denis and Marion's home in Birmingham. The prisoners were forced to write 'P' and 'W' on their trousers to mark them out in society, as can be seen on the man on the right.

time: competitive sport was male-dominated, and promoted for men and boys, like the books Denis was given at school. Sporting 'pink' papers existed all across the country and were an important way to share the news and continue to grow the wider football supporter community. People who had not been at a particular event could get up to speed with the latest results and dominant players, which also helped with betting. Those who had been there could relive every action and see if their perspective matched those of the journalists. Players, managers, and pundits all took a copy, including Andy Gray, Ron Atkinson, and Jon Motson. My mother also recalls asking her father each Saturday, 'Can we get the *Argus*?'

In the 1949/50 season, Aston Villa played Birmingham City at Villa Park. The match pitched Trevor Ford against Gil Merrick, the Blues' goalkeeper. As biographer Neil Palmer notes, there was no love lost between the two. He

The cover of the Sports Argus back in its first year in 1897, including the strapline 'A Journal Of All Manly Pastimes'. Image: Reach.

also recalls that clashes were considerably rougher at the time with shoulder barging legal and the tendency of some keepers to grab some sand before a corner and chuck it into a forward's eyes.[51] If the early days of Villa had been marked by Scottish style, the early 1950s brought Irish cleverness. Ford departed and, with the money, Villa were able to bring in Irish centre-forward Dave Walsh from West Bromwich Albion and a young Danny Blanchflower, the Northern Irish star who would go on to great success at Tottenham Hotspur.

Despite the prevailing impression that football was a man's game, Denis and Marion both went to Villa games regularly before their girls were born. Denis tried taking his first daughter (my aunt) but she was less enthusiastic. It was my mother who caught the football bug.

The 1957 FA Cup Final was played on 4 May at Wembley Stadium. It was nearly a Birmingham derby to add to the excitement; however, Manchester United beat Birmingham City in the semi-final and Aston Villa beat West Bromwich Albion in their semi-final replay. The final was controversial from the start when Villa forward Peter

---

51 Palmer, Neil, *Trevor Ford: The Authorised Biography* (Amberley Publishing Limited, 2016).

McParland collided with United goalkeeper Ray Wood, who was knocked unconscious and had to leave the pitch with a broken cheekbone. He eventually made it back into goal for the last seven minutes of the game, this being before head injury assessment protocols.

The team lists for the 1957 FA Cup Final and the programme of entertainment in the pre-match build-up.

Villa won 2-1, with both of their goals scored by McParland, making it Villa's seventh FA Cup title and their first major trophy for 37 years. Denis apparently returned home to Birmingham much later that evening and somewhat buoyed by elation and alcohol. He gleefully presented his daughter (my mother), then aged eight, with a 10s note, which is around £10 in today's money. The exact amount is subject to some debate depending on how my mother tells the story, but it was certainly much more than her pocket money at the time. This made a lasting impression on my mother, who suddenly came to the realisation that 'there must be something good in this Aston Villa obsession'.

The more sombre record is that six of the 11 players who took to the field for United in this game lost their lives in the Munich air disaster nine months later, as did a further two players who did not appear in the match, while two others who both played were injured to such an extent that they never played again.

Aston Villa triumphant at the end of the 1957 FA Cup Final. Somewhere in the crowd is my grandfather. Image: PA Images.

Denis started taking his second daughter, my mother, to games. He was often in work on a Saturday morning so they travelled straight from the garage and car showroom that he owned, picking up a neighbour from over the road. As a teenager it was also worth the wait at the garage on a Saturday morning if any of the young salesmen were working. They went in the family car, and parked in the street. My mother remembers that boys would approach and say, 'Can I mind your car, sir?' for a few coins, as they have done for years since, although the price has risen. Not as many people had or needed cars so it was easier to park, she recalls, and

Denis's programme and match ticket.

she remembers walking down through Aston Hall grounds and Witton Lane. They sat in the Witton Lane stand, in the second tier on the halfway line, almost exactly where our season tickets are now in the refurbished and renamed Doug Ellis stand. If it was an evening match – which became possible after the installation of new floodlights in 1958 – she was picked up straight from school in Edgbaston. My mother remembers it being very exciting, even if she was a little young to fully understand everything. She was simply aware that, if they won, then everyone was happy, therefore winning was important.

They also went to away games, often cup games. She remembers going to somewhere like Bristol City or Charlton Athletic; an unfamiliar ground. Denis went first through the turnstile. My mother hesitated. Those enormous metal gates can be quite a challenge, never mind for a young kid. A man behind said, brusquely, 'Move along, lad.' He would have thought nothing of it because women and girls were a rarity but my mother was so embarrassed – and still is – to be mistaken for a boy. She did not turn round to the man and say, 'But I'm a girl!' as she wanted to; she just kept quiet and shuffled quickly though after her father. It was a fleeting moment in a lifetime of watching sport but she still remembers it. Denis used to call his daughter 'Jackson' as an affectionate nickname. Perhaps he felt he had a son in a way, but the reality did not spoil the father–daughter bond, especially on matchday.

A happier memory for my mother was travelling to Anfield for a Liverpool game by train. It would have been either a steam train or one of the new diesel locomotives and a particular highlight was having lunch in the dining carriage. The original Birmingham New Street Station was opened by London and North Western Railway in 1854 and the station was rebuilt in the 1960s as part of postwar development. The West Coast Main Line has been hugely important since the 19th century in connecting goods and people, including football players and fans, between Birmingham, Liverpool, Preston and Glasgow.

A steam train heading north from Birmingham in 1961. Image: Trinity Mirror/Mirrorpix.

Travelling around was part of leisure time, either by train or car. It was not just a way to get somewhere, it was part of the event. Denis secured the loan of a Jaguar to drive the family along the new M1 motorway when it opened in the 1950s. It had no speed limits, crash barriers, or lighting; nor much other traffic in those early days. He took my mother by car to the ferry for her French student exchange visit, aged 12 years old. They sailed together but then he left her to get the train alone from Boulogne to Paris. Such was the confidence in public transport and complete strangers in a bygone era.

Denis still wrote letters during the long three weeks to say how much he missed her. The family car was Denis's own pride and joy. He drove the family all the way to Lake Geneva in Switzerland. Such was Denis's enthusiasm that he continued all the way up the mountain to a ski resort. Where Denis went impetuously, mishap generally followed and the car was damaged on the steep and winding roads, necessitating a quick repair job by some generous mountain mechanics in order to get down again.

After the war, Denis's new father-in-law James Cunningham – himself being friends with the McGregor family and no doubt willing to support another Villa man as much as his own daughter – had bought Denis a share in Taylor's garage which then became a partnership and the family business.

The pairing 'Taylor and Grainger' was not to be confused with two successful Sunderland players of the same name at the time. With local radio, print media and word of mouth the only 'social media' marketing options, it was a simple but no less stressful campaign to grow a city business. In the late 1950s and early 1960s, the *Birmingham Daily Post* often carried adverts for cars to buy or sell. Denis's garage and showroom were particularly proud of their Austin collection, calling the general public to 'See all the '65 models at Taylor

Taylor and Grainger garage in Pershore Road, Birmingham, 1951. To the left of the garage lay Cannon Hill Park. The house to the right has since disappeared to become the access to Riverside Drive. Image: The Geoff Thompson Archive/photobydjnorton.com.

and Grainger Ltd', 'See us for early delivery', and 'See the Austin Maxi'.

'Put a tiger in your tank' was a slogan created in 1959 by Emery Smith, a young Chicago copywriter who had been briefed to produce a newspaper ad to boost sales of Esso Extra. This made it on to the orange and black promotional pencils that Taylor and Grainger had made for their business and sat proudly on the front desk. In an *Esso* trade newspaper interview that Denis gave, the journalist asked Denis to reflect on building his business, to which he replied that, despite the long hours invested and lack of holidays, he had a great sense of fulfilment, 'like a hole in one', which he was quick to point out to the journalist that he had also achieved. Ever the sports fan, he undoubtedly tried his best to get as many sporting analogies into his marketing as possible.

The site was taken over for a similar business after Denis passed away in the early 1970s and is now a vast Esso petrol station and car wash, next to the Selly Park Tavern. If you are ever passing that way to or from the south, feel free to smile and think of the peaceful, passionate football fan who made his own little bit of Birmingham trade there.

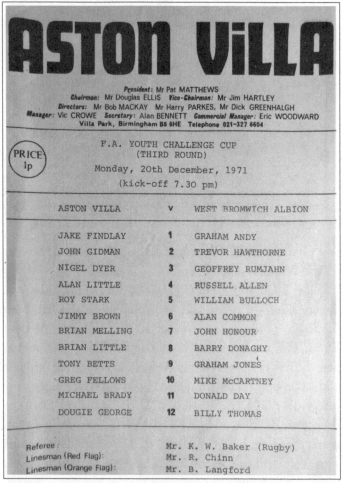

ASTON VILLA

President: Mr Pat MATTHEWS
Chairman: Mr Douglas ELLIS **Vice-Chairman:** Mr Jim HARTLEY
Directors: Mr Bob MACKAY Mr Harry PARKES, Mr Dick GREENHALGH
Manager: Vic CROWE **Secretary:** Alan BENNETT **Commercial Manager:** Eric WOODWARD
Villa Park, Birmingham B6 6HE Telephone 021–327 6604

PRICE 1p

F.A. YOUTH CHALLENGE CUP
(THIRD ROUND)

Monday, 20th December, 1971

(kick-off 7.30 pm)

ASTON VILLA	V	WEST BROMWICH ALBION
JAKE FINDLAY	1	GRAHAM ANDY
JOHN GIDMAN	2	TREVOR HAWTHORNE
NIGEL DYER	3	GEOFFREY RUMJAHN
ALAN LITTLE	4	RUSSELL ALLEN
ROY STARK	5	WILLIAM BULLOCH
JIMMY BROWN	6	ALAN COMMON
BRIAN MELLING	7	JOHN HONOUR
BRIAN LITTLE	8	BARRY DONAGHY
TONY BETTS	9	GRAHAM JONES
GREG FELLOWS	10	MIKE McCARTNEY
MICHAEL BRADY	11	DONALD DAY
DOUGIE GEORGE	12	BILLY THOMAS

Referee : Mr. K. W. Baker (Rugby)
Linesman (Red Flag): Mr. R. Chinn
Linesman (Orange Flag): Mr. B. Langford

A single-page programme for an Aston Villa youth team game in 1971, belonging to Denis. He would support all of Villa's teams and also attend matches of other teams he did not typically support. The youth team line-up, who went on to win the FA Youth Cup, includes a young Brian Little, later playing for and managing Villa. It also features his brother, Alan.

Chapter 14

Family duty and a football legacy

Glasgow, Lanarkshire, Birmingham,
Warwickshire (1919–1960s)

1800s	William Cunningham and Mary Scott	Cornelius Russell and Marion Henry	John Grainger and Elizabeth Coton	Samuel Swann and Elizabeth Cox
1900s	James Cunningham and Helen Russell		John Joseph Grainger and Amy Swann	
	Marion Cunningham and Denis Grainger			

BEING 'IN the club' can be a joyous thing: pursuing the same goals; enjoying time with like-minded people; feeling supported by a community who will always have your back, no matter what. It goes a step further than just being a social collection of individuals. There are usually some conditions or an invitation to join; some expectations or rituals of behaviour; and possibly a visual marker – a badge, a tie, a jersey – that only the certified members are permitted to wear with pride. Of course, the word 'team' does not just define opposition players in a competitive sports match. A team can be two or more humans (or animals) working together on the same task. In the run-up to elections, those working to promote a candidate may be referred to as 'Team [insert last name of politician]'. Club and team can also have a less positive connotation, depending on one's position. To say 'join the club' can mean an expression of empathy for someone who is struggling or unhappy in the same way as you. 'I am not in their little club' can mean a person feels ignored or excluded from the activities of others. To 'take one for the team' means to undertake an unpleasant task or make a personal sacrifice for the benefit of friends or colleagues, who may or may not be grateful afterwards.

There is no doubt that the concept of a club or team is important to us. Most of us are born into ready-made units – families – but we still spend our lives seeking out or forming new units without blood ties that we might feel that we love just as much; that we would happily do our duty towards. If we travel to an away fixture, we know we are among kin if they are wearing the club kit or singing the same songs. If we go on holiday to escape home, we can bond with complete strangers over a shared interest and where you come from becomes another point of reference, 'Oh I know someone from there. Do you know so-and-so?' The answer is usually no, but with a polite smile.

Although from a Scottish family, Marion was born south-west of Sheffield. It was 1919 and the furthest south that the Cunningham family had lived, more than 200 miles from their native Ayrshire and Lanarkshire. Here the steel industry was booming and Marion's father was doing well at the Vickers works. Her parents socialised with other manufacturers, including William McGregor, the Birmingham man whose Scottish father had led the founding of the Football League and was heavily involved in Aston Villa. No doubt the shared heritage and shared interest in both business management and sport created an instant social bond. As she grew up, the families remained friends and Marion referred to Mr McGregor as 'Uncle Willy', even though they were not actually blood-related.

When she was still young, the family moved back to Wishaw, Lanarkshire. Marion was sent by train into Glasgow to attend Laurel Bank School. This had been founded at the beginning of the century to give girls educational opportunities which until then had been offered only to boys. The archive photographs portray a stereotypical British girls' school in the 1920s and '30s: uniform gym slips, hockey sticks, and stern schoolmistresses in black gowns.

Hockey players at Laurel Bank School, 1914. Image: Noisy Brain Blog (www. noisybrain.blog)

Marion was intelligent and particularly good at mathematics. She kept a school embroidery, which Laurel Bank girls were encouraged to do, listing her subjects and achievements: drawing, writing, and numerous stars for music (singing and piano) and mathematics. She was also active in outdoor sports, playing tennis and going swimming in the fresh waters of Scotland's coastline.

Along with hockey played in the girls' schools, women's football was becoming increasingly popular in the industrial north of England and Scotland. One particularly successful team of the interwar years was Dick, Kerr Ladies of Dick, Kerr and Co Ltd engineering works, Preston, England. They had formed in 1894 and had played in front of 53,000 at Goodison Park in 1920. They played in international matches in 1920: four against Femina Paris and then making

A hand-embroidered strip of material listing Marion's school achievements.

An outdoor adventure with cousins that typically included a dip in the cold water.

up most of the England squad against a Scottish Ladies XI, winning 22-0. Just as the men had for decades, the women thrived within the support network of their own clubs and wore both their local and national jerseys with pride.

And then, all of a sudden in 1921, the Football Association outlawed the playing of the women's game on association members' pitches, on the grounds that 'the game of football is quite unsuitable for females and ought not to be encouraged'. This decision would stand until 1971. Not to be halted, the English Ladies' Football Association was formed. Twenty-four teams entered the first competition in the spring of 1922, eventually won by Stoke Ladies, beating Doncaster and Bentley Ladies 3-1. Women's football desperately tried to continue in Scotland. In the 1924/25 season, three clubs – Aberdeen, Queen of the South, and Raith Rovers – made separate requests to the Scottish FA for their grounds to be used for women's football matches. Each request was denied.

One club that girls could join was their local company of Girl Guides, also known as Girl Scouts in other parts of the world. In 1908, a British soldier, Lieutenant-General

Dick, Kerr Ladies football team.

Robert Baden-Powell, published a book called *Scouting for Boys: a handbook for instruction in good citizenship*. It was a manual on observation, tracking and woodcraft skills, but also on self-discipline and doing one's duty in the wider community. It was based on Baden-Powell's own boyhood and army experiences, which meant it was more targeted at the children of families who supported king and country.

What Baden-Powell had not imagined was the popularity of the book with girls. They registered their own Patrols (small groups of scouts) in the boys' organisation. In 1909, a Boy Scout rally was held at Crystal Palace – the same venue for the FA Cup finals at the time. A group of girls without tickets begged to be let in and created some negative publicity. The *Boy Scouts Headquarters Gazette* even wrote, 'If a girl is not allowed to run, or even hurry, to swim, ride a bike, or raise her arms above her head, how can she become a Scout?' This was a similar attitude that had led to the witch trials of generations earlier (see Chapter 2). Women moving quickly, dancing vigorously, or behaving wildly was viewed with suspicion and was therefore discouraged by society for centuries.

Marion's own photographs from her adventures with the Girl Guides in 1938: (clockwise from top left) a competition to pitch a tent blindfold; hiking in the snow; girls from a Polish company posting a letter from the international camp; girls from a Norwegian company in their version of the uniform tunic, cap, neckerchief and various badges.

Just a year after the boys, in 1910, a Girl Guides organisation was formed, led by Baden-Powell's sister, Agnes, and similar organisations were created around the world. They shared the same motto as the boys – Be Prepared – but had their own uniform. They also had the three-part promise (respecting certain values or religious beliefs; duty to the monarch or country; and helping other people, keeping the Guide or Scout Law). The young members became bound together in their groups, learning together and going on adventures. They were constantly reminded by their leaders to 'lend a hand' and to 'do your best'.

Marion joined the 6th Wishaw, 132nd Lanarkshire company. She stayed throughout her teenage years and rose to the rank of lieutenant. They had weekly meetings where they would practise skills while also chatting about their favourite singers and film stars. She attended camps across Scotland in the 1930s with her Wishaw company. She travelled to the international chalet in Switzerland with girls from all over the world in July 1938, all in their different uniforms and singing songs in different languages. She even went to a 50-year reunion in the 1980s, which signifies her happy memories and dedication to the organisation. We still have all of her numerous badges, commendations, and lanyards. Incidentally, my mother still has all of hers and I still have mine.

Badges – and club training or playing kit – are worn with pride, never mind if you are a professional at international level or a junior turning out for the under-12s in your home town. Jerseys and (sometimes very smelly) training bibs serve a very practical function of indicating who is currently on which team. Badges, kit, uniform, and a whole range of other items we now have today, also say to the wider world that 'I belong' and often that 'I have achieved something'. These two sentiments are crucial to us, as individuals and as communities.

No doubt William McGregor would have told Marion that Aston Villa were also proud of their club badge and the motto, 'Prepared', similar to the Scouts' and Guides' motto. The Lion Rampant forms the central part of the Royal Banner of Scotland and records of its use go back to the early 13th century. The complete banner of a red lion on a yellow background with a floral border is actually restricted to be used only by the monarchy and other great officers of state by an Act of Parliament. However, the lion itself is a recognisable symbol of Scotland and is also used on one of the two crests of Glasgow Rangers, who celebrated 150 years of existence in 2022. It is in the centre of the badge of the Scotland international football team and on the logo of the Scottish Football Association.

The lion was brought to the Aston club in the 1870s by their Scottish members, who included William McGregor, George Ramsay, and Fergus Johnstone. At first, the badge was only used on club headed paper and envelopes. Soon they decided that their sombre shirts needed brightening up a bit. This is where a more skilful hand was needed and so it was that Miss Midgeley, the sister of the club secretary, was drafted in to sew a lion on each shirt.

Unfortunately, the typical hand-scrubbing laundry process that was regularly required to separate the mud of Aston Lower Grounds from the jerseys (the same being worn every Saturday) meant that the lion quickly lost its colour and faded away. The decision was made that the club should send an order up to Scotland for 13 lions on fabric shields that could be detached and reattached each time. No doubt the poor sister raised an eyebrow. 'You men want me to spend ev-er-y Friday – day and night – sewing your football badges,' Miss Midgeley likely exclaimed, 'on top of all my other chores and never mind if I want to go out and enjoy myself?'

Luckily for her, it was not to be. As Fergus Johnstone described, 'They came – about the size of a dessert plate! When they were duly attached – you could hardly see the man for the lion – we were each as self-conscious as a bride in a wedding dress. We went on to the field but the gorgeous lion got us down. We had a most awful whacking and the lion was relegated to the club notepaper and flags.' After this, the lion did not reappear on the club shirts until just before the FA Cup run of 1957, but seemed to bring the players just the strength and good fortune that they needed.[52]

Despite the engineering genes in the family, despite the investment in her education and Girl Guiding skills,

---

52 Brown, Paul, 'From the archives: Origins of Villa's rampant lion' (Aston Villa Football Club website, 20 May 2016).

Aston Villa headed paper, 1920, with the club badge and motto. This is from a letter from the chairman to Huddersfield Town FC. Villa had just defeated them in the FA Cup Final and the chairman writes to compliment the players and club of Huddersfield on their season. Image with permission of Aston Villa Football Club.

and despite her obvious aptitude for mathematics, a career was no pursuit for a young lady. Not according to Marion's mother, anyway.

After school, Marion was instead enrolled in the Glasgow and West of Scotland College of Domestic Science. It seemed a terrible deal and Marion was bitterly disappointed. If there was one ray of hope, it was that Scotland's colleges, particularly those in and around Glasgow, were training electrical appliance demonstrators 'on the fringe of the technical world', according to engineer Caroline Haslett in 1919. With the reduction in house servants, such appliances were targeted toward housewives, which could be understood

Students in a sewing class at Glasgow and West of Scotland College of Domestic Science, 1931. Sewing was one of the subjects taught on the 'Engaged Girls' Course', popularly known as the 'Brides' Course', where future wives were taught how to run a family home. Image: Glasgow Caledonian University, Research Collections, Archives.

as reinforcing the stay-at-home role or increasing female autonomy and skills in a modern world.[53]

After a seemingly very innocent and idyllic childhood, life was about to change. Even before Marion's trip to Switzerland in 1938, Germany had annexed Austria to become a federal state of Germany. Soon after she returned home, with her song book and camera documenting her many new European friends, British Prime Minister Neville

One of Marion's 'Housewife' certificates, 1937.

Chamberlain signed the Munich Agreement which agreed for Germany to occupy the Sudetenland, the German-speaking part of then Czechoslovakia, in order to avoid another war. Some people in Britain felt that Germany had been treated very harshly after the First World War. Others were worried that Germany was trying to expand its territory again and that this move would result in more fighting. Rumours of the persecution of Jews and other groups were gradually filtering through to the British newspapers, but the extent was not fully known and visas for immigrants were limited. The ruling party in Germany, the National Socialist German Workers' Party – informally shortened to Nazi – were viewed with some suspicion.

The world had already witnessed the straight-arm Nazi salute at the Berlin Olympics in 1936, which were the first to be televised and the first to have a torch relay. Jewish

---

53 Eleanor Peters (2022), 'On the fringe of the Technical World: female electrical appliance demonstrators in interwar Scotland', *Women's History Review*, 31:2, pp.230-254

athletes had been banned from swimming pools and training centres, and several countries considered boycotting the event. However, such discrimination was not only happening in Germany as the United States had their own restrictions for African-Americans, who had fewer opportunities as athletes and could not enter many restaurants and hotels. The Olympic Games went ahead but with more than sport in the spotlight.

In the summer of 1938, both the England and Aston Villa football teams travelled to Germany for matches. Before the England fixture against Germany, a Football Association representative went to the changing room and told the players that they had to give the Nazi salute during the German anthem. The players refused but the FA official came back minutes later with a message from the British Ambassador: if they did not do it, the consequences for Europe could be very serious. The players obeyed. The next day, the Villa players were preparing to face an even stronger German Select XI. They refused to salute and there were criticisms in the press the next day. In their following

England players give the Nazi salute before playing against Germany in 1938. Image: PA Images.

match, the FA and the Foreign Office were more insistent. The Villa players made the salute but they followed it by raising two fingers afterwards, which the German players apparently laughed at.

Even though her parents probably resisted again, Marion was permitted to move to London at a time when legal adulthood did not start until age 21. She acquired a position as a house assistant in a girls' hostel. These would be young female students who were away from home but not socially connected or trusted enough to live in their own apartment. They would be sent to the city to study for qualifications (secretarial, domestic, nursing) and it was Marion's task to look after their welfare and behaviour. It was probably something that her Girl Guiding leadership experience set her up perfectly for.

The great advantage – and probably the reason she was allowed to go – was that her older brother, Bill, was also in London at the time. Unbeknown to the parents, this actually meant more social freedom. He was supposedly able to closely supervise her but, in reality, it guaranteed her fair share of parties and access to clubs and other places she would not have experienced before. Her box of memories contains programmes for social and entertainment venues as well as an autograph book full of notable names from the era.

In September 1939, war was declared. Marion would eventually join the RAF, after her older brother Bill had already enlisted with the army, but she still had to wait a year or two. The only other excitement that year, apart from her time in London, was that Edinburgh City Girls beat the dominant Dick, Kerr Ladies 5-2 in Edinburgh. They then beat Glasgow Ladies 7-1 in Falkirk to take the impressively named 'Championship of Great Britain and the World' title. Women's wartime service on a par with the men was not

(Clockwise from top left) Cary Grant's autograph; Bing Crosby's autograph; Marion's card from the glamorous Dolphin Square residence near the River Thames in Westminster, where visitors could join in the evening dinner dances for 6 shillings and 6 pence, with Eddie Carroll and his band as the resident musicians; Eddie Carroll's autograph on the front of the card.

immediately available. In June 1939, King George VI had established the Women's Auxiliary Air Force (WAAF) for duty with the RAF in time of war. It was initially only a kind of satellite organisation, intended for substituting any needed roles in the main RAF. Finally, in 1941, the WAAF became part of the Armed Forces of the Crown, subject to the Air Force Act, although they had a separate ranking system and pay which was two-thirds of their RAF colleagues'. With conscription for women introduced from December 1941, the ranks swelled further so that by July 1943 a peak strength of 182,000 had been reached. By 1945 a quarter of a million women had served in the WAAF in over 110 different trades around the world.

With her mathematical skills and Girl Guiding experience, Marion was the ideal candidate for surveillance and she enlisted in 1941. She was finally able to do something more exciting than domestic duties, even though the whole idea of war did not sit right in her mind. Radar operators kept a constant watch for enemy aircraft and plotted their location for station officers to respond to. Rotating aerials transmitted a narrow radio beam, like an invisible searchlight. It could not measure height but could detect aircraft flying at 152m (500ft) at ranges up to 177km (110 miles). The traces were displayed on a circular screen much like modern radar displays.

Marion met the young army driver, Denis (Chapter 13), while she was stationed at the WAAF base called Castle Kennedy, which lies three miles east of Stranraer in south-west Scotland. This was a modern airfield built to house No. 3 Air Gunnery School. Other units

WAAF radar operator Denise Miley plotting aircraft on the CRT (cathode ray tube) of an RF7 receiver in the Receiver Room at Bawdsey CH. Her right hand has selected the direction or height-finding and her left hand is ready to register the goniometer setting to the calculator. Image: Imperial War Museum CH 15332.

based there during the war specialised in torpedo training and target towing. Denis worked for the Army Service Corps, which dealt with the various logistics of keeping all ports and bases stocked with supplies, and one can imagine that he found many excuses to keep delivering to that particular base.

They were married in Birmingham in October 1944. In wartime it was very difficult for couples to get leave at the same time or in the same place. There was also rarely time for the normal waiting time of three weeks to have the banns read in church on Sundays. Instead of being married in the bride's home town, many took advantage of a short rendezvous at a local registry office; in this case it would have been while Denis was visiting his home town (and beloved football team).

Marion's service record describes a 'conscientious character'. However, the family story goes that she did her best to try and leave the RAF as soon as possible – unsurprising as both Denis and Marion were pacifists – which meant that she was one of the first to be demobilised

Marion in RAF uniform, 1943.

the very day after the war ended when many were kept on for months or years afterwards. Initially they lived in Manchester, where Denis was still working for the Army Pay Office. In the 1930s, Manchester had been active in anti-war activities and both Denis and Marion became members of the Peace Pledge Union, which they continued when they moved

to Birmingham. In line with their Peace Pledge Union ideals, Marion and Denis invited German prisoners of war to their home for lunch or tea (see Chapter 13) as well as to watch football matches. Many of the soldiers were young, like Marion had been at the start of the war, and had been members of the Hitler Youth, the organisation similar to the Scouts that was compulsory for German children in the 1930s along with the League of German Girls.

Marion still retained her own active Girl Guiding spirit, playing golf with her husband and going to watch football at Villa Park together on Saturdays, until it was time to start a family of her own. By the 1950s they were living in the King's Heath area of Birmingham with their two daughters. After the way their own families had worked their way up with middle-class aspirations, and after all the chaos and uncertainty of wartime Britain this was the 1950s idyll: a detached house with driveway for a car and a large garden at the back. Chesterwood Road was an enormous suburban horseshoe with a wide road and pavements for the children to go out and play 'until it's time for tea' or it got dark, whichever came first.

Until the 18th century, the King's Heath area of Birmingham was an unoccupied moorland that was part of the Royal Manor of King's Norton and then developed into a village in the 19th century. *Lord of the Rings* author J.R.R. Tolkien was living there in Westfield Road in the early 1900s before attending King Edward's School and creating the Tea Club and Barrovian Society with his friends, meeting regularly at Barrow's Stores. A century later, soul singer Laura Mvula wrote the 2013 song 'Green Garden' as a eulogy to her former home in King's Heath. Her own journey mirrors many of my ancestors' attempts to find a better life further and further into the suburbs:

'When we moved to our new house, for us kids it was a big deal to have trees in the back garden. Where we had lived in Selly Park, the back garden was more concrete than grass, so it felt like we were in a forest. Some of my happiest memories are of endless summer holidays where it seems like we spent most of the time in the garden, making up dance routines or having mammoth water fights. The song is a celebration of that.'[54]

Marion and Denis sent their children to King's Heath High School, owned by Major Dean Davis and his wife who lived in a large house in whose grounds the school buildings stood. Past pupils remember the brown and gold

---

54 An interview with Business Live, published by Alison Jones, 22 February 2013.

King's Heath High Street in a postcard from the early 1950s.

uniform, the corgis in the garden, and that at one time the boys were given coaching at King's Heath Cricket Club behind the school by Derief Taylor. Taylor left Kingston in Jamaica to serve with the British Eighth Army in the war. While fighting in North Africa, he met the Warwickshire batsman Tom Dollery and later decided to try to become a professional cricketer with Warwickshire. Injury forced him into coaching where he became highly respected in the youth game, and then was snapped up as coach of Warwickshire for many years, and also managed one of England women's cricket tours to Jamaica.

In many ways, Marion did play her role as the suburban Birmingham housewife. As the magazine *Woman* recounted in 1963, the aim was to be simply wonderful: effectively and efficiently raising the children and keeping the husband happy. However, as the same magazine suggested in another article, this was not the only interpretation. Women *could* go out and work and gain further education for personal fulfilment, even though society (and the same magazine) was persuading them that the home was their true calling.[55]

---

55 Caitriona Beaumont (2015), 'What is a Wife? Reconstructing Domesticity in postwar Britain before The Feminine Mystique', *History of Women in the Americas*, 3, pp. 61-76.

Housewife *magazine, June 1947, advertising alluring underwear and evaporated milk – essentials to please the hard-working husband. Image: Thom White.*

Even though Marion was at home, raising two young daughters, football was never far away. Next door lived the Wisemans. Jack Wiseman was a Birmingham City man through and through, which would have caused many a debate across the garden fence with Denis and Marion. Wiseman joined the board of the football club in 1956 and went on to be the club's highly respected chairman.

While still running his car business in Birmingham, Denis came home suddenly one day to announce that he had bought a house to the south of the city in the Warwickshire countryside. And that was that: the family were on the move again.

Tanworth-in-Arden village is of Anglo-Saxon origin, with the name derived from 'Tanewotha', meaning the thane's (baron's) 'worth' or estate. In the 19th century the suffix 'in-Arden' was added to the name, in order to avoid confusion with the town of Tamworth in Staffordshire, and it refers to the Forest of Arden in which the village lay. One of the attractions of the house was that it had a garden gate leading straight on to the golf course. Marion, being her independent self, stayed loyal to her club back at Moseley, in Birmingham, playing regularly on ladies' days and winning club medals. She coupled this with keeping house and driving her daughters to Sunday school socials in the village hall. They were not members of the church –

Marion and her neighbour, Gwen Wiseman, with their daughters in 1949.

probably because they preferred an early tee-off at the golf club – although Denis and Marion were finally laid to rest in the churchyard. My mother vividly remembers the horror of leaving her Easter bonnet on the back ledge of the car before one Sunday school event back in Birmingham and seeing her mother speeding off down the road, again rushing off to play golf.

Tanworth-in-Arden, 1957. Image: Warwickshire County Record Office PHN600/622/1

The car and football combine into another family story on the occasion of Marion and Denis's first daughter's 21st birthday.

Contrary to modern annual celebrations, the 21st was traditionally the one birthday that was properly recognised because it was the official beginning of adulthood. A large party had been planned and Marion was furiously busy preparing the house and refreshments in order to welcome their guests. It was April and Aston Villa had been knocked out in the FA Cup fourth round, but West Bromwich Albion and Birmingham City would be playing the semi-final at Villa Park to decide who would represent the Midlands at Wembley. Denis was determined – 'this day of all days' tutted Marion – that he had to go all the way into Birmingham and across town to Aston to get tickets from the Trinity Road ticket office. If Marion had protested that neither of these were 'their' club so why go, she probably realised the benefit of having him out from under their feet. 'And you can take our other daughter and one of the dogs with you.' Incidentally, the two terrier dogs had been another snap decision of Denis's, bought during the chaotic build-up to moving house. They proved to be trouble ever since.

So it was that my mother, her father, and the dog – Bootsie – headed off to Villa Park, leaving Marion to resume her work as domestic lieutenant. They parked in nearby Bevington Road, and, as it was a hot day, left the window open a fraction for the dog to get some air. When they hurried back with the tickets, mindful of the party starting, they discovered that the dog – terriers being of a mischievous and adventurous disposition – had escaped. Panic and worry ensued and Bootsie was reported as missing at the police station. Denis and my mother had to make the long journey back home, rather distraught and casting gloom over the eldest daughter's big occasion. Fortunately, following a lot of tears, Aston police station called later that evening. The dog had been found, handed in to the station, and Denis had to drive all the way back to Aston to claim his lost property. This has now evolved into a standard family cautionary tale of a) not taking dogs on important shopping missions, and b) the way football can ruin a good party if one is not careful.

Denis in one of his cars, with a troublesome terrier behind the wheel.

It was not until the 1980s that Marion could finally realise her ambition of taking university courses, which she did as distance learning by post in the days before laptops and online lectures. She also frequently went travelling later in life to the places that war and home duties had limited, and sent back postcards from Egypt, India, the United States, the Soviet Union and other countries all over Europe.

The football fever continued, long after Denis had passed away, becoming what we did as a family. I would have said that my first game was while at primary school, marvelling at Tony Daley speeding down the wing. In fact, as my mother frequently reminds me, she climbed the stairs of the stands while eight months pregnant. I started young.

Going to Villa Park in the 1980s with my grandmother was approached with the same domestic care as a traditional family picnic and the same sense of adventure as a Girl Guide camp. My brother and I distinctly remember being wrapped up in coats, claret and blue scarves, hats and gloves for matches in winter. We've all had many experiences since of numb feet and frozen backsides, desperate for a Bovril or hot chocolate at half-time. Not so with Granny Marion. She was perfectly turned out in smart clothing underneath a long wax jacket and head scarf. I thought she looked more like the Queen than a regular supporter. Once installed in our seats, she would sometimes produce a rug (Scottish tartan, of course) to place over our knees. At half-time there was no need to fight the rush at the bar with two small children. The phrase 'pie and a pint' was certainly not in Granny's vocabulary. A Thermos of coffee was produced for herself, orange squash for us kids, and KitKat chocolate bars all round. After the game we were efficiently marched back to the car through the cold evening air and tucked up again on the back seat with the same rug for the journey home.

At that age we knew we had become members of a club but we could have no idea of the legacy that history had given us: the generations of work and play that created the beautiful game for us to enjoy; the coalminers, the factory machinists, the soldiers, the teachers, the priests, the shopkeepers, the business entrepreneurs, who all played their part. Marion knew and saw so much social change herself. Out of the whole family tree, she was the one who lived in all of the great industrial and footballing centres – Glasgow, Sheffield, Manchester, Birmingham. She had been born in a time when the authorities said that certain clubs – football, technology, further education, adventure – were not for her, but they were.

Official club photographs of my Aston Villa mascot day, 18 April 1987. Both my mother and grandmother were in the crowd. Image: Terry Weir/ Aston Villa Football Club.

Bibliography

Here is a list of some of the books, journals, and websites used for this research project, in addition to those appearing as footnotes in the chapters. It does not include every source and readers will find many more with useful and interesting information. I also do not list the hundreds of football club websites, many of which have excellent webpages and news articles on their origins and development through the decades.

I am grateful to all of the writers, researchers, archivists, club staff, and sports history enthusiasts who have given me permission to reproduce their work and some extra help along the way.

On the history of sport:

Camanachd Association: history of shinty – www.shinty.com/history

Curling History Blog – curlinghistory.blogspot.com

Dunning, E., Murphy, P., and Williams, J., *The Roots of Football Hooliganism: An Historical and Sociological Study* (London: Routledge & Kegan Paul, 1988)

Faulds, M.H., and Tweedie, Jnr, W.M., *The Cherrypickers: Glenbuck, Nursery of Footballers* (1981, reprinted in 1981 by Cumnock and Doon Valley District Council)

Football Pink – www.footballpink.net

Football Unites, Racism Divides – www.furd.org

Historical Kits – www.historicalkits.co.uk

Holt, R., *Sport and the British: A Modern History* (Oxford: Oxford University Press, 1989)

Inglis, S., *The Football Grounds of Great Britain* (second edition, London: Collins Willow, 1987)

Journal of Sport History – published by University of Illinois Press

Matthews, T., *Birmingham City Football Club* (Tempus Publishing, 2000)

McCarra, K., *Scottish football: a pictorial history from 1867 to the present day* (Glasgow: Third Eye Centre, 1984)

Morris, P., *Aston Villa: The history of a great football club, 1874–1960* (Naldrett Press/Heinemann, 1960)

Morris, P., *West Bromwich Albion: Soccer in the Black Country* (London: Heinemann, 1965)
National Football Museum – www.nationalfootballmuseum.com
Outside Write: football travel, history and culture blog (twitter) – twitter.com/outsidewrite
Page, S., *Pinnacle of the Perry Barr Pets: The Men and Matches behind Villa's Double* (Sheffield: Juma, 1997)
Robinson, R., *The History of The Queen's Park Football Club 1867–1917* (Glasgow: Hay Nisbet, 1920)
Sanders, R., *Beastly Fury: The Strange Birth of British Football* (London: Bantam Press, 2010)
Scottish Football Museum – www.scottishfootballmuseum.org.uk/
Soccer & Society – journal published by Taylor and Francis Online
Sport in History – journal published by Taylor and Francis Online
Sports Heritage Scotland – www.sportsheritagescotland.co.uk
Taylor, R.P., and Ward, A., *Kicking and Screaming: An Oral History of Football in England* (London: Robson, 1995)

Examples of websites and blogs dedicated to the history of particular teams and grounds:

Blyth Spartans AFC – www.blythspirit.wordpress.com
Celtic Wiki – www.thecelticwiki.com
Everton Chronicles – www.bluecorrespondent.co.uk
Hampden Collection – www.hampdencollection.com
Heart of Midlothian Football Club Heritage (twitter) – twitter.com/Hearts_Heritage
Huddersfield Town Collection – www.huddersfieldtowncollection.wordpress.com
Play Up Liverpool – www.playupliverpool.com
This is Glenbuck (twitter) – https://twitter.com/GlenbuckIs
West Bromwich Albion Chronicle – https://www.wbachronicle.com/

On the history of industry:

Bremner, D., *The Industries of Scotland: Their Rise, Progress, and Present Condition* (A. and C. Black, 1869)
Brewery History Society – www.breweryhistory.com
Grace's Guide to British Industrial History – www.gracesguide.co.uk
Griffiths, S., *Griffiths' Guide to the Iron Trade of Great Britain* (Griffith, 1873)
Heritage Crafts – www.heritagecrafts.org.uk
Midlands Pubs – www.midlandspubs.co.uk
Miller, T.R., *The Monkland Tradition* (London and New York: T. Nelson, 1958)
History of Scottish Mining – www.scottishmining.co.uk
Shill, R., *Workshop of the World: Birmingham's Industrial Heritage* (Stroud: The History Press, 2006)
Shill, R., *Birmingham Canals* (Stroud: The History Press, 2013)

On social and cultural history:

A Visitor's Guide to Victorian England (Michelle Higgs Blog) – www. visitvictorianengland.com
Auschwitz-Birkenau Memorial and Museum – https://www.auschwitz.org/en/
British Film Institute National Archive – www.bfi.org.uk/bfi-national-archive
British History Online – www.british-history.ac.uk
British Library – www.bl.uk
British Newspaper Archive – https://www.britishnewspaperarchive.co.uk
English Heritage – www.english-heritage.org.uk
Europeana: art, books, films, and music – www.europeana.eu
Historic England – www.historicengland.org.uk

Historic UK – www.historic-uk.com

History and Policy (research) – www.historyandpolicy.org

Historygirl (twitter) on Victorian and Edwardian Britain – twitter.com/janeyellene

History Scotland – www.historyscotland.com

History Today – www.historytoday.com

Hurt, J.S., *Elementary Schooling and the Working Classes, 1860–1918* (Routledge, 2016)

Journal of Social History – published by Oxford University Press

Larkham, P.J., and Clapson, M., (editors) *The Blitz and its Legacy: Wartime Destruction to Post-War Reconstruction* (Routledge, 2013)

Labour History – journal published by Liverpool University Press

Migration Museum – www.migrationmuseum.org

Museums Victoria (Australia) – www.collections.museumsvictoria.com.au

National Archives – www.nationalarchives.gov.uk

National Library of Scotland – www.nls.uk

National Library of Australia – www.nla.gov.au

National Museums Scotland – www.nms.ac.uk

Office for National Statistics – https://www.ons.gov.uk/

Peace Pledge Union – www.ppu.org.uk

Hansard (official report of all British parliamentary debates) – www.hansard. parliament.uk/

Undiscovered Scotland – www.undiscoveredscotland.co.uk

University of Glasgow Library Blog – www.universityofglasgowlibrary.wordpress.com – and Story – https://universitystory.gla.ac.uk/

Whyte, I., *Scotland and the Abolition of Black Slavery, 1756–1838* (Edinburgh University Press, 2006)

On local history:

A history of Birmingham places and place names from A to Y – www.billdargue. jimdofree.com

A Tour of Lost Birmingham – mappingbirmingham.blogspot.com

Ayreshire History – www.ayrshirehistory.com

Balsall Heath Local History Society – www.balsallheathhistory.co.uk

Bird, V., *A Short History of Warwickshire and Birmingham* (London: B.T. Batsford Ltd, 1977)

Birmingham Hippodrome Heritage – www.birminghamhippodromeheritage.com

Birmingham History Forum – www.birminghamhistory.co.uk

Birmingham Museums – www.birminghammuseums.org.uk

Birmingham Old Prints, Photographs and Maps 1600-1900's (facebook.com)

Black Country Living Museum – www.bclm.com

Chinn, C., *Peaky Blinders: The Real Story of Birmingham's most notorious gangs* (London: Kings Road Publishing, 2019)

Connecting Histories (Birmingham and the West Midlands) – www. connectinghistories.org.uk

Cotton Town: Blackburn with Darwen – www.cottontown.org

Digbeth, Birmingham – www.digbeth.com

Gender and Legal History in Birmingham and the West Midlands – University of Birmingham blog – blog.bham.ac.uk/legalherstory/

Handsworth Historical Society – www.handsworth-historical-society.co.uk

Herefordshire Through Time – www.htt.herefordshire.gov.uk

History West Midlands – www.historywm.com

Dudgeon, J.P., *Our Liverpool: Memories of Life in Disappearing Britain* (Headline Book Publishing, 2011)

Jamieson, B.A)., *North Berwick Between the Wars* (*East Lothian Courier* and East Lothian Council, 1996

John Gray Centre, East Lothian – www.johngraycentre.org
King's Heath Local History Society – www.kingsheathhistory.co.uk
Lower Severn Vale Levels – www.aforgottenlandscape.org.uk
Midlands Pubs – www.midlandspubs.co.uk
North Lanarkshire Museums – www.culturenlmuseums.co.uk
Northampton Museums – www.northamptonmuseums.com
Perry, N., *A History of Stourbridge* (Stroud: The History Press, 2019)
Pilning and Severn Beach Area History Group – www.stedders108.wixsite.com/mysite
Rushden and District History Society – www.rushdenheritage.co.uk
Scotland's Places – www.scotlandsplaces.gov.uk
Sheroes of History – sheroesofhistory.wordpress.com
The Collection: art and archaeology in Lincolnshire – www.thecollectionmuseum.com
The Iron Room: Blog of the Archives and Collections at the Library of Birmingham –
    theironroom.wordpress.com
The Workhouse – www.workhouses.org.uk
Understanding Scottish Places – www.usp.scot
Upton, C., *Back to Backs: Guidebook* (The National Trust, 2004)
Upton, C., *A History of Birmingham* (reprinted, Andover: Phillimore and Co. Ltd, 2011)
West Bromwich Local History Society – www.westbromwichhistory.com
Wolverhampton History and Heritage website – www.historywebsite.co.uk

Examples of family history blogs:

Walker, M. – www.afamilyhistoryblog.wordpress.com
Scobbie, J. – www.noisybrain.wordpress.com

On the history of war – sport and society:

Breuil, X., Le football en Belgique pendant la seconde guerre mondiale: entre normalité,
    unité et continuité (1939–1947) *Guerres mondiales et conflits contemporains*,
    268, 7-20 (2017)
Brown, P., *The Ruhleben Football Association: How Steve Bloomer's Footballers Survived
    a First World War Prison Camp* (Goal Post, 2020)
Football and the First World War – www.footballandthefirstworldwar.org
Football and War Blog (University of Wolverhampton) – www.wlv.ac.uk/research/
    institutes-and-centres/centre-for-historical-research/football-and-war-network/
    football-and-war-blog
Forces War Records – www.forces-war-records.co.uk
Imperial War Museum – www.iwm.org.uk
Kuper, S., *Ajax, the Dutch, the War: Football in Europe during the Second World War*
    (London: Orion, 2003)
National Army Museum – https://www.nam.ac.uk/explore/boer-war
Nottinghamshire Great War Roll of Honour – www.nottinghamshire.gov.
    uk/RollOfHonour
Operation Market Garden – www.ww2marketgarden.com
Royal Air Force Museum – www.rafmuseum.org.uk
Ruvigny and Raineval M.H.M., *De Ruvigny's roll of honour 1914–1918: a biographical
    record of members of his majesty's naval and military forces who fell in the Great
    War, 1914–1918* (Naval & Military Press, 2003)
Taylor, P.H., *Enemies become friends: a true story of German prisoners of war* (Lewes:
    Book Guild, 1997)
The Great War (1914–1918) Forum – www.greatwarforum.org
The Long, Long Trail – www.longlongtrail.co.uk
The Wartime Memories Project – www.wartimememories.co.uk
Voices of War and Peace – www.voicesofwarandpeace.org

Indexes

Index of topics
and chapters

Alcohol; alcoholism and temperance 5, 10

Amateur clubs, leagues 11

Badges, club crests, mottos 11, 14

Basket-making 6

Behaviour (of players, supporters); crowds, hooliganism 6, 13

Betting, gambling, match-fixing 7, 9

Books, comics 13

Brewing; breweries 5

Bull Ring 6, 7, 11

Charity; funds, missions, matches 5, 7, 10, 11, 12, 13

Childbirth; rates, midwife 7, 10

Clans (Scottish); clan feuds 2, 3

Clothing; uniform, supporters, replica kit 13, 14

Commentary, live scores; radio, boards 9

Cricket 4

Crime 6

Curling 3, 10

Decorating, house painting 9

Dogs 14

Domesday Book 4

Drinking establishments, public houses 3, 5

Economic depression; The Great 3

Education; schools, colleges, university 4, 5, 7, 10, 11, 12, 14

Electroplating 4, 11

English Civil Wars 2, 3, 4, 8

Farming 2, 6

Fives (sport) 12

Food manufacturing 12

Footwear; boot and shoe trade, football boots 11, 12

Gaelic football 2

Gangs; street violence, 'Peaky Blinders' 6, 7

Gold and silver; trade, standards, marks, jewellery 4, 8

Golf 2, 10

Great Exhibition of 1851 8

Grocers 11

Guns; making, viewing 8

Hat-making 4

Health; diseases, medicine, nutrition, welfare, suicide 5, 7, 8, 11, 12, 13

Horses; and carts, military 6, 9

Housing; provision, conditions, overcrowding, back-to-back, suburban 2, 3, 4, 5, 7, 11, 12, 14

Identity documents; passport, driving licence 9

Industrial impact on landscape 2, 3

Iron and steel work; puddling 2, 3, 5, 6, 10, 11

Italian 'Calcio Fiorentino' (sport) 6

Japanning, Japan-ware 5

Knights Templar 2

Leagues; creation, structure 8, 9, 10, 11

Malt; trade, maltings, maltster 5

Marketing; sponsorship, product advertisements 11

Marriage; process, weddings, morals 2, 4, 5

Migration; into Britain from Ireland, Continental Europe, Pakistan, and the West Indies 2, 7, 12

Migration; from rural to urban, urban to rural 2

Migration; from Britain to Europe, North America, Australia 7, 10, 12

Mining 2, 3

Motor trade, tyres 12, 13

National Socialist German Worker's Party (NSDAP); salute 14

Newspapers; news, sports reports, advertisements, magazines 5, 6, 9, 11, 13, 14

Olympic Games 8, 14

Pawnbroking 8, 11

Peace Pledge Union 13, 14

Poetry, folk songs 2, 3, 4

Prisoners of War 11, 13, 14

Public (political) meetings, declarations 3, 7

Public recreation spaces; parks 4, 6, 9

Punishment; prisons 2, 3, 6

Quoits (sport) 3

Rationing; food, clothes 11, 12

Rebellion, Scottish against English 2, 3

Referees, umpires 6, 11

Religion; beliefs, morals, religious tension 2, 3, 4, 7, 10, 11

Roma, Traveller and Fairground; families, culture 9

Rugby football 2, 4, 10

Rules (of football); Association rules 4, 6, 10, 11

Scouts and Guides movement; creation, girls, camps, international 14

Shinty, shinny, bandy, hurling 2, 7

Singing, chanting 9

Slavery 2, 4, 13

Spanish Flu epidemic 13

Stadium; design, use, disasters 7, 13

Strikes; work protests 5, 9, 12

Suffrage; voting rights, women 7

Surveillance, radar operators 14

Textile trade; mills, owners, cotton trade, garments 9, 10

Theatres; music, dance, dinner-dance, pantomime, cinema 12, 14

Tickets; admission prices, income 5

Tolls, toll-keeping 3

Town and village football, feast-days 2, 4, 6, 10

Trains; travel, spotting 8, 12, 13

Trams, tramways 6

Wages, salaries 8, 9, 10

War, military service; 19th century, Boer 6, 8

War, 1914-1918; recruitment, fighting, convalescence 7, 8, 9, 10, 11, 12

War, 1939-1945; service, fighting, air raids 7, 10, 11, 12, 13, 14

Waulking (of cloth) 2

Weaving, weavers 3

Welsh 'Cnapan' (sport) 6

Witchcraft; witch trials 2, 14

Women's factory work 12

Women's football 2, 7, 12, 14

Woodwork, joinery, carpentry 2

Worker unions, associations 5

Workhouses 7

World Cup 8

Index of teams and clubs (football except where another sport is mentioned) and chapters

Abercorn 10

Aberdeen 14

Accrington Stanley 13

Alloa 10

Alnwick, Northumberland (parishes) 2

Arsenal (formerly Woolwich Arsenal) 2, 11

Ardrossan Seafield 5

Aston Brook St Mary's Rugby 4

Aston Villa 3, 4, 5, 6, 7, 8, 9, 10, 13, 14

Ayr United 3, 7

Barcelona 12

Bath City 10

Beardmore's Forge (ladies) 7

Birmingham City (formerly Small Heath Alliance and Birmingham FC) 3, 5, 6, 7, 8, 9, 11, 12, 13, 14

Blackburn Olympic 9

Blackburn Rovers 5, 7, 8, 9, 10

Blyth Spartans Ladies 7

Bolckow Vaughan Ladies 7

Bolton Wanderers (formerly Christ Church) 7, 8, 9

Bootle 6

Borussia Dortmund 11

Bournville 12

Bradford City 7

Bright Sparks (Ladies) 12

Bristol City 13

British Ladies'

Burnley 6, 8, 9

Burslem Port Vale 5, 6

Burton Swifts 6

Bury 7

Calthorpe (formerly Birmingham Clerks) 4, 8

Cambuslang 10

Carlisle Munitions Ladies 7

Celtic 2, 3, 5, 7, 10

Charlton Athletic 13

Chelsea 7, 9, 13

Christopher Brown's Ladies 7

Clydesdale 10

Coventry City 12

Cowlairs 10

Crewe 6

Crystal Palace 8

Darlington 11

Darwen 6, 8, 9

Derby County 4

Dick, Kerr's Ladies 14

Doncaster and Bentley Ladies 14

Dumbarton 10

Dumbreck 10

Dundee 10

Eastern 10

Edinburgh City Girls 14

FC Eindhoven 11

PSV Eindhoven 11

Entente Anversoise 11

Enville (Staffordshire) Cricket Club 4

Everton 6, 8, 10

Femina Paris 14

Foster Tank Girls 12

General Electric Company 13

Genoa Cricket and Football Club 12

Glasgow Ladies 14

Glenbuck Cherrypickers 3, 10

Granville 10

Great Guns (ladies) 12

Grimsby 6

Hamilton Academical 10

Hampden Bowling Club 10

Harrow School 9

Heart of Midlothian 10

Hibernian 7, 10

Highland Light Infantry 10

Huddersfield Town 13

Hudson's (soap factory) 5

Kilmarnock 10

King's Heath Cricket Club 14

Leeds United 2

Leicester City 9

Leith Golf Club 2

Lincoln Munition Girls 12

Lincoln 6

Liverpool 3, 7, 9, 10, 13

Manchester City (formerly Ardwick) 6, 9, 13

Manchester United (formerly Newton Heath L&YR FC) 9, 13

Middlesbrough 3, 8

Middlesbrough Ironopolis 5

Mitchell St. George 5

Monymusk (village) 2

Motherwell (merged Glencairn and Alpha) 2, 10

Muirkirk (Athletic and United) 3

Newcastle United 2, 7, 8

New Monkland Curling Club 10

North Berwick Golf Club 11

Northampton Town 11, 12

Northwich Victoria 6

Norton (village) 10

Norwich City 8

Nottingham Forest 2

Old Etonians 9

Palmer's Shipyard Ladies 7

Partick 9

Partick Thistle 10

Pelsall 6

Preston North End 3, 5, 6, 8, 11, 13

Queen of the South 14

Queen's Park 8, 10

Queen's Park Rangers 8

Raith Rovers 14

Rangers 2, 8, 10, 14

Renton 10

Rotherham Town 11

Rovers 10

Royal and Ancient Golf Club of St Andrews 2

Royal Antwerp 11

Ruston Aircraft Girls 12

St Mirren 10

Saltcoats Crescent 5

Sheffield (village) 10

Sheffield United 6, 7, 9, 11

Sheffield Wednesday 2, 5, 8

South Wishaw Bowls Club 10

Stafford Road Works 4

Stoke Ladies 14

Sunderland 8, 13
Swansea 12
Third Lanark Rifle
   Volunteer Reserves 10
Thistle 10
Tottenham Hotspur 2, 3,
   8, 11
Turton 9
University of Glasgow
   Cricket Club 4
Ulster 5
Vale of Leven 8, 10
Villa Cross Wesleyan
   Chapel Cricket Club 4

Walsall (formerly Walsall
   Town Swifts, a merger
   of Walsall Swifts and
   Walsall Town) 6, 7
Walsall Cricket Club 4
Warwick County 8
Warwickshire Cricket
   Club 14
Wednesbury Old
   Athletic 4
Western Cricket Club 4
West Bromwich Cricket
   Club 4
West Bromwich Albion

(formerly Salter's
   Spring Works and West
   Bromwich Strollers) 5,
   7, 8, 9, 11, 13, 14
West Ham United
   (formerly Thames Iron
   Works) 5, 9
Wolverhampton Cricket
   Club 4
Wolverhampton
   Wanderers 7, 8, 9, 12
Worcester College,
   Oxford 12

Index of people (not family members) and chapters

Agbonlahor, Gabriel 5
Aldecoa, Emilio 12
Alexander, Field
   Marshall 10
Angus, William 10
Ansell, Joseph 5, 8
Ashton, J.C. 9
Astaire, Fred 12
Aston, Jack 7
Athersmith, Charlie 8
Atkinson, Ron 13
Baden-Powell, Lt-Gen.
   Robert and Agnes 14
Bambridge, Charlie 10
Barnard, John Jervis 7
Beatty, Admiral and
   Lady 8
Blanchflower,
   Danny 13
Bloomer, Steve 4
Bloomer, Steve 8
Bone, Edward and
   William 3

Bone, Jock 3
Bootman, John 9
Bosnich, Mark 5
Boulton, Matthew 5
Bradford, Joe 9, 11
Brearley, John 8
Brown, Albert 4
Buck, Alec 3
Burns, Robert 1, 2, 3
Busby, Sir Matt 2
Cameron, John 8
Cameron, Reverend
   Richard and
   Michael 3
Carrott, Jasper 14
Carson, John 4
Chatt, Robert 8
Cole, Henry 8
Compton, Denis 11
Cowan, James 'Jas' 4, 8
Crerand Pat 1
Cromwell, Oliver 2, 3
Cromwell, Thomas 4
Crosbie, John 3, 11
Daly, Tony 14
Dalzel, Archibald 2
Dewald, Father 11
Dickens, Charles 7
Dickson, Thomas 3
Dixie, Lady Florence 7
Dollery, Tom 14

Douglas, Sir William 3
Earls of Glencairn 2
Eden, Jessie 12
Ehiogu, Ugo 5
Evans, Albert 8
Finlay, James 3
Ford, Trevor 13
Forrest, James 10
Gallacher, Hughie 2
Gardner, Robert 10
Gerry and the
   Pacemakers 9
Gibson, Mel 3
Graham, George 2
Gray, Andy 5, 13
Gregory, Elizabeth 2
Grey, Daniel 5
Grierson, Joe 5
Gunter, Brian and
   Anne 2
Haasz, Johnny 12
Hall, Jack 9
Hodgetts, Dennis 8
Hodgson, Roy 5
Holte, Sir Thomas 2, 4
Houlding, John 10
Howe, Reverend, of
   Oswaldtwistle 13
Hunter, Archie 4
Hutson, Mary (Nettie
   Honeyball) 7

Johnstone, Fergus 14
Kay, John 9
Kimber, William 'Billy' 7
King Charles I of
England 2, 3
King Charles II of
England 2, 3
King Edward I of
England 2, 3
King Edward II of
England 2
King Henry II of
England 13
King James II of
England (James VII of
Scotland) 2
King James VI of Scotland
(James I of England) 2, 3
King Phillip of France 2
King William I (William the
Conqueror) 4
King William III of
England 8
Kinnaird, Arthur 9
Kinsella, Mark 5
Lapraik, John 3
Leonard, Jack 7
Liston, Robert 2
Little, Brian 13
Lowry, Laurence Stephen
(L.S.) 7
McGregor, William (Snr),
William (Jnr) 8, 10,
13, 14
McParland, Peter 13

Malley, Willy 10
Merrick, Gil 13
Miller, Thomas 10
Monck, George, 1st Duke of
Albemarle 2
Moores, John 7
Motson, Jon 13
Mulcaster, Richard 11
Murray, Billy 'Bubbles' 9
Mvula, Laura 14
Nevill, Captain Wilfred 10
Obernkirchen Children's
Choir 9
Oláh, Béla 12
Orr, J. Campbell 4
Pagan, Isobel 'Tibbie' 3
Pankhurst, Emmeline,
Christabel, Sylvia 7
Parkes, Harry 13
Pentland, Fred 8
Pentland, Joseph 11
Prince Albert 4, 8
Queen Victoria of the
United Kingdom of
Great Britain and
Ireland 4, 8
Ramsay, George 4, 14
Reynolds, John 5
Rinder, Frederick 8
Robert the Bruce 2
Saunders, Ron 14
Schmeichel, Peter 5
Shankly, Bill 1, 3
Sheppard, Canon, of St.
Paul's Cathedral 13

Skinner, Reverend John 2
Smith, Emery 13
Spensley, James 12
Stein, Jock 2
Stopes, Marie 7
Sturge, Eliza and Joseph 7
Suter, Fergus 9
Tait, Alec 3
Taylor, Derief 14
Taylor, Gordon 7
Taylor, Graham 5
Templeton, Bobby 10
Tolkien, John Ronald
Reuel 14
Trautmann, Bert 13
Tull, Walter 11
Turnbull, Alexander
'Sandy' 9
Vaughton, Howard 4
Wallace, William 2, 3
Walsh, Dave 13
Walsh, Nathaniel and
sons 9
Warburton, Albert 9
Weir, Jimmy 3
Wheldon, Fred 8
Wharton, Arthur 11
Wilkes, Albert 5
Wiseman, Jack and
Gwen 14
Wolstenholme, Sam 8
Wood, Michael 11
Wood, Ray 13
Yates, Sydney 9
Yorke, Dickie 13